American River College Library
4700 College Oak Drive
Sacramento, CA 95841

IDENTITY THEFT

Selected Titles in ABC-CLIO's
CONTEMPORARY
WORLD ISSUES
Series

American Families in Crisis, Jeffrey S. Turner

Animal Rights, Clifford J. Sherry

Campaign and Election Reform, Glenn H. Utter and Ruth Ann
   Strickland

Climate Change, David L. Downie, Kate Brash, and Catherine
   Vaughan

Corporate Crime, Richard D. Hartley

DNA Technology, David E. Newton

Domestic Violence, Margi Laird McCue

Education in Crisis, Judith A. Gouwens

Emergency Management, Jeffrey B. Bumgarner

Energy Use Worldwide, Jaina L. Moan and Zachary A. Smith

Environmental Justice, David E. Newton

Gangs, Karen L. Kinnear

Gay and Lesbian Rights, David E. Newton

Globalization, Justin Ervin and Zachary A. Smith

Lobbying in America, Ronald J. Hrebenar and Bryson B. Morgan

Mainline Christians and U.S. Public Policy, Glenn H. Utter

Modern Sports Ethics, Angela Lumpkin

Nuclear Weapons and Nonproliferation, Sarah J. Diehl and James
   Clay Moltz

Obesity, Judith Stern and Alexandra Kazaks

Policing in America, Leonard A. Steverson

Renewable and Alternative Energy Resources, Zachary A. Smith
   and Katrina D. Taylor

Rich and Poor in America, Geoffrey Gilbert

Sentencing, Dean John Champion

U.S. National Security, Cynthia A. Watson

U.S. Social Security, Steven G. Livingston

U.S. Trade Issues, Alfred E. Eckes, Jr.

Waste Management, Jacqueline Vaughn

For a complete list of titles in this series, please visit
www.abc-clio.com.

Books in the Contemporary World Issues series address vital issues in today's society, such as genetic engineering, pollution, and biodiversity. Written by professional writers, scholars, and nonacademic experts, these books are authoritative, clearly written, up-to-date, and objective. They provide a good starting point for research by high school and college students, scholars, and general readers as well as by legislators, businesspeople, activists, and others.

Each book, carefully organized and easy to use, contains an overview of the subject, a detailed chronology, biographical sketches, facts and data and/or documents and other primary-source material, a directory of organizations and agencies, annotated lists of print and nonprint resources, and an index.

Readers of books in the Contemporary World Issues series will find the information they need to have a better understanding of the social, political, environmental, and economic issues facing the world today.

IDENTITY THEFT

A Reference Handbook

Sandra K. Hoffman and Tracy G. McGinley

**CONTEMPORARY
WORLD ISSUES**

A B C CLIO

Santa Barbara, California
Denver, Colorado
Oxford, England

Copyright 2010 by ABC-CLIO, LLC

All rights reserved. No part of this publication may be reproduced, stored in a retrieval system, or transmitted, in any form or by any means, electronic, mechanical, photocopying, recording, or otherwise, except for the inclusion of brief quotations in a review, without prior permission in writing from the publisher.

Library of Congress Cataloging-in-Publication Data
Hoffman, Sandra K.
   Identity theft : a reference handbook / Sandra K. Hoffman and Tracy G. McGinley.
      p. cm. — (Contemporary world issues)
   Includes bibliographical references and index.
   ISBN 978-1-59884-143-5 (print : alk. paper) —
   ISBN 978-1-59884-144-2 (ebook)
  1. Identity theft.   I. McGinley, Tracy G.   II. Title.
   HV6675.H64   2010
   364.16'33—dc22   2009043174

   ISBN 978-1-59884-143-5 : paper
   ISBN 978-1-59884-144-2 : ebook

14   13   12   11   10   1   2   3   4   5

This book is also available on the World Wide Web as an eBook.
Visit www.abc-clio.com for details.

ABC-CLIO, LLC
130 Cremona Drive, P.O. Box 1911
Santa Barbara, California 93116-1911

This book is printed on acid-free paper ∞

Manufactured in the United States of America

Contents

Preface, xi

1 **Background and History, 1**
   What Is Identity Theft?, 1
     Personal Identity Theft, 2
     Business Identity Theft, 3
   The History of Identity Theft, 5
     Jacob and Esau, 6
     Cade's Rebellion of 1450, 6
     Sarah Wilson in Colonial America, 7
     Czar Nicholas II and His Family, 8
     The Great Imposter, 9
     The Most Misused Social Security Number
       in History, 10
     The Chicago Debacle, 11
     The First Documented Multinational Internet Bank
       Robbery, 12
     An Early Case of Credit Card Fraud, 13
     The First Internet Murder, 15
   Who Are the Perpetrators?, 16
     Opportunity Takers or Makers, 17
     Gender, 19
     Age, 23
     Ethnicity, 24
     Criminal History, 25
     Country of Origin, 26
     Affiliation with Other Crimes, 27
     Affiliation with Other Criminals, 27
   Who Are the Victims?, 29
     Types of Identity Theft, 29

Geographical Location, 31
Age, 32
References, 34

2   **Problems, Controversies, and Solutions, 41**
The Victims' Experiences, 41
    Methods of Detection and Time Lapse, 42
    Types of Identity Theft and the Restoration Period, 44
    Effects on Relationships, 46
    Emotional and Medical Concerns, 47
    Financial Losses, 49
    The Second Insult, 49
Sources and Methods Used by Perpetrators to Access
        Identities, 51
Trends and Special Issues, 53
    Tax Fraud, 54
    Medical Fraud, 54
    Real Estate Loan Fraud, 56
    Offshoring Identities, 57
    Data Breaches, 59
    The Hidden Costs of the Crime, 62
Solving the Identity Theft Problem, 62
    Responsibility Theories, 63
    Government Responses, 64
References, 83

3   **Worldwide Perspective, 89**
Canada, 89
United Kingdom, 100
Mexico, 107
Russia, 109
South Africa, 112
Asia, 113
The Threat to International and Homeland Security, 115
References, 118

4   **Chronology, 123**

5   **Biographical Sketches, 139**
Abagnale, Frank, Jr. (1948–), 140
Ashcroft, John (1942–) U.S. Attorney General, 140

Bliley, Thomas Jerome, Jr. (1932–) U.S. Representative
(R-Va.), 141
Bowen, Debra (1955–) California Secretary
of State, 142
Calderon, Charles (1950–) State Senator
(D-Calif.), 143
Cantwell, Maria (1958–) U.S. Senator (D-Wash.), 143
Carter, Steve (1954–) Indiana Attorney General, 144
Cogdill, David (1950–) State Assembly (R-Calif.), 145
Cuccinelli, Ken (1968–) State Senator (R-Va.), 146
Feinstein, Dianne (1933–) U.S. Senator (D-Calif.), 146
Foley, Linda, 147
Frank, Mari, 148
Givens, Beth, 149
Gramm, William Philip (1942–) U.S. Senator
(R-Tex.), 149
Kaine, Timothy M. (1958–) Governor (D-Va.), 150
Kyl, Jon (1942–) U.S. Senator (R-Ariz.), 151
Leach, James Albert Smith (1942–)
U.S. Representative (R-Iowa), 151
Leahy, Patrick (1940–) U.S. Senator (D-Vt.), 152
Madigan, Lisa (1966–) Illinois Attorney General, 153
May, Johnny, 153
Oller, Thomas (1958–) State Assemblyman
(R-Calif.), 154
Ostergren, Betty "B. J.", 154
Paterson, David A. (1954–) Governor (D-N.Y.), 155
Petro, James (1948–) Ohio Attorney General, 156
Poochigian, Charles (1949–) State Senator
(R-Calif.), 157
Simitian, Joe (1953–) State Senator (D-Calif.), 157
Specter, Arlen (1930–) U.S. Senator (R-Pa.), 158
Torlakson, Tom (1949–) State Assemblyman
(D-Calif.), 159
Wyland, Mark (1946–) State Senator (R-Calif.), 160

6 **Data and Documents, 163**
Executive Summary Consumer Fraud and Identity Theft
Complaint Data January–December 2008, 163
President's Identity Theft Task Force, 165
Identity Theft and Assumption Deterrence Act, 173
Title V of the Gramm-Leach-Bliley Act, 1999, 180

7 Directory of Organizations, Associations, and Agencies, 199

8 **Resources, 219**
Print Resources, 219
Books, 219
Journals and Magazines, 224
Pamphlets/Booklets, 236
Nonprint Resources, 237

Glossary, 247
Index, 253
About the Author, 263

Preface

*I*dentity Theft: A Reference Handbook is a comprehensive guide to developing an understanding of what identity theft is. The book demonstrates that the crime of identity theft knows no boundaries. Victims and perpetrators of identity theft vary in age, gender, race, socioeconomic status, and occupation. Furthermore, it is a crime of global concern. Incidents of identity theft are escalating in the United States as well as in other countries. Given the far-reaching implications and proliferation of the crime, it is important to develop a thorough understanding of the crime in order to work toward viable solutions to the problem.

Chapter 1 begins by defining identity theft and distinguishing between the different types of the crime. The chapter then offers readers a history of the crime to illustrate its evolution as it has adapted to changes in modern society. After the historical discussion, the chapter focuses on the common characteristics of identity theft perpetrators. In this section, readers are presented with demographic information pertaining to the offenders and their motives for committing the crime. Lastly, Chapter 1 discusses the types of identity theft to which victims are most often subjected and explores the factors that may contribute to the likelihood of victimization.

Chapter 2 addresses the problems, controversies, and solutions surrounding identity theft. This section looks at the elements that go into detecting identity theft, the impact that it has on its victims, and the tactics that perpetrators utilize to commit the crime. Also discussed are various trends in the crime, such as medical identity theft, and issues that put identities at risk of being stolen, including information security breaches. Chapter 2 then focuses on the possible solutions to identity theft. These solutions are discussed from various perspectives. The chapter delves into many of the state and federal government responses to the crime, including legislation to assign an agency the responsibility of collecting and maintaining a database of identity theft complaints. Then, the role of the criminal justice system in responding to victims is explored. The chapter concludes by offering suggestions for protecting personal identifying information.

Chapter 3 takes readers on an exploration of the global implications of identity theft. This chapter examines the connection between identity theft in the United States and other countries. The scope and nature of the problem in Canada, the United Kingdom, Mexico, Russia, South Africa, and Asia is discussed as well as how these countries have responded to it. The chapter closes with an examination of the threats posed by identity theft to international and homeland security.

Chapter 4 provides a chronological overview of the crime of identity theft, its evolution, and the laws that were created in response to it. The chapter offers a listing of federal and state laws, civil lawsuits, criminal cases, security breaches, and other noteworthy events that have shaped the way in which identity theft is addressed in modern society.

Chapter 5 is designed to help familiarize readers with the key activists, thinkers, victims' advocates, researchers, citizens, business leaders, and policy makers in relation to identity theft. It describes each person's role in addressing critical issues pertaining to the crime.

Copies of some of the key pieces of legislation appear in Chapter 6, thereby allowing the reader to review, in detail, the laws that are considered the most significant in tackling identity theft problems. Also included in this chapter is information relating to the latest statistics published by the Federal Trade Commission. Chapter 7 provides a list of the organizations, associations, and agencies that have evolved to deal with the crime of identity theft. The origin, function, and Web site content (if available) of each entity is discussed. An annotated bibliography of key resources on identity theft is offered in Chapter 8. These resources include books, journals, magazines, newspapers, pamphlets, booklets, and Web sites.

At this point, we would like to acknowledge those who made it possible for this book to become a reality. We would like to express our appreciation to the publisher for assisting us through the process of writing this book. Also, we would like to thank our friends and family members for their support. A special thanks to Bryan, Connor, Hannah, Walter, Jason, and Melissa for their patience and encouragement. Finally, we dedicate this book to all victims of identity theft.

1

Background and History

dentity theft is frequently mentioned in today's society; the crime is often reported in the news. Advertisements warn consumers to review their credit reports, and companies offer insurance, credit monitoring, and early detection products. By and large, identity theft is not considered a serious crime, but is often thought of as a nuisance crime in which a person's information, such as a credit card number, is stolen and used to make purchases. Though many may think of it as a new social phenomenon created by increased reliance upon technology, in reality it is a much broader and more complex crime than this, and one that can have serious ramifications for all aspects of society, including the economy and national security.

The purpose of this chapter is to assist readers in developing a better understanding of this complicated, multifaceted crime. First, identity theft is defined in order to build a foundation for the remainder of the book, and then a discussion of the crime's history demonstrates its transformation as it has adapted to changes in modern society. Lastly, an assessment of existing research on the subject is undertaken in an effort to discern the characteristics most commonly associated with the perpetrators and their victims.

What Is Identity Theft?

Identity theft is a modern name for an ancient crime. Identity theft did not become a federal offense, however, until 1998. Although they vary from state to state, identity theft-related statutes have been enacted in every state. Thus, the following definition is based upon a compilation of these established laws. Simply stated, identity theft is fraud. There are many types of identity theft, and thieves target both businesses and individuals.

Personal Identity Theft

Personal identity theft is the use of an individual's personal identifying information without his or her knowledge and with the intent to aid or abet in any unlawful activity such as the fraudulent obtaining of services, merchandise, money, and/or credit. It also occurs when an individual's identifying information is used to file for bankruptcy or to aid in the commission of other felonies and/or misdemeanors.

Personal identifying information distinguishes a person from all other people. It includes, but is not limited to, a person's name, address, telephone number, birth date, Social Security number (SSN), driver's license number, passport number, health insurance policy number, employee identification number, employment history, student identification number, mother's maiden name, financial account numbers, account passwords, biometric data, e-mail address, and instant messaging screen name. Once a thief has access to this information, there are several ways the information may be used.

The most severe form of identity theft is a complete identity take over. This occurs when a key piece of personal identifying information is stolen and used by a thief to take control of every aspect of the victim's life. A complete identity take over usually begins with a stolen SSN or mother's maiden name. Either piece of personal information can be used to obtain a breeder document, a government-issued identification record that leads to the issuance of additional identification documents.

A common scenario of a complete identity take over involves a stolen mother's maiden name. This is a critical piece of information that is required to apply for a duplicate birth certificate (i.e., a breeder document). Once obtained, a duplicate birth certificate can be used as identification for getting a Social Security card and driver's license in the victim's name. Then, these fraudulent government identity documents can be presented as identification for opening financial accounts, applying for a passport, securing employment, procuring utilities, and acquiring an array of goods and services. In essence, the thief can now live under the newly assumed identity as if he or she actually is that person.

Social Security numbers are another key piece of personal identifying information. Each number is unique and permanently assigned to one individual. A stolen SSN can facilitate a complete identity take over in the same manner as a stolen mother's maiden name. Unfortunately, victims have very few options if their numbers are stolen and used to commit fraud and/or other crimes. They may request a new number (SSA 2002). However, the process for securing a new number requires an extensive amount of time and paperwork. In addition, identity theft issues may resurface in the future. Problems may arise when the old and new numbers are associated in various databases, such as those maintained by the credit bureaus.

Business Identity Theft

Thieves also steal the identities of businesses. The term *businesses* refers to small companies, corporations, financial institutions, healthcare related organizations, and government entities. Business identity theft involves the use of a business identifier without permission and with the intent to aid or abet in any unlawful activity such as fraudulently obtaining services, merchandise, money, and/or credit. This also occurs when business-identifying information is used to file for bankruptcy or to aid in the commission of other felonies and/or misdemeanors. Business identifying information distinguishes one business from all others and includes the name of the business, its address, telephone number, e-mail address, logo, trademark, Web site, corporate credit card number, checking account number, and tax identification numbers.

In some cases, the identifying information of businesses is stolen in order to gain access to the company's financial accounts (Collins and Hoffman 2004). Business checking accounts are often targeted by identity thieves. For example, criminals may steal a business check and duplicate it electronically. The checks are often cashed or used to make purchases without being detected because they bear a legitimate account number or business name. The business owner may not find out about the fraud until they balance the accounts, verify the account activities online, or receive notification that the account is overdrawn. The following case illustrates how businesses are victimized in this manner.

According to reports, Justine Coppolino was the ringleader of a network of Utah-based identity thieves (Deseret News 2008). The indictment states that she stole the identities of both businesses and individuals (U.S. Attorney 2007). The identities were used to manufacture payroll checks that Coppolino and her co-conspirators cashed at Salt Lake City-area businesses. Over 80 computer-generated payroll checks were printed, each displaying the names and logos of legitimate businesses stolen from many sources, including telephone books. To ensure that the checks appeared legitimate, Coppolino scanned the signatures belonging to real people into her computer and affixed them to the checks. For her role in the counterfeit check scheme, she was sentenced to almost six years in prison and ordered to pay over $50,000 in restitution (Desert News 2008).

This case is representative of thousands of similar incidents that occur in the United States every year. However, identity thieves target business credit card accounts as well as checking accounts. A thief may make unauthorized charges on an existing account, open a new account, or add themselves as an authorized user of a business credit card. Why do criminals seek out this account information? It is simple. Business credit cards usually have higher credit limits than personal accounts, and business checking accounts are more likely to carry a higher balance than personal accounts. To help avoid detection, thieves typically strike swiftly, using stolen account information during a short span of days or weeks and may make several transactions per day. Thus, business accounts are often targeted because of the high returns that can be obtained quickly.

Another form of business identity theft occurs when a company's employer identification number (EIN) is stolen and used to obtain credit, take out loans, or to file tax returns. The Internal Revenue Service (IRS) assigns EINs for tax purposes. As a business identifier, it is comparable to an SSN, a personal identifier. Both numbers are associated with credit reports, taxes, and financial accounts.

Most cases of business identity theft are committed, however, to gain access to one of the most important assets of any business: the identifying information of the business's customers, clients, employees, patients, or vendors (Collins and Hoffman 2004). Many methods are employed to steal these assets. Owners may even use their legitimate businesses as the source for stealing personal identifying information. For example, the owner of several

Los Angeles–area tax preparation businesses was sentenced in January 2009 to 11 years in prison after admitting to an elaborate fraud scheme (U.S. Attorney's Office 2009). Abdul Wahid pled guilty to several felonies, one of which was aggravated identity theft, after stealing the identities of several of his clients, including businesses and individuals. In one case, Wahid filed a bogus tax return in another person's name. The IRS sent the refund check to Wahid, who then deposited it in his own account.

Dishonest employees also steal identities from their workplaces. Sometimes the stolen information is passed on to other people. In one case, a hotel clerk stole the credit card numbers of several customers and exchanged them for a gift card. Noel Miller was employed as a clerk at a Hilton Hotel (U.S. Attorney 2006). During the course of her employment, she stole 25 credit card numbers belonging to guests. Miller gave the account information to another person instead of using it herself. In exchange, the co-conspirator gave her a $300 Wal-Mart gift card. In the end, more than $60,000 worth of fraudulent purchases were charged to the credit cards Miller had stolen. Miller was arrested and pled guilty to fraud charges. In October 2006, she was sentenced to six months in federal prison, six months of house arrest, and ordered to pay $60,000 in restitution.

In summation, identity thieves target both businesses and individuals, and often there is a connection between the two. Sometimes the identities of businesses are stolen. Other times, businesses are exploited in order to gain access to the personal identifying information of individuals related to the business. Identity theft, whether business or personal, is an old crime. The next section explores the history of its evolution so as to help readers gain a better understanding of the consequences of the crime as it relates to modern life.

The History of Identity Theft

Identity theft is a relatively new name for an age-old phenomenon. Early accounts of the crime were a simple form of impersonation. In the legal sense, impersonation is the act of imitating another person with the intent to defraud others for personal gain (Garner 1999). Imposters assumed the identities of others by imitating how their subjects dressed, behaved, and talked. Over time, impersonation became ineffective as other forms of personal identifying information came into being. Forged, stolen, and fictitious identification documents, as well as financial account information, became the catalyst for identity theft. Furthermore, technology has changed the way personal information is used, collected, and stored. As identity theft evolved from simple impersonation to a technology-driven identity, the methods used to commit the crime also evolved. The following incidents span hundreds of years and demonstrate how identity theft evolved into the crime that is known today.

Jacob and Esau

Identity theft is most often committed for personal financial gain. An example is found in early Biblical writings (Tenney 1969). In the book of Genesis, a young man named Jacob imitated his brother so he could inherit the family estate. Jacob and Esau were the twin sons of Isaac and Rebecca. To be precise, Esau was the oldest; he was born a few minutes before his brother. As he aged, Isaac's health and eyesight faded. He realized it was time to prepare for his death. Thus, Isaac made arrangements to transfer the family estate to his oldest son, Esau.

Rebecca found out about her husband's plans, and was determined that Jacob, not Esau, should receive the inheritance (Tenney 1969). Rebecca devised a scheme to take advantage of her husband's failing eyesight by enlisting Jacob to impersonate his brother. On the appointed day, Jacob met with his father and pretended to be Esau. He dressed in Esau's clothing so he would smell like his brother, and since Esau had ample body hair, Jacob applied goatskins to his hands and arms to fool his father's sense of touch. He imitated Esau's manner of speech and spoke about the topics that were important to his brother. The guise was successful, Jacob received his father's blessing, and inherited the family estate.

Cade's Rebellion of 1450

A person suspected of committing a crime may use identity theft to avoid detection by authorities. One incident that occurred during the late Middle Ages is an example of how a murder suspect can imitate another to avoid apprehension. John Aylmer practiced medicine in England during the 1440s (Miller 2003). He fled to France in 1449 after being accused of murdering his mistress, and about a year later, Dr. Aylmer resurfaced in Kent, England. He did not use his real name, but instead he claimed his name was Jack Cade.

Aylmer began organizing an army of dissidents to overthrow King Henry VI (Miller 2003). Perhaps to appear more credible to potential recruits, he changed his name again, this time claiming to be John Mortimer, a relative of Richard, Duke of York. Aylmer and his army of knights, squires, merchants, poor farmers, and small property owners successfully defeated the king's soldiers in a skirmish at Kent. From there, they marched into London and briefly seized control of the city. Mayhem, pillaging, and murder followed. As a result, most rebels disassociated themselves from Aylmer. The army collapsed. The king pardoned all who took part in the uprising. Nevertheless, Aylmer was killed by the Sheriff of Kent.

Some historians conclude that the rebel leader was an opportunist who was motivated by his need for personal glorification (Miller 2003). Nonetheless, it is clear that the imposter took advantage of England's economic conditions and political climate for reasons that have been lost to history. Although Aylmer's attempt to oust the king failed miserably, he achieved notoriety; William Shakespeare preserved the rebel's exploits in the play *Henry VI* by basing one of the characters upon him (Ross 2001).

Sarah Wilson in Colonial America

At times, identity theft is committed to escape an unpleasant situation and to avoid one's obligations. One documented case in early American history demonstrates how an indentured servant, motivated by her desire for a lavish lifestyle, used identity theft to escape servitude and begin a new life. Sarah Wilson was born in 1754 in the county of Staffordshire, England (Haughton 2002). At the age of 16, she left home, went to London, and secured employment as a maid to Caroline Vernon, lady-in-waiting to Queen Charlotte, the wife of King George III. However, Sarah was caught stealing the queen's personal belongings and was sentenced to death. Vernon, lady-in-waiting, liked Sarah and begged that her life be spared, thus her sentence was reduced to transportation to the colonies.

Sarah, designated as an indentured servant, arrived in Baltimore, Maryland in 1771 aboard a prison ship (Haughton 2002). She was sold to a Virginia plantation owner, Mr. Devall, who took

Sarah to work on his estate. Much to her owner's chagrin, she ran away. Sarah fabricated a new identity for herself, and resurfaced as Princess Susanna Caroline Matilda. She pretended to be the sister of Queen Charlotte. Sarah dressed as if she was a princess, as she somehow had managed to steal a dress and ring from the queen and smuggle them across the ocean. By sharing intimate details about the royal family, Sarah convinced many Virginia aristocrats of her noble heritage, and they lavished her with money and gifts.

While Sarah was fashioning a new life for herself, Devall wanted her back (Haughton 2002). He circulated advertisements debunking Sarah's claim of royalty, identifying her as a servant, and offering a reward for her return. Eventually, she was found and brought back to the plantation. When Devall left to fight in the Revolutionary War, Sarah seized upon the opportunity to escape again. She was too well-known in Virginia to travel there, so she fled north. This time, she assumed the identity of a real person, an indentured servant who had recently arrived in Maryland. Both women shared the same name, Sarah Wilson.

Sarah traveled to New York where she met and married a British Army officer. After the Revolutionary War ended, Sarah's husband opened a business financed with the money Sarah had stolen from the Virginia aristocrats during her masquerade as Princess Susanna. Sarah lived the remainder of her life in the style that she had longed for since her youth.

Czar Nicholas II and His Family

From time to time, the identities of deceased persons are stolen. In one fascinating case, identity theft was committed to achieve fame and to obtain the rights to an alleged fortune. Russian Czar Nicholas II was overthrown in a coup in 1917 (Lyzhina 2004). He, his immediate family, their doctor, and household servants were executed by the Bolshevik police in 1918, but rumors immediately spread throughout the world that some of his children had escaped death. Over the next several decades, numerous men and women claimed to be the children and grandchildren of Nicholas II.

The youngest daughter of the czar, Anastasia Nikolayevna Romanova, was imitated most often. Her most convincing imposter emerged in 1920 (Lyzhina 2004). The story began with an apparent suicide attempt when a woman jumped off of a bridge in

Berlin. She was rescued by a patrolman and taken to a mental institution, where she told the doctor that her name was Anastasia. German authorities were skeptical so they issued identification documents to her bearing the name of Anna Anderson.

The incident was reported around the world, and as a result, many friends and relatives of the czar's family traveled to Germany to interview Anna (Lyzhina 2004). Some were convinced she was, indeed, Anastasia, but others were adamant that she was an imposter. The Romanov relatives tried to settle the matter once and for all in 1927 when they declared that Anna Anderson was not Anastasia. Anna tried repeatedly over the years to prove in a court of law that she was Anastasia. Her last effort was in 1970. The court did not find enough evidence to confirm or refute her identity. Fourteen years later, Anna died in the United States.

When a mass grave was unearthed in Russia in 1991, the decades-old mystery finally seemed to be solved (Gill et al. 1994). The grave contained the skeletal remains of nine people; DNA testing identified them as those of Nicholas II, his wife, three of their five children, their physician, and three of their servants. Further testing showed that Anna Anderson was not related to the royal family. She was simply an imposter (CRF 1997). Despite the DNA evidence, debate continues today over the identity of Anna Anderson and she and her case have been the subject of many books, movies, plays, and documentaries.

The Great Imposter

In the previous examples, identities were assumed based upon the imposters' ability to imitate their victims' behaviors, clothing, and so forth. By the 20th century, the creation of and reliance upon identification documents lead to changes in how identity theft was committed. Forged, stolen, and fictitious identification documents became the instruments for perpetrating identity theft. One well-known case is the subject of the book and movie, *The Great Imposter*, which is based upon the life of Ferdinand Waldo Demara, Jr. (Lawrence Public Library n.d.).

Demara was born in Massachusetts in 1921 (Lawrence Public Library n.d.). He dropped out of high school, ran away from home, and joined a monastery (Time 1951). A few years later, Demara abandoned his career as a monk and subsequently held many prestigious positions. He posed as a college instructor, doctor, hospital orderly, and school teacher, but Demara eventually began living as a monk again, this time joining a monastery in Canada (Peate n.d.). It was there where he met and befriended a surgeon, Dr. Joseph Cyr. Unbeknownst to the surgeon, Demara stole Cyr's medical credentials. In March 1951, Demara joined the Royal Canadian Navy posing as Dr. Cyr and was assigned to a ship that was stationed in the midst of the Korean conflict. Even though he had no formal medical training, Demara performed many successful surgeries while onboard (Lawrence Public Library n.d.).

Cyr's mother discovered the fraud when she was reading a story in the newspaper about the doctor's heroic wartime surgical accomplishments and noticed that the picture in the paper was not her son (Peate n.d.). She contacted her son who, in turn, contacted the Royal Canadian Mounted Police. Demara was immediately discharged from the Navy and deported. He returned to the United States where he continued his career of deception (Lawrence Public Library n.d.). Demara's identities included a zoologist, law enforcement officer, scholar, medical researcher, hospital orderly, and school teacher. He was arrested several times over the years for fraud, embezzlement, theft, and forgery, but was not deterred. By his own admission, he did not choose a life of deception for financial gain. Rather, he enjoyed the challenge and expressed his motive as unadulterated mischief.

The Most Misused Social Security Number in History

The advent of Social Security numbers brought about a new type of identity theft. On August 14, 1935, President Franklin D. Roosevelt signed the Social Security Act into law (SSA 2003). At the time, the United States was suffering from the worst economic crisis in history, the Great Depression. The purpose of the act was to help restore economic security and to ensure stability in the future. For record-keeping purposes, the Social Security numbering (SSN) system was developed, and the first Social Security card was issued in November 1936 (SSA n.d.-a). By the end of 1937, about 30 million people had been assigned SSNs (SSA 2005). The program was still in its infancy when an incident foretold how vulnerable SSNs were to being grossly misused.

The E. H. Ferree Company manufactured and distributed wallets to department stores across the United States (SSA n.d.-b). In 1938, the company launched a campaign to market a unique feature of their product, a small slot made specifically to hold a

Social Security card. For demonstration purposes, a sample card was placed in every wallet. The SSN on the card, however, was an actual number that belonged to Hilda Schrader Whitcher, a secretary for E. H. Ferree Company. By 1943, nearly 5,800 people were using Whitcher's number as their own. The Social Security Administration (SSA) cancelled the number and issued Whitcher a new one. Despite these efforts, the number continued to be misused over the next 40 years by more than 40,000 people.

In retrospect, the incident predicted the risks surrounding the use of SSNs as identifiers, but the warning signs went unheeded. SSNs soon became identifiers for employees, taxpayers, patients, and military personnel (SSA 2005). The problems became even more apparent by 1971 when a report was issued by a SSA task force. It recommended that the SSA refrain from encouraging the use of SSNs for identification purposes. Unfortunately, it was too late. SSNs were already being widely used and misused as identifiers in the public and private sectors.

The Chicago Debacle

The introduction of credit cards spurred another new type of identity theft. The first credit cards were issued in the 1920s by gasoline companies, department stores, restaurants, and hotels (Jabaily 2004). Each establishment had their own credit card, which meant that a person had to carry several different cards. The Diners Club issued the first versatile credit card in 1950. It could be used at any restaurant or hotel that was a member of the Diners Club network. Franklin National Bank was the first bank to offer a credit card that could be used to charge purchases at any establishment located anywhere in the nation. A few years later, Bank of America introduced a multipurpose credit card. In 1958, the bank mailed out nearly 60,000 unsolicited cards to people living in Fresno, California (Stein n.d.). Recipients could use the cards right away, as no action was required to activate the cards. The marketing ploy was so successful that it triggered fierce competition among the banks. It culminated in *the Chicago Debacle*.

Prior to the 1966 holiday shopping season, several banks mailed 5 million unsolicited credit cards to addresses in the Chicago area (O'Neil 1970). The banks were immediately swamped with complaints. Individuals who never received the credit cards received bills for purchases they did not make; furthermore, children and pets received cards in their names. Credit cards were mailed to convicted felons who went on shopping sprees and then failed to pay their bills. Many credit cards were stolen out of mailboxes, and postal workers were accused of stealing the cards and selling them. Eventually, organized criminal enterprises got involved in the credit card fraud business. Consumers were outraged (Stein n.d.). Many citizens and legislators advocated banning credit cards altogether. Congressional hearings ensued, but the controversy subsided over the next few years. By 1978, credit cards were commonplace in American households.

The First Documented Multinational Internet Bank Robbery

Identity theft existed long before computers, the Internet, or the World Wide Web. However, one of the most drastic changes in the history of identity theft coincided with the technological developments of the 1990s. Between 1992 and 1995, technology made it possible for financial institutions to offer their services online, and databases became a necessity for managing the exchange of massive amounts of personal information. As technology evolved, criminals devised new methods to exploit its weaknesses. Breaches occurred at the same time financial institutions were trying to persuade customers to conduct their banking transactions online, but one incident eroded customer confidence to the point that the future of online banking was in jeopardy. It involved an international ring which exploited technological weaknesses and resulted in one of the largest known online bank robberies in history.

Vladimir Levin, a 1971 graduate of Tekhnologichesky University, lived and worked in St. Petersburg, Russia (Smart Computing n.d.). At age 23, he discovered a flaw in Citibank's online security that allowed him to transfer money from Citibank's customer accounts to his personal account in Finland. Recognizing the potential for great wealth, Levin recruited several accomplices to help him rob the bank. In July 1994, members of the ring used stolen usernames and passwords to log onto Citibank's computer network and quickly transfer millions of dollars to financial institutions located around the world. In August, bank officials noticed two suspicious wire transfers totaling about $400,000 and reported it to the FBI. With the help of Russian authorities, the FBI traced the activities to Levin's home. Since no extradition agreement pertaining to electronic crimes existed between Russia and the United States, Levin could not be brought to the United States to stand trial, so authorities watched his every move and waited for the opportunity to bring him to justice.

On March 3, 1995, an Interpol agent arrested Levin as he got off of a plane in the United Kingdom (House of Lords 1997). He was extradited to United States to face charges of stealing nearly $12 million (Smart Computing n.d.). Through a plea agreement, Levin pled guilty to stealing a lesser amount of $3.7 million and was sentenced to three years in prison and ordered to pay $240,000 in restitution to Citibank. Although bank customers may have been inconvenienced, they did not experience any direct monetary losses due to the breach.

This was the first time that a breach of this magnitude was publicly acknowledged by a financial institution. However, it may not have been the very first Internet bank robbery. Up until that time, most financial institutions were reluctant to report breaches to law enforcement authorities, their customers, or the media for two main reasons: the publicity could result in a loss of customers or stop customers from entering into online transactions and they feared that the publicity might encourage criminals to compromise databases for the sake of notoriety (Golden 1999).

This incident, in conjunction with others, reinforced many known shortcomings and brought new security issues to light. Although financial institutions were concerned about protecting themselves and their customers from network intrusions, only a small portion of their budgets was allocated to information technology (IT) security (Golden 1999). The long-held belief that insiders, those within organizations, were responsible for the thefts of proprietary information was no longer accurate. Outsiders also posed a threat. Identity theft had evolved into a global crime facilitated by the exploitation of technology.

An Early Case of Credit Card Fraud

During the 1990s, retailers embraced the migration of their businesses to the World Wide Web. This offered convenience to current customers and served as a platform for attracting new ones. Many merchants found that a brick and mortar storefront was no longer necessary. Instead, businesses operated solely on the World Wide Web, but business owners and their customers were confronted with the same issues as those experienced by the financial industry. As e-commerce exploded, security breaches did too. Many of the breaches resulted in credit card fraud, a type of identity theft. As merchants lured customers to their Web sites, an incident occurred that threatened the future of e-commerce.

On March 28, 1997, employees of an Internet service provider (ISP) found suspicious software on one of their servers; the software was designed to steal usernames and passwords (Cryptome JYA Archives 1997). As the employees worked to secure the server, they noticed that the hacker was logged onto the server and in the midst of erasing traces of the intrusion. Also logged onto the server was one of the ISP's legitimate customers. The customer, identified as "C. W." in court documents, was chatting with "Smak," the trespasser. Smak told C. W. that he had hacked into the server and stolen all of the credit card numbers used on an e-commerce site. He offered to sell them to C. W. Smak bragged that he also had another 60,000 credit card numbers that he had stolen from various sources and offered to them to C. W. as well.

With the help of C. W., the FBI launched an investigation (Cryptome JYA Archives 1997). C. W. purchased 710 valid credit card numbers from Smak and later purchased 580 more. When Smak offered to sell an encrypted CD containing over 100,000 stolen credit card numbers, C. W. expressed interest. They met at San Francisco International Airport to finalize the deal, but instead of leaving the airport a wealthy man, 36 year-old Carlos Felipe Salgado, Jr., aka Smak, was arrested. He chose to enter guilty pleas to four federal charges rather than face a trial. Salgado pled guilty to unauthorized access of a computer in furtherance of fraud, unauthorized access of a computer causing damage, trafficking in stolen credit card numbers, and possessing more than 15 stolen credit card numbers with intent to defraud.

This incident was highly publicized, but unlike the banking breach, the names of the ISP and the merchants were never revealed. Consumer advocates voiced their disdain concerning nondisclosure practices. Adding insult to injury, the ISP and the merchants were referred to as "victims" in the court documents. The individuals whose credit card accounts were compromised knew something that no one seemed willing to acknowledge— they were victims, too. Identity thieves learned many lessons from this case and similar ones throughout the 1990s. They no longer had to rummage through dumpsters or purchase identities from insiders; the crime can be committed online, and software could now perform some of the tasks needed to facilitate it (i.e., stealing usernames and passwords). Hardware and software allow identities to be stored in many locations, such as on a CD or in a database. In conclusion, there are many ways to exploit technology, and technology is now firmly established as part of the process of stealing, buying, selling, trading, or giving away proprietary information.

The First Internet Murder

Some crimes are committed online, while others are committed offline but involve the use of online resources. A 1999 case, dubbed "the Internet Murder," shocked the United States as it was the first case of offline stalking and murder involving the online purchase of personal information (Wright 2000). Liam Youens was obsessed with Amy Boyer, and maintained several Web sites where he chronicled his fixation and plotted her murder.

There is no indication that Liam and Amy were friends or that they ever had a conversation (AmyBoyer.org 2004). He wrote on his Web site that they were in the same church group while in the 8th grade, but it appears that his obsession began when they were in a 10th grade algebra class together. After graduating from high school in 1997, Liam left his hometown to attend college in Rochester, New York (Wright 2000). He stalked Amy when he was home on breaks from school. After one year, Liam dropped out of college and returned home to live with his mother. Shortly thereafter, he was convicted of domestic violence upon his mother. In spite of the conviction, Liam was able to purchase several guns and ammunition, and he continued to write about Amy on his Web site (AmyBoyer.org 2004). At one point, he thought he had lost track of her, so he purchased a background check from an online firm, 1-800 US Search. It confirmed Amy still lived at home, but Liam wanted to know where she worked. He was ecstatic about the information he bought from another online information broker, Docusearch. Liam purchased her SSN, the name of her employer, and her employer's address. On October 15, 1999, he made his last Web site entry and then got into his car and drove to where 20-year-old Amy was employed (Wright 2000). He waited in his car for her to leave work, and when she got into her car, Liam pulled up to the driver's side and shot her numerous times before shooting and killing himself.

Two days after her death, Amy was victimized again when she became a victim of identity theft (AmyBoyer.org 2004). Her loved ones were devastated, outraged, and frustrated. Prior to the murder, Amy's purse had been stolen. It contained checks, a credit card, and her Social Security card. Amy reported the theft to the police, cancelled her credit card, and put a stop payment on the checks. When her murder was reported in the news, the thieves took advantage of the situation. They manufactured a driver's license in her name and used the information to make fraudulent credit card purchases. They also cashed nearly $5,000 in counterfeit checks in her name.

Amy's mother sued Docusearch. Almost four years after Amy's murder, the Supreme Court of New Hampshire issued their findings (*Helen Remsburg v. Docusearch*). The court ruled that, when an information broker or private investigator receives a request from a client for a third party's personal information, the identity of the client and the purpose of the request must be determined before selling the information. The court also ruled that an information broker or private investigator is intruding upon a person's privacy if they obtain and sell his or her SSN, without permission, to a client. Docusearch settled the lawsuit by agreeing to pay $85,000 to Amy's estate, however the heinous crime brought to the forefront the privacy, legal, moral, and ethical issues surrounding the role of technology, including online data brokers, in supporting criminal activities (Ramer 2004). These same issues are still debated today.

History is replete with incidences of identity theft. Although only a few are cited here, they provide a brief profile of the people who commit this crime. Identity theft, however, cannot be prevented unless the characteristics of the perpetrators, motive, and modus operandi are addressed.

Who Are the Perpetrators?

Information regarding the perpetrators of identity theft is limited because most research focuses on victims of the crime. This section reviews existing data in order to better understand who commits identity theft and why and how they commit it. Motives explain why individuals commit crimes and are the underlying needs that compel an individual to act in a manner that will satisfy those needs (Casey 2001). The underlying needs may be material, emotional, and/or psychological. Historically, the motives for committing crimes have not changed.

In contrast, the modus operandi change and evolve over time (Casey 2001). A modus operandi (MO) refers to how individuals commit crimes. They are the actions taken by perpetrators to ensure that the crime can be carried out successfully, to guarantee they will not be caught during the act(s) of preparing for and committing the crime, and to avoid being identified as the person who committed the crime. Given that MOs change and evolve over time, further discussion of those methods most commonly used to obtain identifying information is presented in chapter 2, but the following case illustrates why and how one woman committed identity theft.

According to reports, a background check would have revealed that Shovana Sloan was on probation and had a history of identity theft and fraud-related convictions at the time she applied for a job through a temporary employment agency (Seal 2006b). The agency placed Sloan in the billing department of a hospital in Manassas, Virginia. She was given access to the patients' personal identifying information in order to perform her job's tasks. In 2003, she stole and used the SSN of a patient named Susanne Sloane (*Suzanne Sloane v. Equifax Information Services*). For months, Sloan pretended to be Suzanne and incurred over $30,000 of fraudulent debt in her victim's name.

Sloan was arrested in March 2004 (Seal 2006a). Her written confession reveals not only her motives for committing identity theft but also her methods. Since she had unfettered access to the identities of many patients, one might wonder how she chose her victim. She explained that she stole Suzanne's identity because their names were similar. Perpetrators often choose a victim with a similar or the same name to minimize the risk of slipping up and getting caught. Sloan also admitted that she needed assistance with reestablishing her financial stability and to afford the lifestyle she wanted. She understood that it was highly unlikely that a recently released convicted felon could obtain over $30,000 of credit in her own name.

Sloan was convicted once again and sentenced to prison (Virginia Department of Corrections). One question remains unanswered: did Sloan accept the job at the hospital intending to steal identities, or did she take advantage of an opportunity that presented itself to her?

Opportunity Takers or Makers

A typology developed by Robert Morris II at Sam Houston University in Huntsville, Texas, suggests that identity thieves take advantage of opportunities that are present or create opportunities when none exist (Morris 2004). In the exploratory research titled "The Development of an Identity Theft Offender Typology: A Theoretical Approach" and published in *The Graduate Research Journal*, Morris divides identity thieves into four major categories: the circumstantial identity thief, the semi-pro, the professional, and the survivalist.

The first category, the circumstantial identity thief, is the starting point for most identity thieves (Morris 2004). Several circumstances must exist in unison for the crime to take place. The offender must be presented with an opportunity to perpetrate the crime, such as finding a wallet containing a credit card. Then, he must have an opportunity to use the card. For example, the offender might be a clerk at a store where he can process credit card transactions. It is important to note that under different circumstances the offenders, such as the clerk, may not commit identity theft. If they do, it could be limited to one incident. On the other hand, offenders who continue to perpetrate identity theft progress to the next category.

The semi-pro identity thief learns new techniques from each experience (Morris 2004). They find that the incentives for committing identity theft outweigh the incentives for not committing the crime and that the financial and nonfinancial benefits are substantial because identity theft is easy to commit and there is little chance of apprehension by law enforcement. Perpetrators in this category do not wait for opportunities to arise; instead, they intentionally engage new methods for acquiring and using stolen personal identifying information. Offenders tend to commit the crime with more and more frequency as time passes. For example, offenders in this category may recruit others to steal personal information from their workplaces. As the offender finds new ways to use the information, the recruits are called upon to steal more and more frequently. The offender might also develop a network of customers to purchase stolen information. Unsold information is used in new ways such as opening utilities, telephone, and cell phone accounts. After a while, the perpetrator acquires the skills, methods, and knowledge needed to advance to the next category.

The professional identity thief may regard identity theft as an occupation (Morris 2004). Offenders in this category utilize a vast array of methods, ranging from stealing mail to hacking databases, to obtain personal information. They are adept at hiding their true identities. In order to remain invisible for long periods of time, some professional identity thieves completely take over the identities of other people and often enlist others, called co-op identity thieves, as partners in carrying out the crimes.

The last category is the survivalist identity thief (Morris 2004). Those in this category jeopardize the safety and security of U.S. citizens and law enforcement personnel. The survivalist may hide behind another person's identity to avoid being arrested. He may be a suspect in a criminal case or an escapee from jail. If a survivalist is arrested, he may use another person's information to conceal his true identity and may even resort to violence in order to keep his true identity concealed. Terrorists are also classified as survivalist identity thieves. They may be in the United States illegally, and their purpose for utilizing identity theft is often to conceal their identities as they plan or carry out terrorist acts with the intent to kill or injure others.

The research typology outlined here is useful for understanding the differences between a one-time offender and a terrorist who perpetrates identity theft. Nonetheless, other personal characteristics, such as age and gender, must also be taken into consideration when building a comprehensive profile of an identity thief.

Gender

Existing research can help to ascertain if there is a link between certain demographic characteristics and the likelihood of committing crime. Statistics demonstrate, for instance, that one gender is more likely to carry out a crime than the other. The "Sourcebook of Criminal Justice Statistics" contains information derived from over 100 criminal justice sources (Pastore and Maguire n.d.). Even though it does not contain statistics explicitly for identity theft offenders, it provides the gender of persons arrested and charged with all types of crimes. According to the statistics, more males than females are arrested and charged with committing crimes. From 2002 through 2006, 76.5 percent of all arrestees were male; only 23.5 percent were female. Given these statistics, one would expect available research to confirm that more males than females commit identity theft. Interestingly, research results are mixed. Two studies found that more males than females commit identity theft; yet a third study shows more females commit identity theft.

The most recent study, "Identity Fraud Trends and Patterns: Building a Data-Based Foundation for Proactive Enforcement," was conducted at Utica College's Center for Identity Management and Information Protection (CIMIP) in Utica, New York (Gordon et al. 2007). The results of the research were released in October 2007 at a conference held by the Economic Crime Institute of Utica College. Researchers analyzed 517 cases that were investigated by the United States Secret Service (USSS) from 2000 through 2006. The study found that 67.4 percent of identity theft perpetrators were male.

Exploratory research conducted by the Identity Theft Partnerships in Prevention, an outreach initiative at Michigan State University (MSU), School of Criminal Justice in East Lansing, Michigan, showed similar findings. The unpublished study, "Identity Theft: Predator Profiles," ascertained that 64 percent of identity thieves were male (Collins and Hoffman 2004). The study examined randomly selected reports of arrests or convictions of 1,037 perpetrators from 1999 to mid-April 2002. The data were retrieved from the Web sites of state, local, and federal law enforcement agencies, other government entities, and media reports.

The third study, "Exploring the Crime of Identity Theft: Prevalence, Clearance Rates, and Victim/Offender Characteristics," used a case study approach. It was conducted by researchers at the University of South Florida (USF) who used information collected from a sizeable police agency for cases that resulted in an arrest (Allison et al. 2005). This analysis found that females were more likely to commit identity theft than males. Of the 52 offenders in the study, 63 percent were female.

Given the differences in the methodologies of the three studies, more research is needed to determine if, indeed, gender plays a significant role in the commission of identity theft. However, there may be other factors that contribute to the statistical differences such as where the cases originated. The data used in the Utica College study were collected from a federal agency, while the data used in the USF study were collected from a police department. Cases investigated by the USSS are generally referred to them by state and local law enforcement agencies located across the United States and must meet stringent USSS thresholds. The cases in the USF study are concentrated in specific area of one state.

Available research also suggests that while females commit fewer crimes than males, females commit identity theft more often than most other types of crimes. The research conducted at Utica College found that 32.6 percent of offenders were female (Gordon et al. 2007). "Identity Theft: Predator Profiles," a study done at MSU, concluded that 36 percent of perpetrators were female (Collins and Hoffman 2004). Both studies indicate that more females commit identity theft as compared to overall crimes attributed to women. According to the "Sourcebook of Criminal Justice Statistics," females accounted for 23.5 percent of those arrested and charged with crimes in general from 2002 through 2006 (Pastore and Maguire n.d.). The study conducted at Utica College shows that the number of females committing identity theft is 9.1 percent higher than the overall crime rate for women, 32.6 percent compared to 23.5 percent; while MSU's numbers exceed the overall crime rate by 12.5 percent. Hence, research indicates that females commit identity theft more frequently than all other crimes in general.

The findings of the Utica College and MSU research are substantiated in a report released by the U.S. Department of Justice, Bureau of Justice Statistics. The report, "Women Offenders," does not provide specific identity theft conviction statistics (Greenfeld and Snell 1999). However, property offenses such as burglary, larceny, and fraud are discussed. Stolen identities are often an element of many types of fraud, including forgery and embezzlement (U.S. Congress 2002). "Women Offenders" suggests that more females were convicted in state courts of property felonies than violent and drug felonies between 1990 and 1996 (Greenfeld and Snell 1999). Within the category of property felonies, the number of females convicted of fraud rose 55 percent (Greenfeld and Snell 1999). The statistics for one year, 1996, show that women made up 41 percent of the felons convicted of fraud, forgery, and embezzlement.

Identity theft is considered not only fraud but also a white-collar crime. Although the definition of white-collar crime has been debated since the late 1940s, it is widely accepted that it occurs when an individual or entity violates a position of trust or responsibility and the violation results in personal gains or benefits a particular organization (Helmkamp et al. 1996). White-collar crime statistics, therefore, must be taken into account when determining the role of gender in identity theft.

A report issued by the National White Collar Crime Center (NW3C), "White Collar Crime Statistics," contains detailed data on arrests and case dispositions from 1990 to 2005 (NW3C 2007).

White-collar crimes are divided into three categories: fraud, forgery/counterfeiting, and embezzlement. In the report, the fraud category is divided into 18 types of offenses: tax; financial institutions; securities and exchange; mail; wire, radio, or television; bankruptcy; Social Security; false impersonation; citizenship and naturalization; passport; identification documents and information; false claims and services–government; false statements; conspiracy to defraud the United States; unauthorized access devices; computer; health care; and other. Arrestees are delineated by gender as well as by the category and type of white-collar crime associated with the arrests.

According to the report, there were 182,752 fraud arrests in 1990 compared to 231,721 in 2005 (NW3C 2007). Males accounted for over half of the arrests in both 1990 (54%) and 2005 (55%). Forgery/counterfeiting arrests totaled 50,403 in 1990 and 87,346 in 2005. In 1990, 64 percent of the arrestees were men. That number declined to 60 percent in 2005. Conversely, the number of women arrested for forgery/counterfeiting increased 4 percent between 1999 and 2005 from 36 percent to 40 percent. There were 7,708 embezzlement arrests in 1990 compared to 14,097 arrests in 2005. Nearly 60 percent (58%) of the arrestees in 1990 were male compared to 50 percent in 2005. In other words, females were arrested for embezzling at the exact same rate as males in 2005. The report clearly shows that although more males are arrested for white-collar crimes, arrests among females have risen over the 16-year period. The only category representing a decline in women arrestees is in the category of fraud. The number of arrestees decreased from 46 percent in 1990 to 45 percent in 2005.

It is important to note that although identity theft is a white-collar crime, not all white-collar crimes are identity theft or even involve identity theft at all. Perjury, lying under oath in a legal proceeding, is an example of a white-collar crime that is not identity theft. However, the 18 types of fraud offenses recognized in the report, "White Collar Crime Statistics," are very similar to the identity theft fraud offenses that are tracked by the Federal Trade Commission (FTC). Complaints of identity theft are collected by the FTC from victims of the crime. The complaints are classified by the type of fraud reported by the victims, that is, credit card, government documents or benefits, employment-related, phone or utilities, bank, loan, other, and attempted identity theft.

In summation, research suggests that gender plays a role in the likelihood of committing identity theft. More research, however, is warranted to determine if males tend to commit identity theft more often than females and if females commit identity theft more frequently than other types of crimes.

Age

Research indicates that age is a factor in identity theft as well as in other crimes. The "Sourcebook of Criminal Justice Statistics" contains data on the ages of individuals at the time they were arrested (Pastore and Maguire n.d.). It suggests that the number of arrests tends to decrease as the age of the perpetrators increases. In 2002, 5.2 percent of all arrestees were 14 years old and younger. The largest number of arrests (41.2%) occurred in the 15- to 24-year-old age group. There were fewer arrests (12.3%) in the next age group, 25- through 29-year-olds, and even fewer (10.9%) persons aged 30 to 34 years. Arrests declined to 10.4 percent in the 35- to 39-year-old age group. There was a substantial decrease in the age group of 40- to 44-year-olds, which accounted for 8.9 percent of the overall arrests. Arrestees in the 45- to 49-year-old age group fell to 5.5 percent. Those in the 50- to 54-year-old age group dropped to 2.9 percent. The number of arrests in the remaining age groups also declined, that is, 55- to 59-year-olds (1.4%), 60- to 64-year-olds (0.6%), and 65-year-olds and older (0.6%). As the groups advanced in age, the number of arrests declined significantly. However, the relationship of age to perpetrators when it comes to identity theft seems to differ from the pattern as it relates to crime in general, and research suggests that the aging-out process does not pertain to identity theft offenders. Essentially, perpetrators may begin committing identity theft at an older age and continue it later in life as compared to other types of crime.

In the study conducted at MSU, "Identity Theft: Predator Profiles," identity thieves ranged in age from 17 to 67 years , and 20 percent of those arrested or convicted were between 17 and 24 years (Collins and Hoffman 2004). However, most of the offenders (43%) were in the 25- to 34-years-old age group. One third (33%) were 35 to 49 years old. Fourteen percent of the offenders were between 50 and 67 years old.

The results of the study conducted at Utica College, "Identity Fraud Trends and Patterns: Building a Data-based Foundation for Proactive Enforcement," were similar. This study found that perpetrators ranged in age from 18 years to 65 years and older

(Gordon et al. 2007). About 19 percent of the offenders were between the ages of 18 and 24 years old. The 25- to 34-year-old age group represented the highest number of offenders (42.5%). One third (33%)of the offenders were 35 to 49 years old. A significant decline was seen in the 50- to 64-year-olds (5.1%), and the numbers continue to decrease among those age 65 and older (0.09%).

A study from USF, "Exploring the Crime of Identity Theft: Prevalence, Clearance Rates, and Victim/Offender Characteristics," found a slightly older age range for offenders, but followed the same pattern as the previous two studies. In this study, the age of offenders ranged from 28 to 49 years of age, and the mean, or average, age of the perpetrators was 32 years old (Allison et al. 2005).

In sum, research suggests that perpetrators begin committing identity theft at an older age and continue committing the crime later in life when compared to overall crimes in general. Those 15 to 24 years old constitute the majority of arrests for crimes in general; however, this age group is not the largest for identity thieves; rather, most identity thieves are between the ages of 25 and 34. Arrests for all crimes in general begin to decline significantly with the 25 to 29 age group; whereas the most active identity thieves encompass and surpass these ages.

Ethnicity

Very little research is available regarding the ethnic background of identity thieves. According to the "Sourcebook of Criminal Justice Statistics," the majority (69.7%) of those arrested in 2006 for crimes in general were Caucasian (Pastore and Maguire n.d.). Arrests among the Hispanic population are included in this figure. African American arrestees accounted for less than a third (28%) of all those arrested that year. The remainder included American Indians and Alaskan Natives (1.3%) and Asian or Pacific Islanders (1.1%). These numbers are consistent when compared to statistical data for those arrested for fraud. The ethnicity of persons charged with fraud offenses was comprised of 68.7 percent Caucasian, 30 percent African Americans, 0.6 percent American Indians and Alaskan Natives, and 0.7 percent Asian or Pacific Islanders. In contrast, the results of two identity theft studies differ from these statistics.

The study done at USF, "Exploring the Crime of Identity Theft: Prevalence, Clearance Rates, and Victim/Offender Characteristics," concluded that only 27 percent of the offenders were Caucasian, while 69 percent were African American (Allison et al. 2005). Furthermore, Asians and Hispanics each comprised only 1 percent of the offenders. The study also pointed out that Hispanics were underrepresented in the numbers of perpetrators, as they comprised 19 percent of the city's overall population where the research was conducted.

The research done at Utica College, "Identity Fraud Trends and Patterns: Building a Data-based Foundation for Proactive Enforcement," found that over half (53.8%) of the identity theft offenders were African American (Gordon et al. 2007). Caucasian (38.3%) and Hispanic (4.8%) defendants accounted for 43.1 percent of the perpetrators, and Asians made up 3.1 percent of identity theft offenders. None of the defendants were classified as American Indian or Alaskan Native. When compared to the 2006 data in the "Sourcebook of Criminal Justice Statistics" for all fraud arrests, an obvious disparity emerges. The number of Asian defendants (3.1%) in the study was over four times more than the number arrested for fraud in general (0.7%), as indicated by the "Sourcebook of Criminal Justice Statistics." In the study, Caucasian offenders were 26.2 percent scarcer than the number of total fraud arrests among the Caucasian and American Indian or Alaskan Native ethic groups combined (i.e., 43.1%, compared to 69.3%, respectively). Conversely, African American offenders (53.8%) greatly exceeded the number of those arrested for fraud offenses in general (30%).

It is interesting to note that two studies indicate that there is a correlation between the ethnicity and gender of those who commit identity theft. According to the research conducted at Utica College, more African American females (61.6%) commit identity theft than Caucasian females (30.8%), Asian females (2.9%), or Hispanic females (4.7%) (Gordon et al. 2007). The study conducted at USF found that identity thieves are most likely to be African American females (Allison et al. 2005). Still, more research is needed to establish if ethnicity is a factor in determining the likelihood of committing identity theft. Moreover, further research is needed to ascertain if there is a correlation between gender, ethnicity, and identity theft.

Criminal History

Law enforcement agencies nationwide have noticed a steady rise in identity theft committed by offenders with prior criminal histories (White House 2006). Additionally, many of the offenders have an extensive record of major crimes such as drug offenses. The study, "Identity Fraud Trends and Patterns: Building a Data-Based Foundation for Proactive Enforcement," found that 29.9 percent of identity theft offenders had prior criminal histories (Gordon et al. 2007). Of those, the most common offense was larceny/theft (26.6%) followed by fraud (15%), forgery (12.8%), violent crimes (12.6%), and drug offenses (9.4%). Over 5 percent (5.4%) had identity theft offenses on their records. A few offenders had prior criminal histories of terrorism (2.2%) and immigration violations (2%).

Another study, "Identity Theft: Predator Profiles," found that 13.9 percent of the perpetrators had prior identity theft convictions (Collins and Hoffman 2004). The study, however, did not take into account prior arrests or convictions for other crimes. Even so, both studies indicate that the majority of offenders have no prior criminal record of identity theft convictions. Since very little research is available in this area, more research is needed to determine if, indeed, most identities thieves do not have criminal histories at the time they are arrested or convicted of identity theft.

Country of Origin

Research indicates that the majority of U.S. identity theft offenders are born in the United States. The study, "Identity Fraud Trends and Patterns: Building a Data-Based Foundation for Proactive Enforcement," found that 75.9 percent were born in the United States (Gordon et al. 2007). Excluding the United States, the most often reported countries of origin were Mexico, Nigeria, the United Kingdom, Cuba, and Israel. The study, "Identity Theft: Predator Profiles," found that only 9 percent of those arrested or convicted were either illegal immigrants or foreign nationals, however offenders' countries of birth were not provided in the study (Collins and Hoffman 2004).

Since the study, "Identity Fraud Trends and Patterns: Building a Data-Based Foundation for Proactive Enforcement," found that nearly a quarter of the offenders were born outside of the United States, more research is recommended in this area. Nonetheless, both studies seem to indicate that the majority of identity thieves in the United States are U.S. citizens.

Affiliation with Other Crimes

Identity theft is often used to facilitate other crimes, both violent and nonviolent, and stolen identities are used to conceal criminals' and terrorists' true identities to help them avoid detection by law enforcement authorities. Identities are used to purchase services, such as cell phones, needed to carry out all types of crimes. Cash obtained by identity theft is used to purchase drugs and finance terrorist acts. Sometimes, the merchandise procured by identity thieves is sold to raise funds for these purposes.

The "Identity Theft: Predator Profiles" study found that, at the time of their arrest, 30 percent of perpetrators were charged with other crimes in addition to identity theft (Collins and Hoffman 2004). Fifteen percent were charged with violent crimes such as homicide or assault; another 15 percent were charged with drug-related offenses. On the other hand, "Identity Fraud Trends and Patterns: Building a Data-Based Foundation for Proactive Enforcement" discovered notably lower numbers (Gordon et al. 2007). According to that study, drug possession and drug trafficking combined accounted for 1.9 percent of offenses facilitated by identity theft; about 1 percent (0.9%) of the offenses involved weapons. Given the disparity between these findings, additional research is needed to determine the frequency and types of crimes that are facilitated by identity theft.

Affiliation with Other Criminals

Nationwide, law enforcement agencies have reported a continuous rise in identity thefts attributed to motorcycle clubs, terrorist groups, street gangs, and organized criminal enterprises (President's Identity Theft Task Force 2007). Although the structure of these organizations ranges from loosely knit to highly organized, there is evidence that identity theft often involves more than one individual. "Identity Theft: Predator Profiles," the research conducted at MSU, found that the majority (60%) of identity theft cases involved a network (Collins and Hoffman 2004). For clarification, a network is defined as two or more individuals working together to perpetrate a crime. Since the study was conducted shortly after the 2001 terrorist attacks on the United States, researchers analyzed the connection between Al Qaeda and identity theft. Five percent of those arrested or convicted had ties, or were suspected of having ties, to the terrorist group. While this number may seem insignificant, it is important when the magnitude and nature of the attacks are considered.

Other research indicates that identity thieves do not belong to organized rings or that no evidence of networks was detected during the investigation of the cases. The study done at Utica College, "Identity Fraud Trends and Patterns: Building a Data-Based Foundation for Proactive Enforcement," concluded that the number of offenders per case ranged from 1 to 45 (Gordon et al. 2007). However, the majority of cases (57.6%) involved one perpetrator who worked alone in committing identity theft. Cases involving two offenders totaled 22.8 percent. The number of cases involving three individuals dropped significantly, to 7.9 percent. Only 1 percent of the cases involved 13 to 45 defendants.

The results of the research "Identity Fraud Trends and Patterns: Building a Data-Based Foundation for Proactive Enforcement" is corroborated by the findings of a study conducted at USF, "Exploring the Crime of Identity Theft: Prevalence, Clearance Rates, and Victim/Offender Characteristics." USF researchers found that 64 percent of identity theft cases were committed by a lone perpetrator, 33 percent of the cases involved two perpetrators, and only 3 percent of the cases involved three perpetrators working together to commit identity theft (Allison et al. 2005).

One can devise a profile of an identity thief based upon the available research and statistical data, which suggests that most identity thieves operating in the United States are born in the United States, and that the majority are males between the ages of 25 and 34. However, males tend to commit identity theft less frequently than they commit other types of crimes. Females, on the other hand, tend to commit identity theft more often than all other types of crimes. In addition, there seems to be a correlation between thieves' age, gender, and ethnicity. Although more research is needed in this area, indications are that most perpetrators are African American males.

Current research shows that most identity thieves do not have a criminal history of identity theft convictions. However, it is a crime that is often linked to other types of crime. More research is needed to determine the extent to which identity theft facilitates violent and nonviolent criminal acts. Research also indicates that the majority of identity thieves are not part of a criminal network. It is important, however, that more studies be done in this area given the impact the acts of criminal organizations can have upon the United States, such as terrorism. It is imperative to determine how and why these networks are formed as well as how they are sustained over time.

This section has explored one aspect of identity theft, the perpetrators of the crime, but is equally important to develop an understanding of those victimized by this crime. The next section focuses on the statistics and research pertaining to identity theft victims.

Who Are the Victims?

Victims were overlooked in the criminal justice system and in society prior to the 1970s. Since that time, however, there has been a growing interest in addressing their needs. This interest was prompted by the conservative, crime control nature of our society and by advancements made by the women's movement (Karmen 2003). One of the most alarming aspects of identity theft is that anyone can become a victim at any moment in time. Age, race, gender, and economic status do not deter the crime. Everyone, ranging from infants to the deceased, is at risk. Some people, however, may be at greater risk for victimization than others. This section begins by addressing the types of identity theft perpetrated upon victims, followed by a general victim profile based on victimology theories. The study of victimology provides vast insight into crime and prevention and helps to determine who is most likely to be a target of crime, how to meet the needs of victims, and what steps can be taken to prevent the crime from happening in the future. For these reasons, examining identity theft victimization is important.

Types of Identity Theft

The FTC's annual report, "Consumer Sentinel Network Data Book for January–December 2008," states that 313,982 victims reported the theft of their identities during 2008 (FTC 2009). The number of complaints has increased by 282,842 since 2000 (FTC 2001). As stated previously, there are eight types of identity theft: credit card fraud, government documents or benefits fraud, employment-related fraud, phone or utilities fraud, bank fraud, loan fraud, other identity theft, and attempted identity theft. Some victims experience several types of identity theft simultaneously. For example, victims may discover that new credit card accounts have been opened in their name while at the same time withdrawals have been made from their checking accounts.

According to the FTC, credit card fraud was the most often reported type of identity theft (20%) in 2008 (FTC 2009). Of these cases, 12.3 percent of victims stated that their imposter opened new accounts in their name, as opposed to compromising an existing account (8%). Although the incidence of this specific type of identity theft has declined significantly in recent years, credit card fraud remained the most prevalent complaint filed every year from 2000 through 2008. As incidents of credit card fraud decreased, other types of identity theft increased; for example, complaints of employment-related fraud and government document or benefits fraud grew in 2008 (FTC 2009). Government document or benefits fraud is now the second-most common type of identity theft, as complaints of this nature more than doubled between 2001 and 2008, from 6 to 15 percent (FTC 2002). Fraudulent tax returns, a sub-type of government or benefits fraud, increased from 1.9 percent in 2001 to 12.2 percent in 2008.

Employment-related fraud accounted for 15 percent of the total complaints filed by victims in 2008 (FTC 2009); this represents an increase of 6 percent since 2001 (FTC 2002). Reports of phone or utilities fraud decreased significantly during this same time. In 2008, 13 percent of victims reported this type of identity theft, as compared to 20 percent in 2001. Bank fraud also slightly declined over the last eight years, accounting for 13 percent of the complaints filed with the FTC in 2001 as compared to 11 percent in 2008. However, it is important to mention that bogus electronic funds transfers (EFT), a sub-type of bank fraud, rose over the last eight years, climbing from 1.9 percent in 2001 to 4.6 percent in 2008.

Another type of identity theft, loan fraud, has also declined in recent years. Fewer victims experienced loan fraud in 2008 (4%) than did in 2001 (7%). The FTC also received fewer complaints of attempted identity theft in 2008. Only 6 percent of victims reported that an unsuccessful attempt was made by another person to use their personal identifying information; this represents a 4 percent decline in this form of theft since 2001. The last type of identity theft, those crimes that cannot be classified as any of the types discussed thus far, includes, but is not limited to, victim reports that their identities were used to evade law enforcement, obtain medical care, rent a house or apartment, buy insurance, avoid paying child support, purchase magazines, and file for bankruptcy. Other identity theft cases made up 24 percent of the complaints filed in 2008; in 2001, 19 percent of victims experienced this type of identity theft.

To summarize, credit card fraud is the most prevalent type of identity theft, and based on FTC statistics, there is good reason to believe it will remain an issue in coming years, even though the volume of complaints has dropped over the last eight years. At the same time, more victims are finding that false tax returns are being filed in their names. Incidents of employment-related fraud are also on the rise; this is disconcerting, given that tax return fraud and employment-related fraud usually involve the abuse of SSNs. Although the numbers of complaints of EFT fraud have fluctuated over the last eight years, it remains the most reported sub-type of bank fraud. On a daily basis, thousands of financial transactions are processed electronically. EFT fraud, especially in the form of debit card misuse, continues to pose problems for victims.

The FTC's statistics provide valuable information about the types of identity theft to which victims are subjected and offer insight into the needs of victims following victimization. They also provide a framework for developing prevention guidelines. These issues are discussed in depth in chapter 2. However, there are other factors which may contribute to the likelihood of victimization. The next section examines one of those factors, victims' states of residence.

Geographical Location

Identity theft occurs in every state in the nation, but some states report higher victimization rates than others. In 2008, the 10 states where the most victims of identity theft resided were Arizona, California, Florida, Texas, Nevada, New York, Georgia, Illinois, New Mexico, and Colorado (FTC 2009). Of these, five states ranked in the top 10 every year from 2001 through 2008; they are: Arizona, California, Florida, Nevada, and New York. Additionally, Arizona surpassed all other states for the number of victims reporting to the FTC from 2003 through 2008. Texas ranked in the top 10 for seven years, 2002 through 2008. Colorado and Washington appeared on the list for six years. One state, Georgia, was in the top 10 for a total of five out of eight years. Other states that appeared on the list at some time between 2001 and 2008 are Illinois, Oregon, New Mexico, Maryland, and the District of Columbia.

Research conducted by the Identity Theft Resource Center (ITRC) confirms that residents of some states may have a differential risk of victimization. The data revealed in the study "Identity Theft: The Aftermath 2004" was derived from surveys of confirmed victims who sought assistance through the center (ITRC 2005). Victims were invited to take part in the online survey. The 197 respondents resided in virtually all of 50 states. The study found that almost 19 percent of the victims lived in California, 9 percent were in Florida, 6 percent in Texas, and 5 percent in New York. These results are consistent with the FTC data for 2004 (FTC 2005). Each of these states was ranked in the top 10 for the number of victim complaints filed with the FTC; in addition, they were also in the top 10 in 2008 (FTC 2009).

Although there appears to be a correlation between geographic residency and victimization, many other issues warrant consideration. Perhaps some states have greater victim assistance resources available to their citizens, or law enforcement agencies are more actively involved in programs that teach citizens about the crime. Thus, a heightened level of awareness may account for the elevated numbers of victim complaints in those states. Another factor to consider is the population density in the states most affected by identity theft. Identity thieves who favor stealing mail, for example, may target victims living in populous states versus those in a less populated one, like South Dakota. In 2008, South Dakota ranked last (50th) for the number of victim complaints (FTC 2009). Residents of states that have the highest rates of illegal immigration may also experience increased incidents of identity theft. In summation, more research is needed in order to fully assess the relationship of geographical location to victimization.

Age

Age may be a factor in determining one's likelihood of becoming a victim of identity theft. According to FTC statistics, victims aged 70 and older accounted for only 5 percent of the complaints filed in 2008 (FTC 2009). This group was victimized less often than all other age categories. In contrast, 20- to 29-year-olds were the most common targets of identity thieves (24%), followed by 30- to 39-year-olds (23%). Seven percent of the complainants were age 19 or younger. Another 7 percent were 60 to 69 years old. Victims aged 40 to 49 comprised 19 percent of all identity theft complaints. Lastly, 14 percent of the complaints were filed by victims 50 to 59 years old.

The ITRC study, "Identity Theft: The Aftermath 2007," found similar results (ITRC 2008). Seven percent of the victims who responded to the ITRC's annual survey reported they were 61 years old or older, compared to 12 percent reporting the same in the FTC data. The ITRC suggests that individuals under 18 years old are less likely to be victimized (4%) while young adults, those between the ages of 18 and 29, are more likely than all other age groups (28%) to be victimized. Those 30–39 years old ranked second in reporting the theft of their identities in both the ITRC study (26%) and according to the FTC data (23%). Victims between 40 and 59 years old comprised one third of the complaints received by the FTC, compared to nearly 35 percent of the respondents in the ITRC survey.

When the age groups are combined, a clearer picture of victimization emerges. According to the FTC, 54 percent of complainants were 39 years old or younger (FTC 2009). The remainder of victims (45%) was 40 years old and older. The results of the ITRC survey were similar. The majority (58%) of victims were 39 years old or younger (ITRC 2008). Respondents 40 years and older accounted for 42 percent of victims.

Although everyone is at risk, those aged 39 and younger may be at greater risk of becoming victims than their elders as, in general, the FTC statistics for an eight-year period show that those between the ages of 18 and 39 were most often victimized. More research is needed to determine why this age group is more vulnerable than others, though financial lifestyles may contribute to vulnerability. Between the ages of 18 and 39 years, people are laying the financial foundation for the rest of their lives. They may be taking out student loans, submitting job applications, applying for car loans, using credit cards, purchasing their first homes, and starting families. The level of financial activity is the highest amongst those in this age group, and all of these activities require applicants to divulge personal identifying information. Since credit reports are an important tool for detecting identity theft, research is needed to determine the age at which those in this group should begin reviewing the reports for fraudulent transactions.

Individuals in this age group may also take more risks than their older counterparts. Perhaps they are more open to changes in technology, even if it means that they may be exposed to greater risk. For example, downloading music and movies is a very popular online activity. One of the dangers of downloading these files to one's computer, known as file-sharing, peer-to-peer, and P2P, is that it can lead to identity theft. Those engaging in file-sharing may unintentionally expose the files stored on their computer to others. If the files contain personal information, it can be stolen and used to commit identity theft.

More research is recommended to ascertain the specific reasons why 18- to 39-year-olds experience a higher rate of identity theft as compared to those age 40 and older. Despite this, a broad victim profile emerges from available research combined with FTC statistics. Most victims of identity theft tend to be young adults. They are more likely to experience credit card fraud as opposed to other types of the crime. Those residing in Arizona, California, Florida, Nevada, and New York may be at greater risk than people who live in other states.

References

Allison, Stuart F. H., Amie M. Schuck, and Kim M. Lersch. 2005. "Exploring the crime of identity theft: prevalence, clearance rates, and victim/offender characteristics." *Journal of Criminal Justice* 33 (1): 19–29.

AmyBoyer.org. *In loving memory of our daughter, sister and friend.* October 10, 2004. Internet Archive Database. http://web.archive.org/web/20041010044045/www.amyboyer.org/index.html. Accessed April 28, 2009.

Casey, Eoghan. 2001. *Digital Evidence and Computer Crime.* San Diego: Academic Press.

Collins, Judith M. and Sandra K. Hoffman. 2004. Identity theft: Predator profiles. Unpublished Paper, School of Criminal Justice, Michigan State University.

Constitutional Rights Foundation (CRF). 1997. "Forensic evidence: The riddle of the Romanovs." *Bill of Rights in Action* 13 (3). http://www.crf-usa.org/bill-of-rights-in-action/bria-13–3-a.html. Accessed April 28, 2009.

Cryptome JYA Archives. 1997. USA v. Carlos "Smak" Salgado. http://jya.com/smak.htm. Accessed April 28, 2009.

Deseret News. "Woman gets 6 years in fed prison for ID theft." August 11, 2008, http://www.deseretnews.com/article/content/mobile/1,5143,700249935,00.html?printView=true. Accessed April 28, 2009.

Federal Trade Commission. 2001. Identity theft victim complaint data: Figures and trends on identity theft, January 2000 through December 2000. http://ftc.gov/bcp/edu/microsites/idtheft/downloads/clearinghouse_2000.pdf. Accessed April 2, 2009.

Federal Trade Commission. 2002. Identity theft victim complaint data: Figures and trends on identity theft, January 1–December 31, 2001. http://www.ftc.gov/bcp/edu/microsites/idtheft/downloads/clearinghouse_2001.pdf. Accessed April 3, 2009.

Federal Trade Commission. 2003. Identity theft victim complaint data: Figures and trends on identity theft, January 1–December 31, 2002. http://www.ftc.gov/bcp/edu/microsites/idtheft/downloads/clearinghouse_2002.pdf. Accessed April 3, 2009.

Federal Trade Commission. 2004. National and state trends in fraud & identity theft, January–December 2003. http://www.ftc.gov/sentinel/reports/sentinel-annual-reports/sentinel-cy2003.pdf. Accessed April 3, 2009.

Federal Trade Commission. 2005. National and state trends in fraud & identity theft, January–December 2004. http://www.ftc.gov/sentinel/reports/sentinel-annual-reports/sentinel-cy2004.pdf. Accessed April 3, 2009.

Federal Trade Commission. 2006. Consumer fraud and identity theft complaint data, January–December 2005. http://www.ftc.gov/sentinel/reports/sentinel-annual-reports/sentinel-cy2005.pdf. Accessed April 3, 2009.

Federal Trade Commission. 2007. Consumer fraud and identity theft complaint data: January–December 2006. http://www.ftc.gov/sentinel/reports/sentinel-annual-reports/sentinel-cy2006.pdf. Accessed April 3, 2009.

Federal Trade Commission. 2008. Consumer fraud and identity theft complaint data: January–December 2007. http://www.ftc.gov/sentinel/reports/sentinel-annual-reports/sentinel-cy2007.pdf. Accessed April 3, 2009.

Federal Trade Commission. 2009. Consumer sentinel network data book for January–December 2008. http://www.ftc.gov/sentinel/reports/sentinel-annual-reports/sentinel-cy2008.pdf. Accessed April 3, 2009.

Federal Trade Commission. n.d. Consumer Sentinel/Military. http://www.ftc.gov/sentinel/military/index.shtml. Accessed April 6, 2009.

Garner, Bryan A., ed. 1999. *Black's Law Dictionary*. 7th ed. St. Paul, MN: West Group.

Gill, Peter, et al. 1994. "Identification of the remains of the Romanov family by DNA analysis." Abstract. *Nature Genetics* 6 (2): 130–35. http://

www.nature.com/ng/journal/v6/n2/abs/ng0294–130.html. Accessed April 28, 2009.

Golden, Peter A. 1999. "Dangers without, dangers within. Network security in the age of e-commerce." In *Electronic Business*, May. http://www.petergolden.com/Articles/PAG-Network%20security.htm. Accessed April 28, 2009.

Gordon, Gary R., et al. 2007. "Identity fraud trends and patters: Building a data-based foundation for proactive enforcement." (October): 1–74. Presented at a conference at the Economic Crime Institute, Utica College. http://www.utica.edu/academic/institutes/ecii/publications/media/cimip_id_theft_study_oct_22_noon.pdf. Accessed February 27, 2009.

Greenfeld, Lawrence A. and Tracy L. Snell. 1999. Women offenders. Revised October 3, 2000. U.S. Department of Justice, Bureau of Justice Statistics. NCJ175688. www.ojp.gov/bjs/pub/pdf/wo.pdf. Accessed February 29, 2008.

Haughton, Brian. 2002. "Weird People—Impostors , Eccentrics & Hoaxes: Sarah Wilson—The Princess Susanna Hoax." *Mysterious People.* http://www.mysteriouspeople.com/princess_hoax.htm. Accessed April 28, 2009.

Helen Remsburg, Administrator of the Estate of Amy Lynn Boyer v. Docusearch, Inc., d/b/a Docusearch.com. (Sup. Ct. February 18, 2003). U.S. District Court Case No. 2002–255. http://www.nh.gov/judiciary/supreme/opinions/2003/remsb017.htm. Accessed April 28, 2009.

Helmkamp, James, Richard Ball, and Kitty Townsend, eds. 1996. "Definitional dilemma: Can and should there be a universal definition of white collar crime?" Proceedings of the academic workshop of the National White Collar Crime Center and West Virginia University, West Virginia. http://www.nw3c.org/research/site_files.cfm?mode=p. Accessed April 3, 2009.

House of Lords, "Opinions of the Lords of Appeal for Judgment in the Cause in re Levin," *Session 1997–98*, June 19, 1997, http://www.publications.parliament.uk/pa/ld199798/ldjudgmt/jd970619/levin.htm. Accessed April 28, 2009.

Identity Theft Resource Center. 2005. Identity theft: The aftermath 2004. http://www.idtheftcenter.org/artman2/uploads/1/The_Aftermath_2004_1.pdf. Accessed April 29, 2009.

Identity Theft Resource Center. 2008. Identity theft: The aftermath 2007. http://www.idtheftcenter.org/artman2/uploads/1/Aftermath_2007_20080529v2_1.pdf. Accessed April 29, 2009.

Jabaily, Bob, ed. 2004. Credit history: The evolution of consumer credit in America. *The Ledger*, Spring/Summer. http://www.bos.frb.org/

education/ledger/ledger04/sprsum/credhistory.htm. Accessed April 2, 2009.

Karmen, Andrew. 2003. *Crime Victims: An Introduction to Victimology.* 5th ed. Belmont: CA. Thomsom Publishing.

Lawrence Public Library. n.d. "Ferdinand Waldo Demara Jr. (1921–1982)." http://www.lawrencefreelibrary.org/english/demara.htm. Accessed April 28, 2009.

Lyzhina, Svetlana, and Zaghid Yusoupov, trans. 2004. The unsolved riddle of princess Anastasia. *Pravda* (Russia), July 13. http://english.pravda.ru/main/18/90/363/13367_Nicholas.html. Accessed April 3, 2009.

Miller, Michael D. 2003. Jack Cade's rebellion 1450. In *Wars of the roses: An analysis of the causes of the wars and the course which they took.* http://www.warsoftheroses.co.uk/chapter_39.htm. Accessed April 28, 2009.

Morris, R.G., II. 2004. "The development of an identity theft offender typology: A theoretical approach." *The Graduate Research Journal.* 1–20. http://www.shsu.edu/~edu_elc/journal/research%20online/re2004/Robert.pdf. Accessed April 29, 2009.

National White Collar Crime Center. 2007. White collar crime statistics. http://www.nw3c.org/. Accessed February 27, 2008.

O'Neil, Paul. 1970. "A little gift from your friendly bank." *Life Magazine* (March 27, 1970). Reprinted in *Frontline.* http://www.pbs.org/wgbh/pages/frontline/shows/credit/more/life.html. Accessed April 28, 2009.

Pastore, Ann L. and Kathleen Maguire, eds. n.d. *Sourcebook of Criminal Justice Statistics.* Table 4.8 [Online]. http://www.albany.edu/sourcebook/tost_4.html#4_l. Accessed August 27, 2009.

Peate, Les. n.d. "The case of the spurious sawbones." *Esprit de Corps Magazine.* http://www.kvacanada.com/stories_lpimposter.htm. Assessed April 28, 2009.

President's Identity Theft Task Force. 2007. *Combating identity theft: A strategic plan.* http://www.idtheft.gov/reports/StrategicPlan.pdf. Accessed May 3, 2007.

Ramer, Holly. 2004. "Mother of slain woman settles lawsuit against info-broker." *USA Today* (March 3). http://www.usatoday.com/tech/news/internetprivacy/2004–03–10-boyer-suit-settled_x.htm. Accessed April 4, 2008.

Ross, David. 2001. "English history: Jack Cade's Rebellion—1450." *Britain Express: The UK Travel and Heritage Guide.* http://www.britainexpress.com/History/medieval/cade.htm. Accessed April 28, 2009.

Seal, Rob. 2006a. "A family fights for identity." *InsideNoVa.com*, http://www.timesdispatch.com/servlet/Satellite?pagename=WPN%2FMGArticle%2FWPN_BasicArticle&c=MGArticle&cid=1137833576776&path=!news. Accessed November 19, 2006.

Seal, Rob. 2006b. "Identity theft hits local home." *Potomac News* (January 22). http://www.potomacnews.com/. Accessed November 19, 2006.

Smart Computing. n.d. *Smart computing encyclopedia: Vladimir Levin.* http://www.smartcomputing.com/editorial/dictionary/detail.asp?guid=&searchtype=&DicID=19495&RefType=Encyclopedia. Accessed April 28, 2009.

Social Security Administration. 2002. What can I do in a case of identity theft? http://ssa-custhelp.ssa.gov. Accessed June 11, 2007.

Social Security Administration. 2003. Historical background and development of Social Security. http://www.ssa.gov/history/briefhistory3.html. Accessed April 28, 2009.

Social Security Administration. 2005. Social Security numbers: Social Security number chronology. http://www.ssa.gov/history/ssn/ssnchron.html. Accessed April 28, 2009.

Social Security Administration. 2007. Birth of a child. http://www.ssa.gov/gethelp2.htm. Accessed June 11, 2007.

Social Security Administration. n.d.-a. Social Security numbers: The first SSN & the lowest number. http://www.ssa.gov/history/ssn/firstcard.html. Accessed April 28, 2009.

Social Security Administration. n.d.-b. Social Security numbers: Social Security cards issued by Woolworth. http://www.ssa.gov/history/ssn/misused.html. Accessed April 28, 2009.

Stein, Robin. n.d. The ascendancy of the credit card industry. *Frontline.* http://www.pbs.org/wgbh/pages/frontline/shows/credit/more/rise.html. Accessed April 28, 2009.

Suzanne Sloane v. Equifax Information Services, LLC. Case No. 062044.P (Va. Ct. App., 4th Cir. Dec. 27, 2007). http http://pacer.ca4.uscourts.gov/opinion.pdf/062044.P.pdf. Accessed August 27, 2009.

Tenney, Merrill C., ed. 1969. *The Zondervan Pictorial Bible Dictionary.* Grand Rapids, MI: Zondervan Publishing House.

Time. 1951. "All at sea." December. http://www.time.com/time/printout/0,8816,889381,00.html. Accessed April 28, 2009.

U.S. Attorney's Office, Central District of California, "Tax preparer sentenced to 11 years in prison for running scheme that led to millions in losses." Press release. January 12, 2009. http://www.usdoj.gov/usao/cac/pressroom/pr2009/002.html. Accessed April 25, 2009.

U.S. Attorney, District of Utah, "Grand jury returns indictments in identity theft cases." Press release. August 29, 2007. http://saltlakecity.fbi.gov/dojpressrel/pressrel07/identitytheft082907.htm. Accessed April 25, 2009.

U.S. Attorney, Eastern District of California, "Hilton clerk sentenced to federal prison for stealing credit card numbers from hotel guests." Press release, October 18, 2006. http://www.usdoj.gov/usao/cae/press_releases/docs/2006/10–18–06Miller.Noel.j&s.pdf. Accessed April 21, 2009.

U.S. Congress. House. *Identity theft: Greater awareness and use of existing data are needed.* June 2002. GAO-2–766. Available at: http://www.gao.gov/new.items/d02766.pdf. Accessed June 27, 2007.

Virginia Department of Corrections-Inmate Status Information Center. http://www2.vipnet.org/cgi-bin/vadoc/doc.cgi/ (object name Sloan). Accessed June 24, 2007.

White House, "Fact sheet: The President's Identity Theft Task Force." News release. May 10, 2006. http://www.whitehouse.gov/. Accessed June 10, 2006.

Wright, Chris. 2000. "Murder.com: What happened last fall on this tiny New Hampshire street triggered a national debate on Internet crime. But was the Web really to blame for the death of Amy Boyer?" *Boston Phoenix*, August 10–17. http://www.bostonphoenix.com/archive/features/00/08/10/MURDER.html. Accessed November 18, 2005.

2

Problems, Controversies, and Solutions

This chapter is designed to acquaint readers with many of the complex issues surrounding identity theft. It discusses the problems faced by victims of the crime and demonstrates the methods utilized by perpetrators to gain access to identities; it also explains how stolen identities are exploited. Next, the chapter addresses potential solutions, including the efforts undertaken by the judicial system, legislators, private businesses, law enforcement agencies, victims' advocates, and private individuals working to combat identity theft. Although the crime cannot be completely prevented, information about personal and workplace security is provided to aid in minimizing the risk of becoming a victim. While this chapter focuses primarily on the United States, it offers some possible global solutions to the crime. A detailed discussion of the international implications of identity theft is offered in chapter 3.

The Victims' Experiences

Many variables determine the affects that identity theft has upon victims. Financial, social, medical, psychological, and familial costs may be associated with victimization. Upon discovery of the crime, victims are forced to confront and resolve the problems surrounding the theft of their identities. They must act quickly to stop the victimization, to clear their names of fraudulent activities and to reduce the risks of being victimized again. A great deal of time is often spent collecting information to help in investigations. Many victims must fill out numerous forms and/or write letters to credit bureaus, collection agencies, creditors, and governmental agencies. At the same time, victims are making many telephone calls. Sometimes, victims have to take time off from work to handle problems in person. One of the effects of victimization, therefore, is lost productivity in the workplace. This section examines the problems that contribute to the difficulties most often encountered by victims. It is important to understand the impact of identity theft in order to implement viable solutions.

Methods of Detection and Time Lapse

Studies indicate that there is a greater likelihood of law enforcement apprehending an offender if the crime is discovered shortly after its committed (Walker and Katz 2005). As a result, the least amount of time that elapses between a criminal act and discovery often leads to a reduction in the damage sustained by victims. This is especially true in identity theft cases. Additionally, research indicates that the time spent resolving problems may depend upon the amount of time that elapses between onset and discovery. A study conducted by the Identity Theft Resource Center (ITRC), "Identity Theft: The Aftermath 2007," suggests that more fraudulent activities are committed when it takes longer to discover the crime (ITRC 2008). In turn, victims spend more time interacting with organizations such as creditors and collection agencies.

How do victims find out about the theft of their identities? There are many methods of discovery. In an earlier study done by ITRC, "Identity Theft: The Aftermath 2004," victims were asked how they found out about the crime (ITRC 2005). A few (15%) were contacted by a business that had instituted early detection procedures. A subsequent study, "Identity Theft: The Aftermath 2007," found that the number of victims notified by a proactive business decreased from 15 percent in 2003 to 10 percent in 2007 (ITRC 2008). Consequently, the overwhelming majority of victims do not discover the crime until it negatively impacts their lives.

Some victims discover the theft when they notice charges on their credit card statements that they did not authorize, and many find out upon receiving a telephone call from the fraud department of their credit card company (Collins and Hoffman 2003). A collection agency may demand payment of delinquent bills that the victims did not incur. Some learn of the theft when they find unauthorized activity on their cell or telephone bills. Others find out when their utility services are interrupted. Victims may discover the crime when they receive: credit cards for which they did not apply, telephone calls and letters from creditors about overdue bills that do not belong to them, or notification that checks have bounced when there should be sufficient funds in the account. Many find out about the crime after applying for a loan and it is denied because of a low credit score. Victims may also discover the crime when they find unauthorized withdrawals on their retirement account statements. Some learn of the theft when they are denied employment or were not promoted in their current jobs. A few victims are arrested for crimes they did not commit.

A single case of identity theft may involve several instances of abuse of the victim's personal information over time. The first time a victim's identity is used is considered the first incident. For example, a thief may steal a credit card and use it to make several purchases. First, the card is used to buy gasoline. The next day, the imposter charges clothing to the victim's credit card. The first time the card was compromised, to purchase gasoline, is considered the first incident. The time period between the first incident and discovery by the victim may be a determining factor in the amount of damage sustained. It may also contribute to the amount of time victims spend restoring their names.

The study, "Identity Theft: The Aftermath 2007," analyzed the time lapse between the first occasion an identity was used and discovery by the victim (ITRC 2008). In addition, data gleaned from previous annual surveys, conducted from 2003 to 2006, was provided by researchers. In 2003, 47.7 percent of respondents indicated that they realized they were victims in three months or less following the onset of the crime. However, 5.7 percent fewer victims discovered the crime in the same time frame in 2007 (42%) than in 2003.

The 2007 survey shows that 22 percent of the victims reported that 4 to 12 months elapsed between the initial victimization and discovery, compared to 2003, when 24.6 percent of respondents discovered the crime between 4 to 12 months after the first incident occurred (ITRC 2008). More victims in 2007 (17%) than in 2003 (13.3%) learned that their identities were stolen more than one year, but less than two years, following the initial episode. Additionally, more victims reported that it took two years or longer to discover the crime in 2007 as compared to 2003 (20% and 14.4%, respectively).

In conclusion, research indicates that fewer victims in 2007 than in 2003 discovered the crime because of early fraud detection methods used by proactive businesses. Victims also reported that more time elapsed between the initial victimization and discovery of the crime in 2007 than in 2003. These findings are surprising given the heightened level of community awareness, legislative actions, strengthened business practices, and law enforcement efforts since 2003. Although the economic recession may be a contributing factor in the latter year, many unknown variables may also be contributing to the problem. Further research, therefore, is necessary to determine the relationship between the onset of the crime, discovery of victimization, and the extent of damages sustained by victims.

Types of Identity Theft and the Restoration Period

There is evidence that the time required to restore one's name depends upon the type of identity theft committed. For example, it generally takes significantly longer for a victim to clear a criminal charge from his or her record than it does to resolve a fraudulent charge on a credit card account. The study, "Federal Trade Commission-2006 Identity Theft Survey Report," found that victims settled problems quicker when an existing credit card account was compromised as compared to other types of identity theft (Synovate 2007). Random telephone surveys were used to gather data for the study. Adults age 18 and older were interviewed between March 27, 2006 and June 11, 2006. Of the 4,917 respondents, 559 stated they had been victims of identity theft between 2001 and the survey date. Their responses were categorized according to the severity of repercussions they experienced. As a result, researchers found three distinct types of identity theft. The first and most severe type was labeled *new accounts and other frauds*. This included the use of victims' identities to: open new bank, credit card, cell phone, and telephone accounts, rent properties, obtain loans, health care, automobile insurance, government documents, and employment, and to commit misdemeanors and felonies. The second type of identity theft, *existing non-credit card accounts*, involved the misuse of victims' existing accounts, excluding credit card accounts. The last type, *existing credit cards only*, pertains to victims whose credit card accounts were compromised.

Regardless of the type of identity theft, 23 percent of the respondents indicated that they did not encounter difficulties clearing their names or that they were able to do so within a day of finding out that they had been victimized (Synovate 2007). Of those, 38 percent were victims of *existing credit card only* identity theft, as compared to victims of *existing non-credit card accounts* (18%) and victims of *new accounts and other frauds* (10%). Eleven percent of all respondents stated that it took three months or more from the date of discovery to handle the problems associated with the theft of their identities. Of those, 15 percent were victims of *new accounts and other frauds,* as opposed to victims of *existing non-credit card accounts* (10%) and victims of *existing credit card fraud only* (8%). Thus, victims whose existing credit card accounts are compromised are more likely to experience a quicker resolution than victims of other types of identity theft.

Research conducted by the Identity Theft Resource Center (ITRC) confirms that victims spend more time resolving problems arising from new account fraud than they do handling existing account fraud issues (ITRC 2008). On average, the "Identity Theft: The Aftermath 2007" study found that it took victims 116 hours to restore their names after their existing accounts were misused. Clearing up problems resulting from new account fraud, criminal records, government document fraud, and medical fraud took much longer. The study also concluded that more victims were able to settle problems quicker in 2007 than in the previous three years. Nearly half of all respondents (49%) in 2007 stated it took them between one and six months to clear their names. In 2004, only 12.7 percent of victims were able to restore their names in the same amount of time. Thirty-three percent reported it took between 7 and 23 months in 2007 to attain resolution, as compared to 26.5 percent in 2004. The number of victims stating it took from two and more than five years to undo the damage caused by thieves dropped significantly (i.e., from 39% in 2004 to 19% in 2007).

The amount of time that victims devote to resolving problems associated with the theft of their identities varies. Research shows that there is a correlation between the type of identity theft experienced by victims and the length of the restoration period. Moreover, there may be other interrelated contributing factors. Available research indicates that the time lapse between the initial victimization and discovery, the type of identity theft committed, and the method of detection may determine how quickly victims clear their names. In addition to the time required for problem-solving, other aspects of a victim's life are also affected. The following sections address some of these problems.

Effects on Relationships

Many victims must contend with issues affecting their personal relationships as a direct result of identity theft. As stated previously, victims are typically preoccupied with the crime. They are busy stopping fraudulent activities, restoring their identities, and protecting themselves from being re-victimized. Thus, relationships with friends, co-workers, and family members are often impacted. The study, "Identity Theft: The Aftermath 2007," found that nearly half (49%) of the respondents indicated that the crime produced stress within their families (ITRC 2008). Twenty-three percent reported a lack of understanding by family members, and 22 percent of the respondents stated that the crime had an effect on their children. Some victims (12%) reported that their relationships with significant others were in trouble or that the relationships were over. At the same time, the majority (51%) of respondents indicated that their family members supported them as they worked through problems.

The relationship between the victim and the offender must also be considered. Research shows that victimization by an immediate family member, significant other, ex-spouse, relative, or friend presents unique challenges for victims. The study, "Federal Trade Commission-2006 Identity Theft Survey Report," found that the majority (84%) of victims did not have a personal connection to the thief (Synovate 2007). Sixteen percent reported that the thief was a member of their family, a relative, friend, co-worker, neighbor, or household employee. The study suggests that a victim/offender relationship may also influence the type of identity theft perpetrated. The respondents who knew their offenders experienced *new accounts and other frauds* or *existing non-credit card account* fraud more often than *existing credit card only* identity theft. In other words, victims who knew their perpetrators were most likely to be subjected to the types of identity theft that take longer to detect and resolve.

Victims of familial identity theft are confronted with problems exclusive to their situation, and emotions often influence their decisions. Since the bond between the victim and offender has been violated, it may be more difficult for victims to deal with the emotional aspect of the crime. As victims try to decide what to do about the crime, other family members may pull them in many different directions. Thus, victims of familial identity theft may experience conflicting emotions that directly impact their decision-making process.

In the research, "Identity Theft: The Aftermath 2007," the effects of the crime on victims whose perpetrator was a member of their family were assessed (ITRC 2008). Victims were asked to respond to a list of questions. The number of answers was unlimited, depending upon the victim's particular case. The majority (58%) of victims responded that the offender used identity theft as a means to spoil their reputation. Over half (52%) indicated that other family members were victimized by the same offender. In addition, 52 percent of the thieves were reported to have an addiction. Fifty-two percent of victims also stated that their perpetrator had committed other crimes in addition identity theft.

Victims were asked questions about their interactions with other family members as they tried to decide how to remedy the situation (ITRC 2008). Fewer than half (42%) indicated that family members would back their decision to hold the imposter accountable for the crimes. The same percentage reported that their families were in favor of filing a complaint with a law enforcement agency. Twenty-seven percent indicated they were uncomfortable filing a complaint against a member of their own family. A few victims (18%) were concerned about becoming outcasts in their own families if they took steps to resolve the situation. Some victims (12%) stated that family members discouraged them from pursuing the case.

Emotional and Medical Concerns

Research suggests that most victims of identity theft experience emotions comparable to victims of violent crimes. Some victims endure these emotions for a longer period of time than others. A few victims experience deteriorating physical health. The study, "Identity Theft: The Aftermath 2007," found that the majority (80%) of victims become outraged or angry upon discovering the crime (ITRC 2008). Other common responses were feelings of frustration (74%) and annoyance (66%). These emotions are not surprising, since victims are thrust into the position of having to prove that they are innocent and that a crime has been committed against them (Collins and Hoffman 2003). Over half (56%) of the victims in the study indicated that they were worried about their financial security (ITRC 2008). The majority (57%) felt powerless. It is important to note that victims often feel that they are totally at the mercy others, such as the perpetrators, creditors, and credit bureaus. The study also found that nearly half (48%) of the respondents reported feeling betrayed. This is especially true if the offender is someone the victim knows personally.

Some victims experience lasting emotional repercussions. In addition, medical problems may develop or preexisting conditions may be exacerbated. The following case illustrates how identity theft impacted one victim who was dealing with health problems at the time of discovering the crime.

Shortly after Phillip retired, he suffered a heart attack. He had bypass surgery and returned home to recover. He grappled with mild depression and was physically weak. One day, Phillip opened his retirement account statement and discovered that his life savings was almost gone. He tried to deal with the problems created by his imposter, but his depression worsened. Eventually, he was diagnosed as clinically depressed. Brenda, Phillip's wife, tried frantically to take care of the problems, but she soon realized that she could do very little. The organizations Brenda had to contact would not cooperate with her because, she was told, Phillip was the victim and she was not, as Phillip's retirement account was in his name only, therefore, the company could not discuss the account with her. It took a legal power of attorney and several weeks of due diligence to have his account restored.

In addition to depression, many victims also report lingering sleep disorders . The survey, "Identity Theft: The Aftermath 2007," found that 40 percent of the respondents suffered sleep disorders for two or more months following victimization (ITRC 2008). The majority of victims were still experiencing feelings of being frustrated (63%), annoyed (58%), and fearful for their financial security (50%). Two months or more following victimization, 29 percent of victims indicated that they stopped trying to clear their names. In 2006, 34 percent of victims gave up trying to resolve the problems associated with the crime. Although the number was down in 2007, this may be an indication of an acute systemic problem when over a quarter of the victims give up trying to restore their names. More research is needed to identify the obstacles that cause some victims to surrender rather than complete the process of restoration. In addition, research should continue in the area of the emotional and medical impact of identity theft, in order to learn how to assist victims more effectively and efficiently. There are other issues associated with identity theft victimization. One of them is the monetary expenses that may be incurred as a direct result of the crime.

Financial Losses

Victims are generally not held responsible for the debts incurred by their imposters, yet there may still be costs associated with the crime. Victims may have expenses for long distance telephone calls, photocopies, certified mailings, travel, babysitting, lost wages, and attorneys' fees. Sometimes, victims decide to pay the debts incurred by their imposters. The research, "Federal Trade Commission: 2006 Identity Theft Survey Report," found that 59 percent of all respondents did not incur any expenses (Synovate 2007). Of those, 80 percent reported that their existing credit card accounts were compromised. Twenty-five percent of victims who incurred expenses of $1,000 or more were in the *new accounts and other frauds* category. Another study confirms that expenses are greater if new accounts are opened in the victim's name, as opposed to the use or take over of an existing account. The study, "Identity Theft: The Aftermath 2007," concluded that victims of new account fraud spent an average of $1,826.27 clearing their names (ITRC 2008). Conversely, victims whose existing accounts were compromised spent an average of $550.39.

Although the amount of expenses incurred by victims differs, there seems to be a direct correlation between expenses and type of identity theft involved. There is evidence that it costs victims more to resolve problems associated with new account fraud than it does those who suffered existing account fraud. More research is warranted to determine the connection between expenses incurred by victims and the variables discussed in this chapter (e.g., the amount of time victims devote to clearing their names, time lapsed between initial victimization and discovery, the method of detection, relationship of victim to perpetrator, and the emotional and medical issues associated with the crime). In summation, identity theft impacts victims in many ways and to varying degrees. Some victims, however, are victimized again by those they rely upon to help them through the process of restoring their good names.

The Second Insult

Victimology theories provide evidence that victims are often victimized twice for the same crime. The first victimization takes place when the actual crime occurs. The second victimization is referred to as *the second insult*. Historically, the second insult describes the victim's experience within the criminal justice system. In the past, victims were not afforded the level of support or information they needed (Doerner and Lab 2005). Today, identity theft victims often encounter similar responses. However, the second insult is not limited to the criminal justice system. Creditors, credit reporting bureaus, collection agencies, and governmental entities may also be less than supportive of victims. These organizations sometimes make it difficult, or even impossible, for victims to remove fraudulent financial and/or criminal information from their records, and even if it is removed, the information often reappears on records in the future. Adverse information eventually ends up in private and government databases, and as a result, the second insult reverberates throughout every aspect of victims' daily lives.

Research indicates that victims are generally dissatisfied with the treatment and services they receive following an incident of identity theft. The majority (64%) of respondents surveyed in the "Identity Theft: The Aftermath 2007" study indicated that they were refused credit (ITRC 2008). Over half of the victims (53%) were pressured by collection agencies to pay the debts incurred by their imposters. Thirty-six percent reported that their credit card interest rates rose. Twenty-seven percent stated that credit cards companies cancelled their cards for no reason. Some victims had trouble obtaining employment (18%) or housing (14%), and 14 percent indicated that their insurance premiums increased. Seven percent were unable to clear fraudulent misdemeanors or felonies from their records.

Overall, 63 percent of the respondents were unable to get adverse information permanently removed from their credit bureau files (ITRC 2008). Nearly one third (32%) indicated that the credit bureaus simply refused to take the fraudulent information off their records. Almost one third (31%) were able to get the information removed only to have it reappear on their files at a later date. Many other problems prevented victims from clearing their names: the offenders continued to obtain credit in the names of the victims, creditors refused to give victims copies of documentation related to bogus accounts bearing their names, and some victims stated that a police report was not accepted as proof of victimization.

The research to date shows that victims of identity theft may be victimized twice for the same crime. It is evident that more can be done to assist victims, beginning at the moment of discovery through the restoration process. However, the problems surrounding identity theft cannot be addressed without understanding where identities are found and how identities are stolen in the first place.

Sources and Methods Used by Perpetrators to Access Identities

Personal identifying information is an integral part of modern society. It is required in order to, among other things, accept employment, open a bank account, purchase a home, turn on utilities, acquire phone service, receive health care, vote in elections, and obtain credit. In short, identities are valuable. When personal information is required to open a credit card account, for example, the card company is tasked with keeping it safe. The problem is that sensitive information is vulnerable to theft wherever it is stored. Thieves steal identities from many sources and use a variety of techniques to gain access to them.

In the survey, "Federal Trade Commission-2006 Identity Theft Survey Report," victims were asked if they knew how their identities were stolen (Synovate 2007). Over half (56%) of the respondents were unable to determine how their imposter gained access to their personal identifying information. A few victims (1%) reported that their identities were stolen after answering a phishing e-mail. Another 1 percent stated that their computer had been hacked. Mail theft was cited as the point of compromise by 2 percent of the respondents. Five percent knew that their information was stolen from business records' point of storage. Another 5 percent reported that their purse or wallet had been stolen. Seven percent became victims after doing business in a store, through the mail, or on the Internet. Seven percent reported their identities were stolen by various other methods. The most frequently cited source of theft, however, was by a person with whom the victim had a personal relationship (16%).

The "Identity Fraud Trends and Patterns: Building a Data-Based Foundation for Proactive Enforcement" study found that 34.1 percent of perpetrators stole personal information from their workplace (Gordon et al. 2007). Of those, 43.8 percent were employed in the retail industry. About 21 percent of perpetrators worked for private businesses. Employment in the financial industry was the source for stolen identities for 23.8 percent of thieves. Other sources for identities included governmental entities (5.1%), educational institutions (3.4%), and the insurance industry (3.4%). The majority (65.9%) of perpetrators, in other words, did not steal identities from their place of employment.

The study, "Identity Theft: Predator Profiles," indicates that 47 percent of perpetrators stole identities from individuals (Collins and Hoffman 2004). In addition to stealing personal information from friends or family members, offenders employed several other low-tech methods. They rummaged through garbage in trash cans, dumpsters, and landfills. They stole purses and wallets from unattended automobiles, backpacks, and shopping carts. Unlocked and unattended mailboxes were another source of identities. However, the majority of perpetrators (51%) were reported as having stolen identities from a workplace. These criminals stole information belonging to customers, clients, patients, employees, vendors, management personnel, co-workers, and the business itself. Two percent stole identities from both individuals and businesses. Furthermore, employers or business owners were the most frequent perpetrators of identity theft in the workplace. However, the research did not delineate between the business owners who used their business as a source for identities and those who created bogus businesses to gain access to proprietary information. The study was conducted before the well-known ChoicePoint incident occurred. Nonetheless, it is a good example of how thieves form bogus businesses to gain access to identities.

ChoicePoint was a data broker that owned and maintained a database of reports on virtually every adult consumer in the United States (United States of America v. ChoicePoint Inc. 2006b). Each report contained an individual's name, address, Social Security number (SSN), date of birth, financial account numbers, property records, criminal history, telephone number, and much more. Over the years, ChoicePoint sold one of its products, background checks, to thousands of private and public entities. In 2005, the company faced a major security breach (United States of America v. ChoicePoint Inc. 2006a). The personal information of over 160,000 individuals had been sold to a network of identity thieves. Approximately 50 fake business accounts were opened by the thieves for the sole purpose of stealing sensitive information, including credit reports. Hundreds of people became victims of identity theft. Consequently, a civil case was filed against ChoicePoint in 2006, and the company was fined $10 million and ordered to provide $5 million to reimburse victims for expenses they incurred in clearing their names (United States of America v. ChoicePoint Inc. 2006b). This case also resulted in tighter controls on access to personal identifying information. Among other security measures, ChoicePoint was mandated to screen potential clients thoroughly before selling them access to their database.

The "Identity Theft: Predator Profiles" study found that identities are most often stolen from financial institutions (15%), healthcare facilities (15%), and government entities (11%) (Collins and Hoffman 2004). Financial institutions include banks, credit unions, mortgage companies, and collection agencies. Healthcare facilities include home healthcare providers, medical laboratories, hospitals, clinics, doctors' offices, and nursing homes. Government entities include driver's license bureaus, post offices, Social Security offices, and so forth. Other sources for stealing identities are: automobile rental agencies and dealerships (5%), retail establishments (3%), insurance companies (3%), credit card companies (2%), eateries and bars (1%), and communications businesses such as telephone companies, cell phone companies, and Internet service providers (1%). Other points of compromise include landlords, real estate agencies, universities, gambling casinos, employment agencies, factories, and so on (14%). Twenty-nine percent of perpetrators stole identities from more than one of these sources.

Even though research results vary, these statistics offer some insight into where thieves find identities and how sensitive information is stolen. Identifying information can be found in a multitude of places, ranging from mailboxes to online databases. Thus, the methods used to steal identities are adapted to exploit weaknesses in security. More research is needed in this area to determine effective measures for securing personal information. However, there are several trends and issues that must be taken into account when considering ways to reduce the incidences of identity theft.

Trends and Special Issues

The Federal Trade Commission (FTC) has collected data from identity theft victims since 1999 to learn more about the crime, and other public and private entities have conducted research on the topic as well. Over the years, developing trends have been identified and many important issues deserving consideration have come to the forefront. The following sections explore trends in how identities are stolen and how they are used. Also discussed are the risks and controversies posed by offshoring identities and data breaches. Lastly, an overview of the hidden costs of identity theft is presented.

Tax Fraud

Incidents of income tax fraud have nearly doubled in recent years (FTC 2009). In 2006, 6.3 percent of the victims who filed complaints with the FTC stated that their identities were used to file fraudulent tax returns. By 2008, that number increased to 12.2 percent. Most victims discover the fraud after they file their own, legitimate income tax returns. In some cases, perpetrators use another person's SSN to obtain employment. The following case is an illustration of this type of identity theft.

Cathy, a resident of Los Angeles, California, filed her 2000 income taxes in a timely manner. But instead of receiving a refund check as she expected, she received a letter from the Internal Revenue Service (IRS) stating that she had not reported the income she earned from her work at a cannery. Furthermore, the letter demanded that she pay taxes on the income. Cathy had never worked in a canning factory; she was employed full-time as a nurse. Many years later, it was discovered that Cathy's SSN was used by an undocumented worker to get the job at the cannery.

In other cases, imposters file income tax returns in the victims' names, so that when the victims file a true return, it is rejected by the IRS. The following case demonstrates this common type of identity theft. After his divorce in 2005, Jim moved from Ohio to a small town outside of Detroit, Michigan. He filed his tax return during the first week of April 2007. A few weeks later Jim received a letter from the IRS stating that a return had already been processed under his SSN. Additionally, a refund check had been issued in his name. An investigation revealed that the imposter was Jim's ex-wife.

Medical Fraud

Medical fraud, also known as medical identity theft, is not a new occurrence. It happens when a person's identifying information is used without his or her knowledge to pay for medical services, equipment, prescription drugs, or doctor visits. According to the

FTC annual report, "Consumer Sentinel Network Data Book for January-December 2008," 4,082 or 1.3 percent of the 313,982 victims reporting identity theft in 2008 complained that their identities were used to commit medical fraud (FTC 2009). Although complaints have decreased from the 2003 rate of 2 percent, this remains one of the most insidious types of identity theft, and the losses sustained because of medical fraud result in increased healthcare costs for all consumers. Additionally, the crime can have a devastating emotional, financial, and physical impact on victims. The following is an account of the ordeal one medical fraud victim endured for over three years.

In 2001 Kathleen Cox, an elderly grandmother, discovered that she was a victim of identity theft (AARP 2004). It began when her imposter was involved in a multiple-car accident. Cox received bills from a hospital demanding payment of $9,000 for injuries she allegedly sustained in the crash, and she was sued for $50,000 by a person who was injured in the wreck. She also discovered that there was a warrant out for her arrest. In reality, she was in her eighties and had not driven a car for over 50 years. In addition, the accident happened in Illinois and Cox lived in Maryland. She told her story to the police, but no investigation ensued. Cox had no choice but to track down the perpetrator by herself. Eventually, she learned that her imposter was a neighbor who happened to have the exact same name as she did. After providing this information to police, the identity thief was finally apprehended.

Victims of medical fraud are also confronted with problems that are unlike those of other types of identity theft. Their health insurance benefits may be depleted by their imposter, and when the victim seeks medical services, payments to healthcare providers may be delayed or denied by their insurance carrier. A victim's medical history may also reflect their imposter's health problems. This can result in higher life and health insurance premiums, or the victim may be denied insurance altogether. Medical identity theft also may cause a victim to lose opportunities for a promotion or employment. When an employer or perspective employer does a background check, it can appear as though the victim is irresponsible and does not pay his or her bills. Thus, it may be determined that he or she is not the right person for the position. Delinquent bills may also result in a lower credit score, which impacts one's ability to obtain credit. Thus, a victim of identity theft may be denied credit altogether or be forced to pay higher interest rates.

Medical identity theft also poses a threat to victims' physical well-being (Dixon 2006). Technology has made it possible for medical records to be maintained and updated instantaneously, and records are now more detailed than ever before in history. This helps healthcare professionals provide the best services possible, however victims of medical fraud are at a disadvantage. Their records often reflect the services, diagnoses, and treatments received by their imposters. Information that is vital during an emergency, such as allergies to medications, might be incorrect. Fraudulent health records may cause the wrong medical treatment to be administered. At best, recovery could be slower; at worst, the wrong treatment could cause death.

Real Estate Loan Fraud

Stolen identities are used to obtain loans. Every year from 2004 through 2007, 5 percent of the complaints received by the FTC stemmed from loan fraud (FTC 2008). Victims reported that their identities were used to acquire real estate, business, personal, auto, and student loans. In 2008, the total number of loan fraud complaints decreased 1 percent, to 4 percent. However, complaints of real estate loan fraud have remained fairly constant from 2003 through 2008. It accounted for 1 percent of the complaints received by the FTC in 2003, compared to 1.2 percent in 2008. Victims of real estate loan fraud, also referred to as mortgage loan fraud, are often challenged to resolve problems involving large sums of money. They may find that mortgages or home equity loans have been obtained in their names, and some victims have even had their homes stolen from them.

A report issued by the Federal Bureau of Investigation (FBI), "2007 Mortgage Fraud Report," found that the problems created by mortgage fraud may cause much deeper and widespread problems; it is a potential threat to the U.S. economy (FBI 2008). The report warned that, if mortgage fraud is left unchecked, it could lead to the collapse of financial institutions which, in turn, would negatively impact the stock market. Since fewer mortgage products are available today, fraudsters are turning to other methods for obtaining real estate loans. The report found that identity theft is reemerging as a trend in the housing market and is being perpetrated to procure home equity and mortgage loans. Home equity loans, often referred to as second mortgages or lines of credit, allow homeowners to borrow money by using the equity in their homes as collateral. The following case is an example of a scheme devised by one perpetrator to obtain both mortgage and home equity loans.

Between May and August 2007, Rory V. Porter targeted individuals who had vacant homes for sale in the Lake City and Gainesville areas of Florida (Attorney General of Florida 2009). He developed friendships with the homeowners in order to get information from them, and then searched public records for the remainder of the data he needed to steal the homeowners' properties. Porter produced counterfeit documents and successfully transferred ownership of the homes, worth over $800,000, into his name. Since it appeared as though Porter was the rightful owner of the properties, he was then able to obtain more than $500,000 in equity loans on the stolen properties. Porter was arrested in November 2007; he pled guilty to charges of grand theft, money laundering, and identity theft.

Offshoring Identities

The offshoring of identities is the practice of employing third-party vendors in foreign countries to perform jobs requiring access to the personal information of U.S. citizens. Current global economic trends have privacy advocates, lawmakers, and corporations locked in a heated debate over the practice. Those in opposition of offshoring are concerned for many reasons, including the following: the United States does not have jurisdiction in countries where identities may be stolen, laws in other countries may change resulting in weaker information security safeguards, many countries have no information protection laws at all, and the obligations of foreign companies to protect personal information may be interpreted in the context of that country's cultural, political, legal, and ethical structure rather than in the context of U.S. law (GalleryWatch 2004).

Supporters of offshoring argue that these fears are unfounded (Atkinson 2004). They claim that U.S. privacy laws are binding regardless of where companies process personal information. Most companies doing business in foreign countries monitor their vendors and insist on stringent security measures; in fact, some countries have stricter privacy laws than the United States.

The number of offshored jobs requiring access to personal information is expected to soar in the coming years. For example, more than 20 percent of employees in the banking industry are expected to be offshore by 2010 (Deloitte Research 2004). Where is personal information processed? Jobs requiring access to the identities of U.S. citizens are being performed in countries around the globe such as Australia, Bangladesh, Brazil, Canada, China, the Czech Republic, Ghana, Guatemala, Hong Kong, Hungary, India, Ireland, Israel, Jamaica, Japan, Korea, Malaysia, Mexico, Pakistan, the Philippines, Russia, Singapore, Taiwan, and Thailand. What types of jobs are offshored? Some of the jobs are: credit bureau record maintenance, human resources functions, including payroll processing, patient record transcription for doctors and hospitals, telemarketing sales, mortgage loan processing, call centers for banks, credit card companies, social service agencies, and product support, account maintenance for banks, credit card companies, investment firms, and insurance companies, and tax processing for accounting firms and some state and federal government entities.

One of the first and most publicized offshore information breaches involved a disgruntled employee in Pakistan. According to reports, the University of California, San Francisco Medical Center (UCSF) outsourced the transcription of its patient records to a firm in the United States (Lazarus 2004b). The U.S. vendor, in turn, hired a woman in Pakistan to handle some of the workload without the approval of the hospital. When the offshore transcriber was not paid as promised, she sent an e-mail to the hospital in October 2003 in which she threatened to expose patient records via the Internet. To reinforce her intent, she attached the confidential discharge records of two patients to the e-mail. This incident highlights the difficulty in controlling who has access to personal information after it is outsourced within the United States and ultimately exported.

U.S.-based entities are also subject to extortion attempts. Heartland Information Services located in Toledo, Ohio, transcribes doctors' dictated notes for several hospitals (Lazarus 2004a). The company sent work to India for processing. Two offshore employees threatened to divulge patient information unless the company met their demands. In this case, Indian authorities intervened and thwarted the extortion attempt.

Infiltration by organized criminal syndicates poses a more worrisome threat to the identities of U.S. citizens (Becker 2005). Foreign criminal organizations have attempted to enter the lucrative market of personal information processing; they have tried to purchase call centers, set up their own call centers, and have attempted to obtain personal information by bribing call center employees. Since call centers are in business to process volumes of personal identifying information, they are in danger of becoming a point of compromise for identity theft.

Putting economic issues aside, two facts remain: offshoring personal information creates unique opportunities for stealing identities while at the same time, the chances of prosecuting the offenders are greatly diminished because the crimes take place beyond U.S. jurisdictional borders. Many lawmakers are concerned that the offshoring of U.S. citizens' personal information poses a threat to national security since identity theft has been utilized in most, if not all, of the terrorist acts perpetrated against the United States (Markey 2004).

Data Breaches

Data breaches are of growing concern to privacy advocates, lawmakers, businesses, consumers, and law enforcement officials. A data security breach is defined as the act of creating the potential for hundreds or thousands of people to fall victim to identity theft due to lost, stolen, unsecured, or mishandled personal information. The Identity Theft Resource Center (ITRC) has tracked disclosed information security breaches since 2005. Once collected, the data is categorized according to the year and type of entity where the breach occurred. As breaches are disclosed, the information is added to the reports and made publicly available. There are five categories of data breaches: *banking/credit/financial, business, educational, government/military,* and *medical/healthcare.* Breaches that occur in the *financial industry* category include banks, credit unions, credit bureaus, credit card companies, finance companies, and investment firms. The category *business* covers all types of private sector enterprises such as automakers, data brokers, insurance companies, stores, hotels, airlines, cell phone companies, telephone companies, and so forth. Breaches occurring in the *educational* category include institutions ranging from elementary schools to universities. The *government/military* category encompasses breaches that occur at all government agencies, including military installations. Breaches in the *medical/healthcare* category include doctors' offices, clinics, laboratories, healthcare insurance providers, and hospitals (ITRC 2009c).

In 2005, there were 157 incidents involving 66,853,201 records containing sensitive information (ITRC 2009a). Breaches occurred most often at educational institutions (47.8%). In 75 separate incidents, 1,996,583 records were exposed, putting individuals at risk of identity theft. Even though the financial industry had fewer breaches (12.7% of all those reported), more records where exposed in this category than all others. There were 20 incidents in which 48,146,173 records were exposed.

In 2006, the number of breaches almost doubled from the previous year (ITRC 2009b). There were 321 disclosed incidents in 2006, compared to 157 in 2005. However, the number of records involved declined from 66,853,201 in 2005 to 19,137,844 in 2006. Most breaches occurred in the *government/military* category, where 98 incidents exposed 7,362,790 records. Breaches occurring at educational institutions ranked second; over 2 million (2,198,830) sensitive records were exposed in 80 incidents.

There were 446 breaches disclosed in 2007 (ITRC 2007). In 2005 and 2006 combined, there were 478 incidents. Thus, disclosed breaches increased dramatically in 2007. There may be two reasons for the increase: more breaches may have occurred in 2007 than in previous years, or more information security breaches may have been disclosed to the public in 2007 than in 2005 and 2006. The *business* category accounted for 28.9 percent of all breaches in 2007. There were 129 incidents in which 105,544,377 records were exposed. In all, 127,717,243 records were exposed in 2007. Educational and government related breaches ranked second and third, with 111 and 110 incidents, respectively. The fewest number of breaches occurred in the *banking/credit/financial* category.

In 2008, disclosed data breaches reached a high of 656 incidents (ITRC 2009c). As a result, 35,691,255 sensitive records were exposed (ITRC 2009c). More than one third (36.6%) of the breaches, or 240 incidents, occurred in the private business sector and exposed 5,886,960 records. Even though there were fewer incidents in the *banking/credit/financial* category, more records were exposed in it than in all other categories; there were 78 breaches in which 18,731,947 records were exposed. Educational institutions ranked second in the number of incidents in 2008, but last for the number of records exposed, with 131 breaches in which 806,142 sensitive records were exposed. Government-related breaches ranked third with 110 incidents, during which nearly 3 million (2,954,373) records were exposed.

A clearer pattern emerges when the data for the last four years is combined. From 2005 through 2008, a total of 1,150 data beaches were disclosed. Of those, 461 were in the *business* category, followed by the *educational* category with 397 breaches. The *government/military* category was third with 339 disclosed incidents. The *medical/healthcare* category ranked fourth, with 223 breaches. The fewest number of breaches occurred in the *banking/credit/financial* category. Overall, the number of reported breaches in each category has risen over the four-year period, but, as stated previously, the actual number of breaches may not have increased. In earlier years, data breaches may have gone unreported. Today, disclosure law requirements may be responsible for the marked increase in known breaches. On the other hand, more breaches may have been voluntarily disclosed.

Between 2005 and 2008, a total of 249,399,543 records containing personal information were exposed. The *business* category ranked first with 119,388,987 records exposed during the last four years. The *banking/credit/financial* category was second with 78,114,369 records exposed. In third place was the *government/military* category, with 31,186,520 records exposed. The *medical/healthcare* category saw 14,523,537 records exposed due to data breaches, and the *educational* category had the fewest, with 6,186,130 records exposed. If each of the 249,399,543 breached records belonged to a different person, nearly 250 million people would have been at risk of becoming victims of identity theft. Should that happen, the FTC, law enforcement agencies, victims' advocates, credit reporting agencies, the entities where the breaches occurred, and the U.S. economy would be overwhelmed.

According to the data, information security breaches have steadily increased over the last four years, and more will certainly be disclosed in the coming years. The data shows that private sector businesses had more breaches than all other categories. In addition, more records were exposed in the business category than in all other categories, accounting for nearly half of all records exposed. In other words, private sector businesses are more likely to put individuals at risk of identity theft than other entities. Although the existing data brings weaknesses to light, it may be better utilized as a tool for developing effective policies and procedures for securing personal identifying information. In order to fully understand the impact of identity theft, however, it is also important to explore the hidden costs of the crime. Some businesses and financial institutions, as well as consumers, bear the financial losses resulting from identity theft.

The Hidden Costs of the Crime

There are costs associated with security breaches even if the personal identifying information exposed is not used to perpetrate identity theft. Likewise, there are costs related to the use of stolen identities. As previously stated, victims of identity theft are generally not held responsible for the debts incurred by their imposters. If an individual's credit card is stolen, the Fair Credit Billing Act limits the cardholder's liability to $50 (FTC n.d.-b). Most credit card companies do not hold victims responsible for the $50 allowable by law. However, many online merchants are at a disadvantage, as they usually absorb the losses created by the crime. If a stolen credit card is used to purchase goods, the fraudulent charge is removed from the individual's account and charged back to the merchant's account. In addition, the merchant may be charged processing fees for reversing the transaction. If the order has been shipped, the merchant loses again, as there is very little chance of recovering the stolen merchandise.

It is impossible to calculate the actual costs of identity theft to businesses, financial institutions, payment processors, and credit card companies, as little information is available from these entities. One study commissioned by the FTC suggests that $47.6 billion were lost due to identity theft in just one year (Synovate 2003). Identity theft, however, is considered one of the expenses associated with doing business. Given this frame of reference, few cases are likely to be investigated. It may be less costly, less time-consuming, and less difficult to absorb the losses than to pursue the criminals. In most cases, the costs are simply passed on to the consumer in the form of higher interest rates, fees, and prices for goods and services. The result is that identity theft takes money out of the pockets of consumers and is a drain on the U.S. economy. This costly crime affects every aspect of modern society. The next section of this chapter examines many of the responses to identity theft.

Solving the Identity Theft Problem

The greatest concern related to identity theft is how to prevent it from happening. The following section focuses on the many possible responses to this crime. First, the debate over whether or not victims play a role in their own victimization is examined, and then legislative responses aimed at combating identity theft are discussed. The last part of this section offers suggestions of identity theft prevention measures to individuals and suggestions for protecting sensitive information in the workplace. It is evident that solving the identity problem depends upon the coordinated efforts of individuals, public entities, and private organizations.

Responsibility Theories

There are several theories defining a victim's responsibility for a crime that is committed against them. Some theories of victimology focus on victim blaming, while others focus on victim defending. Victim-blaming theories concentrate on holding the injured party responsible for what happened to them. Victim-defending theories advocate that the injured party is not responsible (Karmen 2003). When applied to identity theft, these theories can greatly influence the manner in which victims are advised to protect themselves from being victimized again in the future.

The victim-blaming perspective implies that the victim played a role in his or her own identity being stolen. Therefore, the victim is in some way to blame for the crime taking place. This approach often times creates feelings of stress, anxiety, and hopelessness that are fostered by the responses received from others. An identity theft victim may come into contact with law enforcement personnel, prosecutors, and representatives of the credit bureaus, financial institutions, and creditors, and they may respond in a manner that makes the victim feel that no one is going to help resolve his or her identity theft problems. In addition, prevention measures specifically focus on what the victim must do to prevent the crime from occurring again.

The victim-defending perspective of identity theft, on the other hand, implies that the victim is not responsible for the wrongdoing. In this framework, the perpetrator is responsible for committing the crime and should be punished accordingly. Most often, this theory allows for a thorough exploration into the nature of the crime. The victim-defending approach facilitates a discussion on the societal level about how the crime can be prevented from occurring again and encourages victims to examine how the crime happened and how it can be prevented from recurring. This approach, however, does not negate any party's responsibility in the crime.

In part, the President's Task Force on Identity Theft is based upon the victim-defending approach (President's Identity Theft

Task Force 2007). The task force was established on May 10, 2006 to study identity theft and propose solutions for combating it. One of the problems the task force addressed was how personal identifying information is collected, used, and stored. Recommendations included, for example, policies aimed at better protecting SSNs in the public and private sectors. The task force also suggested compensating victims for the time and money they spend resolving their identity theft problems. From a victim-defending perspective, creating a task force implies that government agencies and private entities recognize that victims are not solely responsible for the theft of their identities. However, individuals cannot disassociate themselves from the crime and be careless with their personal information. Likewise, it ought not to be construed that the government is solely responsible for the crime simply because it formed a task force dedicated to identity theft problems.

The victim-blaming and victim-defending theories are very different approaches to understanding the crime of identity theft, however both provide insight into potential prevention measures. Later in this chapter, methods for protecting sensitive information will be addressed.

Government Responses

Much of the legislation that has been enacted regarding identity theft focuses on large-scale governmental and corporate responsibility to protect citizens and consumers. As established in chapter 1, identity theft is not a new crime, and it seemed to be rampant by the late 1990s. Almost daily, the media reported incidents of the crime and the problems it caused for victims. Consumer and privacy groups and victims' advocates fought for tougher laws and victims' rights. Government hearings were held in an effort to assess the problem and recommend solutions, and as a result, a law was passed recognizing identity theft as a felony. What was lacking, however, was statistical data that measured the scope, nature, and prevalence of identity theft in the United States. Later legislation mandated the collection and extrapolation of identity theft incident data and provided assistance to victims of the crime.

The Identity Theft and Assumption Deterrence Act of 1998
The enactment of the Identity Theft and Assumption Deterrence Act of 1998 made identity theft a felony. The Act amended and enhanced existing federal criminal code, 18.U.S.C. § 1028 pertaining

to identity theft and identity theft facilitated crimes. Prior to the Act, legislation only dealt with the manufacture, possession, transfer, and use of fraudulent identification documents such as driver's licenses, passports, and so forth; it did not address the fact that fraudulent documents often contained the stolen personal information of unsuspecting victims. The 1998 Act made it a federal crime for a person to knowingly transfer or use the personal identifying information of another with the intent to commit a crime or to aid in the commission of other crimes. It also enhanced the penalties when identity theft is committed in order to facilitate drug trafficking and violent crimes. The Act recognized that individuals were victims of identity theft, and ordered the creation of an identity theft complaint database.

The Identity Theft Clearinghouse
The Identity Theft and Assumption Deterrence Act of 1998 mandated the establishment of the Identity Theft Data Clearinghouse under the auspices of the FTC. Created in 1914, the FTC is a federal government agency charged with helping protect consumers from fraud and ensuring a fair venue for businesses to sell their goods and services (FTC 2008). In November 1999, the Identity Theft Clearinghouse database was launched to collect identity theft complaints directly from victims of the crime. It is the only national database of its kind.

The information in the database is used for two main purposes. First, all complaints are aggregated into the Consumer Sentinel Network, a database accessible online to authorized officials only (FTC 2009). Those with the right to use it include local, state, and federal law enforcement agencies, state and federal attorney general offices, district attorneys offices, consumer protection agencies, some foreign law enforcement agencies, and U.S. Department of Defense personnel. The Consumer Sentinel Network is a useful tool in case investigations, as it aids law enforcement agencies in identifying potential problems within their jurisdictions. As a result, management decisions can be made to best utilize available resources such as funds, personnel, and time. The FTC also has access to the data, and it is often used as the basis for introducing policies and procedures for dealing with identity theft concerns.

Second, annual statistical reports are generated from the data in the Identity Theft Clearinghouse and are publicly available on the FTC's Web site (FTC 2009). The reports are very detailed and contain both national and state statistics. For example, complaints received in any given year are divided into eight types of identity theft: (1) credit card fraud, (2) phone or utilities fraud, (3) bank fraud, (4) employment-related fraud, (5) government documents or benefits fraud, (6) loan fraud, (7) other identity theft, and (8) attempted identity theft. National data and a state-by-state tally of the complaints received for each type of identity theft are provided. The annual reports are valuable sources for identifying current trends and predicting future trends in the crime. Thus, victims' advocates can implement assistance programs that deliver timely and effective services, and state and federal lawmakers can use the reports as a basis for introducing legislation that targets certain aspects of the crime. Additionally, the information is invaluable to researchers exploring the crime and discussing potential prevention measures.

The annual statistics gleaned from Identity Theft Clearinghouse database are also used for developing consumer educational programs (FTC n.d.-c). To that end, the FTC launched a campaign, "AvoID Theft: Deter, Detect, Defend," whose goal is to promote consumer knowledge by providing the materials needed to establish awareness programs. These materials range from pamphlets to short films and are available to any person or organization interested in informing others about the issues surrounding identity theft. Individuals, law enforcement agencies, churches, clubs, professional groups, and businesses are encouraged to take part in the campaign.

In addition to consumer awareness programs, the FTC offers detailed online victim assistance information (FTC n.d.-a). Step-by-step instructions, forms, and sample letters are provided to guide victims through the maze of re-claiming their identities. Briefly stated, all victims are advised to complete four basic steps as quickly as possible: (1) contact one of the three major credit bureaus, TransUnion, Equifax, or Experian, and place fraud alerts on their credit reports; (2) close the accounts that have been compromised or fraudulently opened in their names; (3) file a complaint with the FTC; and (4) file a complaint with a law enforcement agency. Then, instructions are given for victims of specific types of identity theft such as tax fraud, SSN fraud, driver's license fraud, and so forth.

Since the Identity Theft Clearinghouse database was established, the advantages associated with it have become obvious. The comprehensive annual reports, in conjunction with the online database access, consumer materials, and victim instructions, are helpful tools for determining the prevalence of the crime, identifying current patterns in case investigations, predicting future trends, and guiding awareness programs. Also, these are useful tools for promoting a greater understanding of the nature of the crime, perpetrators, their methods, and victims. These arguments demonstrate the need to continue the initiative and to fund periodic reevaluations and updates. There are, however, some limitations that warrant discussion.

The Consumer Sentinel Network is underutilized. Many eligible agencies have not applied for access to the database (Consumer Sentinel Network 2009). Some agencies have access but use it sparingly at best, and still others are unaware that the database exists. Therefore, ways to increase participation in the Consumer Sentinel Network need to be explored.

The Identity Theft Clearinghouse is also underutilized. One limitation is that all victims do not report the crime to the FTC; in fact, it is fairly common for crimes to go unreported. This phenomenon, called "the dark figure of crime," refers to the number of crimes that are committed that victims never report to police. If victims hesitate to notify police of crimes that occur, than it is logical to believe that in identity theft cases, victims may not notify the FTC. Victims may be unaware that they have the option of filing a complaint with the FTC. At this point, it is important to note that the FTC is not a law enforcement agency; they do not verify or investigate the complaints they receive, but some complaints may be referred to a law enforcement agency.

Victims elect not to file a complaint with the FTC for many reasons. Since the FTC does not investigate cases, some consider it a pointless endeavor. Many others do not consider themselves victims of a crime. For example, this attitude is common in cases of existing credit card account fraud. Research shows that the earlier the fraudulent charges are detected, the easier it is to resolve the problems. Sometimes the issue is resolved with a telephone call. Cardholders, therefore, cannot justify filing a complaint with a law enforcement agency or the FTC. If the crime is not reported, victims may be less likely to use the instructions for clearing their names provided by the FTC. Given the importance of the Identity Theft Clearinghouse, consumer education programs ought to stress reporting the crime to the FTC.

Although the Identity Theft Clearinghouse and the Consumer Sentinel Network are both underutilized, their data is needed to provide better information to consumers, victims, businesses, legislators, and law enforcement agencies. More importantly, the data is useful developing and implementing effective preventative measures.

Identity Theft Penalty Enhancement Act

In 2004, the Identity Theft Penalty Enhancement Act amended 18.U.S.C. § 1028 once again. The Act created the offense of "aggravated identity theft" and introduced mandatory sentences for the crime. Aggravated identity theft is defined as the unlawful transfer, possession, or use of another person's identifying information related to the commission of specific felonies. A conviction for wire, bank, or mail fraud, for example, involving stolen personal information results in two sentences (i.e., one for the fraud conviction and an additional mandatory two-year sentence for aggravated identity theft). A terrorism conviction involving stolen personal information or false identification documents also results in two sentences (i.e., one for the terrorism conviction and an additional five-year sentence for aggravated identity theft). The Act also mandates that those convicted of aggravated identity theft must serve out their sentences in custody, instead of being placed on probation.

The Identity Theft Enforcement and Restitution Act of 2008

The Identity Theft Enforcement and Restitution Act of 2008 was signed into law by President George W. Bush (Krebs 2008). The legislation was designed to help in the investigation and prosecution of cybercrimes, including identity theft, and to provide financial recourse for victims. The new law broadens the federal courts' jurisdiction over computer intrusion cases (Library of Congress n.d.). Prior to the bill's enactment, federal courts only had jurisdiction if the perpetrator crossed state lines to access a victim's personal computer. The new law eliminates the jurisdictional boundaries. Additionally, it removes the limits to monetary damages; it is no longer necessary to prove that a victim sustained at least $5,000 in damages as a result of computer hacking. It also became a felony to damage 10 or more computers associated with the federal government or financial industry over a period of a year. In addition, the new law recommends increasing the penalties for identity theft, hacking, and computer-related fraud offenses. It instructs the U.S. Sentencing Commission to assess and update its guidelines.

Another aspect of the Act addresses the costs incurred by victims of identity theft (Library of Congress n.d.). When the thieves

are convicted, victims may be entitled to restitution for the time
they spend resolving problems. Although the legislation acknowledges that victims sustain monetary losses, it does not address the
entire financial impact of the crime. As discussed earlier in this
chapter, victims are often victimized twice for the same crime, an
event known as the second insult. The new law does not address
these damages. For example, the credit scores of some victims are
adversely affected due to fraudulent financial activities. Consequently, victims are assessed higher interest rates on loans and
credit cards.

State-level Legislative Responses

The majority of identity theft cases are not investigated and prosecuted at the federal level. State Attorney Generals' offices pursue
many cases, but most are investigated by local law enforcement
agencies and prosecuted in local courts. Laws that define identity
theft and assign criminal penalties vary from state to state. Arizona
is credited with being the first state to pass a law criminalizing
identity theft (U.S. Congress 2002). The statute was enacted in 1996.
However, a Mississippi statute, enacted in 1993, could be considered
the first identity theft legislation even though it referred to "false
pretenses" instead of "identity theft" in its title. The statute, Mississippi Code Annotated § 97-19-85, was amended in 1998 to make
identity theft a felony instead of a misdemeanor and expanded the
types of personal identifying information covered under the law.
California and Wisconsin passed identity theft laws in 1997. By
2001, 44 states had enacted legislation under which identity theft
became a criminal offense. Today, all states have passed new laws
or enhanced their existing statutes pertaining to identity theft.

Some statutes define identity theft as the use of another person's identifying information to commit fraud. Conversely, the
laws in some states do not require that the identities be used to
commit crimes; under these laws, it is a criminal offense to possess, buy, sell, or give away the personal identifying information of another person. Depending upon the state, identity theft
is either a felony or misdemeanor. Classification is based upon
the dollar amount of goods, services, and/or money obtained.
Wyoming Statute Article 9, § 6-3-901 maintains that identity theft
is a misdemeanor if the financial gain or attempted financial gain
amounts to less than $1,000. In contrast, Arizona Revised Statute §
13-2008 sets forth that identity theft is a felony even if no financial
gain is realized.

Legislators across the country are constantly amending current laws and introducing new legislation to define identity theft more clearly, update current laws to reflect the evolution of technology and how it is used to commit crimes, increase the penalties associated with the crime under subscribed circumstances, offer consumers and victims more control over their personal information, and provide the tools and resources needed for the investigation and prosecution of perpetrators responsible for identity theft.

Passport Programs

A few states help protect victims from having future problems resulting from the theft of their identities. Approximately 10 states have instituted measures called "passport programs" (FTC n.d.-d). These programs aid victims in clearing their financial and criminal history records of fraudulent activities committed in their names and serve as proof of victimization, should problems occur in the future. Ohio's Identity Theft Verification Passport Program is an example of this initiative.

A victim residing in Ohio must file a complaint with his or her local law enforcement agency in order to be eligible to participate in the program (Ohio Attorney General n.d.). Once the agency confirms that the identity has been stolen, the victim is given a passport application to complete and return. Information from the application, along with biometric data about the victim, is entered into a database by law enforcement personnel, and the passport application and police report are sent to the state Attorney General's office for verification. Once it is validated, the victim is issued a passport identification card. The purpose of the card is to help prevent future problems, as it can be presented to creditors as proof of victimization or presented to law enforcement personnel should the victim be threatened with arrest for crimes committed in his or her name. Creditors and law enforcement officials can verify the victim's status by calling the toll-free numbers provided by the Attorney General's office.

Identity Theft Task Forces

The purpose of a task force is to address a specific problem. It may be a collaborative endeavor between government agencies and private entities, or it may be made up of representatives from one or more government entities. Many states have established task forces to share information leading to the investigation and prosecution of identity theft cases. In June 2008 Georgia became one of the most recent states to pass a law mandating the formation of a task force (State of Georgia 2008). Prior to the passage of Senate Bill 388, identity theft cases were investigated by the Governor's Office of Consumer Affairs. The new bill provided funding to organize an identity theft task force within the Georgia Bureau of Investigation (GBI). In addition to conducting investigations, the GBI concentrates on raising public awareness, aiding victims, and training law enforcement personnel. The GBI also assists other law enforcement agencies with identity theft investigations.

Data Privacy Day

Another response to the identity theft problem is the designation of January 28th as National Data Privacy Day in the United States. The program was founded in Europe in 2007, where it was known as Data Protection Day. In 2009, 27 European countries, Canada, and the United States took part in the international project (Intel Corporation n.d.). The states of Washington, California, Oregon, Massachusetts, Arizona, New York, and Wisconsin declared January 28, 2009 as Data Privacy Day, and North Carolina proclaimed January to be Data Privacy Month. Participants included universities, software vendors, government agencies, privacy advocates, financial institutions, data brokers, and several other types of businesses.

One goal of the program is to encourage a global dialogue regarding privacy issues (Intel Corporation n.d.). In addition, Data Privacy Day provides a forum for increasing awareness among businesses and consumers of the importance of securing sensitive information. To that end, the program also presents an opportunity to educate youth about protecting their personal information online.

Identity Theft Prevention and Mitigation Program

Most states offer information to their residents about how to prevent identity theft and what to do if they become victims of the crime. A recent initiative, an Identity Theft and Mitigation Program, was established in the state of New York as part of the Consumer Protection Board (CPB) (New York State CPB 2009). A portion of the CPB Web site offers privacy protection information for use by businesses and consumers. For example, cell phone security is one of the issues addressed in the consumer section of the site (New York State CPB n.d.). The Web site also contains a section dedicated to assisting victims of identity theft. Under New York law, victims may be entitled to restitution if their imposter is convicted; therefore a worksheet is provided to help victims keep track of the costs they incur as a result of their victimization. They may request restitution for lost wages, time spent resolving problems, attorney's fees, credit counseling, notary fees, financial account losses, and money spent on photocopies and mailings. Another worksheet is available for victims to record information about the contacts they make during the process of clearing their names, including interactions with the CPB. Victims may file a complaint with the CPB online or by calling a toll-free number. The unique aspect of the program, however, is that the CPB has a staff available to assist victims personally in resolving their problems with credit bureaus, businesses, banks, credit card companies, and so forth. In some cases, staff members intercede on behalf of victims.

Criminal Justice System Response

The criminal justice system plays many roles in responding to identity theft victims. Law enforcement agencies, often the first to respond, take complaints and conduct investigations (Collins and Hoffman 2003). Then, offenders are prosecuted in courts of law. Most identity theft cases, however, are not investigated and prosecuted. Why? Law enforcement agencies, prosecutors, and judges across the nation are experiencing increased workloads. At the same time, budgets for personnel and training are shrinking. Identity theft investigations are time-consuming; a single case may involve several perpetrators, victims, and jurisdictions. Likewise, a case may require the talents of several investigators. Simply stated, resources are lacking. Compounding the problem is the perception that identity theft is not a serious crime.

The President's Identity Theft Task Force made recommendations to address these problems (President's Identity Theft Task Force 2007). One suggestion was to develop a centralized database to aid in investigations. This would allow law enforcement agencies to share case data and would be particularly valuable in addressing the jurisdictional issues that are inherent in identity theft cases.

The task force recommended that a universal complaint form be created to standardize the procedures for taking identity theft reports (President's Identity Theft Task Force 2007). The complaint form would be available on the FTC Web site for victims to print, complete, and take to a law enforcement agency for processing. Once the information is confirmed, law enforcement personnel would enter the complaint into the centralized database. This process has several potential benefits for victims as well as law enforcement agencies. It would simplify the procedures for filing complaints. Further, a complaint form that collects specific information about identity theft cases would aid in investigations by making it easier to recognize the connections between cases.

The task force also recommended coordinating and improving training for prosecutors and law enforcement personnel (President's Identity Theft Task Force 2007). First, it was suggested that more training is needed in conducting investigations and assisting victims and should be offered by the FTC. Second, training should be readily available to personnel on the federal, state and local levels. Furthermore, courses should provide up-to-date information.

Private and Public Partnerships

There are many private organizations that work together to provide victims' services, promote public awareness, and offer identity theft insurance protection. Also, public and private entities form alliances in efforts to combat the crime. One such partnership was formed between the International Association of Chiefs of Police (IACP) and the Bank of America (BAC) in 2006 (IACP 2007). This was the first time that the financial industry and law enforcement had collaborated on a nationwide project designed to address prevention, victim assistance, and investigations (ID Safety n.d.). The first phase of the program was complete when a Web site called ID Safety was launched. The site contains prevention suggestions for consumers, advice for victims of the crime and investigative training for law enforcement personnel.

The partnership identified several long-range objectives that must be accomplished (ID Safety n.d.). Its first objective is to prevent identity theft from occurring by: increasing public awareness of the crime and how to prevent it, encouraging local law enforcement agencies and financial organizations to form partnerships, and exploring vendor practices that may be a factor in facilitating the crime. The second objective is to improve methods for investigating identity theft cases by promoting insight into the global aspect of the crime and offering the opportunity for law enforcement agencies nationwide to share investigative techniques and prevention strategies. The last objective is to facilitate a uniform response to the crime among law enforcement agencies and financial institutions and to encourage them to combine their investigative efforts. The partnership, a three-year initiative, was established on solid goals and objectives. It will be reevaluated periodically to determine its effectiveness and future direction.

Protecting Personal Information

Identity theft cannot be prevented entirely. However, individuals can greatly reduce their risk of becoming victims of the crime. As stated in the first chapter, thieves use hundreds of methods to steal identities, and these methods are constantly evolving in response to several factors, such as technological advances and legislation. Preventative measures, therefore, must be continually reassessed. Regardless, individuals can take some basic steps to safeguard their personal identifying information. This section discusses protective measures that are inexpensive or cost nothing at all. In addition, the safeguards can be implemented immediately.

Awareness is the first step in reducing the risk of being victimized. Before sharing personal information, ask several questions. Who is requesting it? Why is it necessary? How will it be used? Who will have access to it? Evaluate the situation and determine if providing the information serves a beneficial purpose. For example, for individuals who are asked to provide their SSNs in order to obtain utility services, the benefits outweigh the risks. On the other hand, providing an SSN as identification for cashing a check puts individuals at great risk. Being aware of how identities are stolen and understanding basic preventative measures are effective tools for reducing the risk of victimization.

Phishing is a common method employed by thieves to steal identities. It is the act of sending deceptive e-mails for the purpose of tricking recipients into providing their personal information. Phishing e-mails usually have five elements in common:

1. The e-mail appears to be from a legitimate source, such as a bank or credit union. The logo of the financial institution is embedded in the e-mail.
2. The message conveys a sense of urgency. Recipients may be instructed to update their information within 48 hours or risk suspension of online account access.
3. Many grammatical and spelling errors may be found in the e-mail.

4. The e-mail might contain a link to a Web page. When recipients click on the link, a Web page appears that looks like it belongs to a legitimate business. However, it is a clone.
5. A form for collecting personal information is provided on the bogus Web page. Once the form is completed and submitted, the information is used to perpetrate the identity theft.

All consumers should learn to recognize phishing attempts and be suspicious of unexpected or unsolicited e-mails. The best practice is to delete these messages, but if an e-mail does appear to be from a legitimate company, financial institution, or government agency, recipients should contact the source by telephone to verify it. Further, consumers should look up the number in a telephone book or on a statement, and never call the number provided in an unsolicited e-mail. To avoid installing a computer virus, recipients should never click on a link provided in an unsolicited e-mail.

There are also risks associated with responding to unsolicited telephone calls. *Vishing,* or voice phishing, is a common method used by identity thieves. It is the act of using a combination of pretexting, phishing, and/or advanced voice technology for the purpose of obtaining personal information under false pretenses. There are many types of vishing schemes. One scheme involves telephone calls made over the Internet using Voice Over Internet Protocol (VoIP) technology. A thief can purchase temporary VoIP numbers and make calls to landline telephones. They often identify themselves as representatives of a credit card company or a financial institution. The caller may state that there has been suspicious activity on the prospective victim's account and may request personal information or provide a toll-free number for contacting the fraud department. Vishers are imitating the fraud notification process used by legitimate credit card companies and financial institutions. The best practice is to hang up the telephone without providing any information and not call the toll-free number the visher provides. Consumers should also ignore the number displayed on caller IDs, as these names and numbers can be forged. Instead, consumers should call the customer service number listed on the back of their credit card or on a billing statement.

Identity thieves can also obtain personal information through face-to-face interactions. Many legitimate businesses employ door-to-door solicitors to sell goods and services; however, no one should ever give personal information to a stranger who knocks at the door. Under no circumstances should a stranger be invited to step inside the residence. There have been many cases of identity theft in which victims allowed strangers into their homes. One thief will find a way to distract the potential customer while another looks for items to steal such as checkbooks, wallets, credit cards, bank statements, or credit card statements. If you are considering doing business with a stranger at the door, do not be pressured into making an immediate decision. Ask for identification and information about the business (e.g., its name, address, and telephone number). End the conversation and take the time to thoroughly research the business. Call the local Better Business Bureau (BBB), or visit their Web site at http://www.bbb.org. If a professional license is required, confirm its status with the state licensing bureau. Consumers should also determine if there are any outstanding complaints or litigation involving the particular business. Finally, if satisfactory answers to these questions are received, call the business to verify that the solicitor is actually their employee.

People must also be careful when purchasing medications over the Internet. As the cost of healthcare rises, the number of online pharmacies increases. It is a quick, convenient service for both customers and providers, however, hundreds of online pharmacies are owned by criminals. In some cases, bogus Web sites are set up for the sole purpose of stealing customers' personal information. In other cases, the pharmacies are not licensed or accredited to sell medications to U.S.-based consumers. Some ship fake, substituted, or weakened medications, while others collect debit and credit card payments but fail to ship the orders. Before purchasing from an online pharmacy, check the National Association of Boards of Pharmacy (NAPB) Web site. There are also two searchable databases available for confirming a pharmacy's validity. The Verified Internet Pharmacy Practice Sites (VIPPS) database consists of pharmacies accredited by the NABP to sell medications for human consumption. The Veterinary-Verified Internet Pharmacy Practice Sites (Vet-VIPPS) database contains pharmacies that are accredited to sell medications for animals. Both databases are available at http://www.nabp.net/index.html?target=/vipps/consumer/search.asp&. In addition, the NABP provides a list of names and URLs of online pharmacies that consumers should avoid.

There are risks associated with using debit and credit cards to conduct in-person and online transactions. When making purchases in person, be aware of who has the card and make sure it is visible at all times. *Skimming* is a common method used to steal identities. Skimming devices are very small and can be easily hidden in a pocket, apron pouch, or under a counter. In a matter of seconds, a card can be swiped through a skimmer, and all of the information on the magnetic strip, including the card's security code, is recorded and stored. When making online purchases, check the BBB Web site before shopping on an unfamiliar merchant's Web site, and write down the merchant's address and telephone number for future reference. Be cautious if the only way to make contact is through a post office box or e-mail address. Look for the security icon, a closed padlock, before entering and submitting an order. Check the URL that appears in the browser bar at the top of the page. Make sure it begins with "https," instead of "http." The "s" indicates that information is encrypted before it is transmitted. Print and keep (or save in a file on your computer) copies of the purchase order, confirmation number, and all e-mail correspondence. In addition to these safeguards, consider having a separate low-limit credit card to use for online shopping, entertainment, and travel.

Protecting incoming and outgoing mail is another way to reduce one's risk of victimization. Identity thieves steal mail hoping to find personal information. The most desirable documents include personal checks written to pay bills, boxes of blank checks being delivered from financial institutions, cell phone, telephone, and utility bills, credit card and bank statements, retirement and investment account statements, preapproved credit card applications, and income tax information such as W2 and 1099 forms. Remove incoming mail from the box immediately after it is delivered. If that is inconvenient, consider purchasing a locked mailbox or renting a post office box. Stop your mail delivery while on vacation. Never put up the red flag on a mailbox and leave it unattended. The red flag tells the postal employee that there is outgoing mail, but it also signals to identity thieves that mail is waiting for them to pick up. The best practice is to take outgoing mail to the post office. Instead of dropping it in the blue curbside receptacle, take the mail inside and deposit it. The curbside mailboxes can fill up, thus making the mail near the top accessible to anyone.

Reducing one's amount of incoming mail also helps prevent identity theft. There are many ways to opt out of receiving unsolicited correspondence. By calling 1–888–5OPTOUT, individuals can temporarily or permanently remove their names from the marketing lists that credit bureaus sell to businesses. Thus, businesses cannot send documents, such as preapproved credit card applications, to those who have chosen not to receive them. Another way to reduce unwanted mail is to complete and return opt-out notices. Financial institutions and other businesses share their customers' information with affiliates, however they are mandated by law to give their customers the opportunity to opt out of having personal information shared with nonaffiliates.

The FTC provides another option to help individuals protect their privacy. Consumers may opt out of receiving telemarketing calls by registering their cell and telephone numbers with the National Do Not Call Registry at http://www.ftc.gov/donotcall. It will not stop all unsolicited calls, but it will drastically reduce the number received.

Shredding obsolete or unwanted documents is another way to reduce the risk of becoming a victim of identity theft. A cross-cut shredder is best because it chops paper into tiny bits that cannot be pieced back together. Shredding prevents dumpster divers from retrieving personal information from recycling containers, dumpsters, trash cans, and landfills. However, some important documents must be retained such as tax returns, insurance policies, stock certificates, and blank checks. Store these in a locked drawer in your home or in a lock box (also called a safe deposit box) at a financial institution.

Passwords should be placed on all financial accounts to help reduce the risk of identity theft. Financial accounts include checking, savings, investment, credit card, telephone, cell phone, and utilities. Passwords identify the account holder when conducting transactions online, in person, or over the telephone. Write these down and keep them with other important documents. To further secure accounts, change all passwords at least once a year. Choose strong passwords that are difficult for another person to figure out. Use a combination of random upper case letters, lower case letters, numbers, and symbols. Avoid using soft passwords such as consecutive letters or numbers. Additionally, passwords should not contain personal information. It is easy to remember a date of birth, a family member's name, full or partial SSN, telephone number, date of graduation, school affiliation, or mother's maiden name; however, a thief may have enough information about an individual to guess his or her password using this very information.

Shoulder-surfing is another method used by thieves to steal personal identifying information. Although it can happen anywhere, it is often associated with the use of an Automatic Teller Machine (ATM). A thief looks over the shoulder of the ATM user, records the numbers selected on the keypad, and uses that information to access the account illegally. When using an ATM, beware of your surroundings. If other people are in the area, shield the keypad and be sure to take your receipt. Another way criminals steal information is by installing skimmers or cameras in ATMs. Thus, it is best to use machines that are located at a financial institution. They are usually placed in high-traffic, well-lit areas, thereby greatly reducing the likelihood that a thief has tampered with the machine. Computer users are also targeted by shoulder-surfers. Take precautions when accessing accounts on public computers such as those located in libraries, coffee shops, airports, hotels, and hospitals. Make sure to shield the keyboard when entering personal information, and do not use a computer if the monitor is positioned where it can be read by others in the room.

Nonexistent, obsolete, or weak computer security increases the risks of identity theft, but though there are many ways to secure computers, some common security measures are often ignored. Keep all software programs, including the operating system, up to date. Regularly check the vendor's Web site for patches and updates. Install antivirus and spyware detection software. Since new viruses are discovered daily, download updates once a week and run a full scan of the hard drive. Make sure that firewall software is installed and turned on at all times; firewalls block intruders from illegally accessing computers. Be aware that the best firewalls are a combination of hardware and software. Read your computer's owner's manual and your Internet Service Provider's (ISP) instructions for securing wireless networks. Criminals are adept at harvesting passwords and personal information by exploiting weaknesses in wireless devises. Consider using a commercial file and e-mail encryption program to further protect personal information. When sharing music and games, make sure that file-sharing software is configured to deny others access to important files on the hard drive, such as income tax returns.

Guard against identity theft when discarding, selling, or donating a computer because data remains on the hard drive even after files, folders, and programs are deleted. Before disposing of an old computer, consider hiring a trusted professional to clean the hard drive or purchasing a *wipe* software program to remove all traces of data. The best option, however, is to remove and completely destroy the hard drive. To maximize protection before disposing of any electronic devise, including cell phones, remove all traces of data.

The basic suggestions offered in this section are effective tools for lessening one's risk of victimization, but if identity theft does occur, it is important to detect the crime as early as possible. To that end, individuals have many options. Scrutinize all bills and account statements as soon as they are received. If unauthorized activities are detected, report them immediately to the company or financial institution involved and close the compromised account. Also, report it if a bill or statement is not received on the date it is expected to arrive.

Another early detection tool is credit reports. Under the Fair Credit Reporting Act (FCRA), individuals are entitled to receive free credit reports every 12 months from the three major credit bureaus (i.e., TransUnion, Experian, and Equifax). Credit reports may be ordered online through the AnnualCreditReport.com Web site at http://www.annualcreditreport.com or they may be requested by calling 1-877-322-8228, a toll-free number.

The reports from all of the credit bureaus contain four basic types of information: personal identifying information, credit history, public records, and inquiries. Personal identifying information includes current and previous addresses, date of birth, SSN, employer, and spouse's name. The credit history section is a record of an individual's debts and payment habits. Public records include bankruptcies, civil judgments, overdue child support, and state or federal tax liens. Lastly, the inquiries section lists all of the entities that accessed the full or partial credit report for a permissible purpose. There are two distinctive types of inquiries: *hard* inquiries are those initiated by the consumer, such as when applying for credit; *soft* inquiries are made by companies for promotional purposes, such as mailing preapproved credit card offers to a preselected group of consumers.

It is evident that credit reports are important because they are a reflection of an individual's activities, ranging from where they live to where they have applied for credit. Equally important, these reports can expose an identity thief's illegal activities. If fraudulent or erroneous information is found on a credit report, consumers should follow the instructions provided by the credit bureau to rectify the situation. However, identity theft victims often need additional help resolving problems. The "consumers" section of the FTC's Web site, Fighting Back Against Identity Theft, offers information to aid victims in clearing their names. The site is located at http://www.ftc.gov/bcp/edu/microsites/idtheft/consumers/index.html.

The successful protection of personal information and early detection of identity theft begins with consumer awareness and knowledge of the crime. Well-informed individuals are more adept at identifying potential risks. Individuals can make better decisions in their personal lives, in the workplace, and in choosing the companies with which they to do business. Ultimately, society is the beneficiary of educated citizens.

Protecting Sensitive Information in the Workplace

Sensitive information is an integral part of doing business. It identifies the business, its customers, and employees. Many state and federal laws govern information security. The Health Information Portability and Accountability Act of 1996 (HIPAA) is an example of a federal law that sets standards for protecting patient information within the healthcare industry (U.S. Department of HHS n.d.). Although laws vary from state to state, most states have enacted legislation that restricts the use of SSNs. In addition to complying with state and federal laws, much more can be done to protect sensitive information. Many of the suggestions in the previous section for protecting personal information can be adapted for the workplace environment, however some issues are unique and warrant discussion. The following section focuses on policies and procedures that can help ensure the security of proprietary information in the workplace.

Customers and employees expect that their sensitive information will be protected once it is entrusted to a business. In addition to physically securing the premises, there are several steps that can be taken to safeguard the information that comes into, flows through, and goes out of a workplace. At this point, it is important to note that everyone in the workplace should be involved in assessing the security measures associated with their job tasks. Even though managers and employees rarely stay with one employer for their entire careers, their input is invaluable. Each position has specific job tasks. Even though personnel changes, the job tasks remain fairly constant over time.

The first step is to be aware of the types of information that the business or organization collects and the purpose for gathering it. Determine if any sensitive information is collected unnecessarily.

For example, it is necessary to use SSNs as identifiers for processing in-house payroll. On the other hand, it is unnecessary to ask customers to use their mothers' maiden names as identifiers when other passwords can serve the same purpose.

The next step is to consider how proprietary information arrives in the workplace, where it is stored, and who has access to it. Sensitive information comes into businesses in several ways, including via fax, telephone, e-mail, Web sites, and by in-person contact. Security measures for each process, therefore, should be taken into account. For example, many businesses take orders for their products by fax. The orders may contain sensitive information, such as debit or credit card numbers. To protect customers' privacy, fax machines should not be located in a public area of the workplace; instead, they should be strategically placed to coordinate with job tasks. Review the job tasks and determine who needs to have access to sensitive information in order to perform their duties. Using the fax machine scenario, follow the orders through the process (i.e., from the receipt of the faxes through shipment of the orders). Determine who must have access to sensitive information as the orders progress through the system and eliminate any steps that expose it to those who do not need it in order to complete their job duties. Then, examine where and how proprietary information is stored. Personnel files, for example, should be kept in locked drawers, and computerized payroll software should be password-protected. Only authorized staff should be given access to sensitive files and computer programs, and their access should be based upon their job functions.

When proprietary information is no longer needed, it should be disposed of in a proper manner. There are several businesses that specialize in shredding or incinerating paper documents for other organizations. Some businesses prefer to shred their unneeded documents in-house. This is a job task assigned to a position within the workplace, therefore document disposal methods should be reviewed for security.

Once current practices have been evaluated and weaknesses in security identified, the next step is to address the findings. Develop company policies and job procedures for protecting sensitive information and include this information in personnel manuals. Provide in-house training programs for the current staff and all newly hired personnel. Insist on compliance. Should an individual violate the organization's trust, have policies in place for dealing with the situation. In addition to training programs, consider offering an assistance program in case a staff member becomes a victim of personal identity theft.

Finally, hiring practices are important when considering ways to protect sensitive information in the workplace. Since some identity thieves seek out employment for the sole purpose of obtaining information, there are many approaches that can be used to screen potential employees for security risks. Examine prior work histories and contact previous employers. Conduct a thorough background check, including criminal records. Check social networking Web sites for information that individuals write about themselves. If hiring through an employment agency, make sure the agency adheres to rigorous screening processes.

Although general in nature, the proactive measures discussed in this section are relatively inexpensive to establish in any workplace. The alternative, such as a security breach of paper or electronic files, can result in a loss of business and can foster a sense of distrust within the workplace. Therefore, the time and money spent on protecting sensitive information can be recouped through customer and employee loyalty.

This chapter discussed numerous measures for preventing identity theft. If incidents of the crime are to be reduced, a concerted effort must be undertaken by the judicial system, individuals, private businesses, legislators, law enforcement agencies, and victims' advocates. Identity theft is still a common occurrence even though progress has been made in some areas. More has to be done to protect sensitive information from being stolen and used by thieves. Perpetrators of identity theft must be held responsible for their crimes, and victims ought to have access to resolution and restoration services that meet their needs.

References

AARP. 2004. "One identity theft victim's 'living hell.'" *AARP Bulletin Today*. http://bulletin.aarp.org/yourmoney/articles/livinghell.html. Accessed June 30, 2009.

Atkinson, Robert. 2004. Meeting the offshore challenge. http://www.ppionline.org/ppi_ci.cfm?knlgAreaID=107&subsecID=123&contentID=252767. Accessed January 15, 2009.

Attorney General of Florida, "Columbia county man pleads guilty to mortgage fraud scheme." Press release, May 7, 2009. http://www.

myfloridalegal.com/newsrel.nsf/newsreleases/93B9C1234B2887B18525
75AF0050B79D. Accessed June 1, 2009.

Becker, Mark J. 2005. "Privacy: Outsourcing and the need for a vendor compliance strategy." In *Expert Commentary*, ed. G. E. Clayton. http://www.irmi.com/Expert/Articles/2005/Clayton03.aspx. Accessed January 16, 2009.

Collins, Judith M. and Sandra K. Hoffman. 2003. *Identity Theft First Responder Manual for Criminal Justice Professionals: Police Officers, Attorneys, and Judges.* Flushing, NY: Looseleaf Law Publications, Inc.

Collins, Judith M. and Sandra K. Hoffman. 2004. "Identity theft: Predator profiles." Unpublished Paper, School of Criminal Justice, Michigan State University.

Consumer Sentinel Network. 2009. Consumer Sentinel Network Members. http://www.ftc.gov/sentinel/members.shtml. Accessed June 20, 2009.

Deloitte Research. 2004. The titans take hold. How offshoring has changed the competitive dynamic for global financial services institutions. http://www.deloitte.com/dtt/cda/doc/content/Offshoring%20Final%281%29.pdf. Accessed January 16, 2009.

Dixon, Pam. 2006. Medical identity theft: The information crime that can kill you. http://www.worldprivacyforum.org/pdf/wpf_medicalidtheft2006.pdf. Accessed April 4, 2007.

Doerner, William G. and Steven P. Lab. 2005. *Victimology*. 4th ed. Cincinnati, OH: Anderson Publishing Company.

Federal Bureau of Investigation (FBI). 2008. 2007 mortgage fraud report. http://www.fbi.gov/. Accessed December 1, 2009.

Federal Trade Commission (FTC). n.d.-a. Defend: Recover from identity theft. http://www.ftc.gov/bcp/edu/microsites/idtheft/consumers/defend.html. Accessed September 7, 2009.

Federal Trade Commission (FTC). n.d.-b. Federal laws: Credit. http://ftc.gov/bcp/edu/microsites/idtheft/reference-desk/federal-credit.html. Accessed June 20, 2009.

Federal Trade Commission. n.d.-c. Fighting back against identity theft: Partnership. http://www.ftc.gov/bcp/edu/microsites/idtheft/become-a-partner.html. Accessed June 20, 2009.

Federal Trade Commission. n.d.-d. State laws: ID theft passport programs. http://www.ftc.gov/bcp/edu/microsites/idtheft/reference-desk/state-crim-passport.html. Accessed June 20, 2009.

Federal Trade Commission. 2008. About the Federal Trade Commission. http://ftc.gov/ftc/about.shtm. Accessed June 20, 2009.

Federal Trade Commission. 2009. Consumer sentinel network data book for January–December 2008. http://www.ftc.gov/sentinel/reports/sentinel-annual-reports/sentinel-cy2008.pdf. Accessed June 20, 2009.

GalleryWatch. 2004. GalleryWatch federal analysis on outsourcing. http://www.gallerywatch.com/. Accessed March 3, 2006.

Gordon, Gary R., et al. 2007. Identity fraud trends and patters: Building a data-based foundation for proactive enforcement. (October): 1–74. Presented at a conference at the Economic Crime Institute, Utica College. http://www.utica.edu/academic/institutes/ecii/publications/media/cimip_id_theft_study_oct_22_noon.pdf. Accessed February 27, 2009.

Identity Theft Resource Center (ITRC). 2005. Identity theft: The aftermath 2004. http://www.idtheftcenter.org/artman2/uploads/1/The_Aftermath_2004_1.pdf. Accessed April 29, 2009.

Identity Theft Resource Center. 2007. 2007 data breach stats. http://www.idtheftcenter.org/artman2/uploads/1/ITRC_Breach_Stats_Report_20071231_1.pdf. Accessed January 14, 2009.

Identity Theft Resource Center. 2008. Identity theft: The aftermath 2007. http://www.idtheftcenter.org/artman2/uploads/1/Aftermath_2007_20080529v2_1.pdf. Accessed April 29, 2009.

Identity Theft Resource Center. 2009a. 2005 data breach stats. http://www.idtheftcenter.org/artman2/uploads/1/ITRC_Breach_Stats_Report_20051231_2.pdf. Accessed June 3, 2009.

Identity Theft Resource Center. 2009b. 2006 data breach stats. http://www.idtheftcenter.org/artman2/uploads/1/ITRC_Breach_Stats_Report_20061231.pdf. Accessed June 3, 2009.

Identity Theft Resource Center. 2009c. 2008 data breach stats. http://www.idtheftcenter.org/artman2/uploads/1/ITRC_Breach_Stats_Report_2008_final_1.pdf. Accessed June 3, 2009.

Intel Corporation. n.d. Data privacy day 2009. http://www.intel.com/policy/dataprivacy.htm. Accessed June 9, 2009.

ID Safety. n.d. About ID safety: A nationwide strategy to prevent and respond to identity crime. http://www.idsafety.org/?fa=about. Accessed June 9, 2009.

International Association of Chiefs of Police (IACP), "International Association of Chiefs of Police and Bank of America offer tax time tips." Press release, March 7, 2007. http://www.theiacp.org/About/PressCenter/tabid/81/Default.aspx?id=820&v=1. Accessed June 9, 2009.

Karmen, Andrew. 2003. *Crime Victims: An Introduction to Victimology*. 5th ed. Belmont, CA: Thomson Publishing.

Krebs, Brian. 2008. New federal law targets id theft, cybercrime. *Washington Post*, October 1. http://voices.washingtonpost.com/securityfix/2008/10/new_federal_law_targets_id_the.html. Accessed June 11, 2009.

Lazarus, David. 2004a. Extortion threat to patients' records. Clients not informed of India staff's breach. *San Francisco Chronicle*, April 4. http://sfgate.com/cgi-bin/article.cgi?file=/c/a/2004/04/02/MNGI75VIEB1.DTL. Accessed January 16, 2009.

Lazarus, David. 2004b. Special report: Looking offshore. Outsourced UCSF notes highlight privacy risk. How one offshore worker sent tremor through medical system. *San Francisco Chronicle*, March 28. http://sfgate.com/cgi-bin/article.cgi?file=/c/a/2004/03/28/MNGFS3080R264.DTL. Accessed January 16, 2009.

Library of Congress. n.d. Thomas. http://thomas.loc.gov/ (object name S2168). Accessed June 10, 2009.

Markey, Edward J. 2004. Offshoring oversight letter—Homeland security. http://www.house.gov/markey. Accessed January 16, 2006.

New York State Consumer Protection Board (CPB). n.d. CPB, Identity Theft, Information Privacy and Internet Security. http://www.nysconsumer.gov/internet_security.htm#Information%20Privacy%20for%20Consumers. Accessed June 9, 2009.

New York State Consumer Protection Board. 2009. "Identity theft prevention and mitigation program to protect New Yorkers." Press release, January 8, 2009. http://www.consumer.state.ny.us/pressreleases/2009/jan82009.htm. Accessed June 9, 2009.

Ohio Attorney General. n.d. Identity theft verification passport. http://www.ag.state.oh.us/victim/idtheft/index.asp. Accessed June 9, 2009.

President's Identity Theft Task Force. 2007. Combating identity theft: A strategic plan. http://www.idtheft.gov/reports/StrategicPlan.pdf. Accessed May 3, 2007.

State of Georgia, Governor's Office of Consumer Affairs. 2008. "Governor Perdue signs consumer protection legislation." Press release, May 13, 2008. http://consumer.georgia.gov/00/press/detail/0,2668,542 6814_94800056_113479898,00.html. Accessed June 9, 2009.

Synovate. 2003. Federal Trade Commission-Identity Theft Survey Report. http://ftc.gov/bcp/edu/microsites/idtheft/downloads/synovate_report.pdf. Accessed April 3, 2009.

Synovate. 2007. Federal Trade Commission-2006 Identity Theft Survey Report. http://www.ftc.gov/os/2007/11/SynovateFinalReportIDTheft2006.pdf. Accessed April 3, 2009.

U.S. Congress. House. 2002. *Identity theft: Greater awareness and use of existing data are needed.* June 2002. GAO-2-766. http://www.gao.gov/new.items/d02766.pdf. Accessed June 27, 2007.

U.S. Department of Health and Human Services (HHS). n.d. Health information privacy: understanding HIPAA privacy. http://www.hhs.gov/ocr/privacy/hipaa/understanding/index.html. Accessed June 9, 2009.

United States of America v. ChoicePoint Inc. 2006a. U.S. District Court for the Northern District of Georgia, Atlanta Division. Case No. 1:06-cv-00198-GET. Civil Complaint. http://www.ftc.gov/os/caselist/choicepoint/0523069complaint.pdf. Accessed March 12, 2008.

United States of America v. ChoicePoint Inc. 2006b. U.S. District Court for the Northern District of Georgia, Atlanta Division. Case No. 1:06-cv-00198-GET. Stipulated Final Judgment and Order for Civil Penalties, Permanent Injunction, and Other Equitable Relief. http://www.ftc.gov/os/caselist/choicepoint/0523069stip.pdf. Accessed March 12, 2008.

Walker, Samuel and Charles Katz. 2005. *The Police in America: An Introduction.* New York: McGraw-Hill Publishers.

3

Worldwide Perspective

Identity theft poses a threat to both foreign and domestic security; therefore it is important to consider the crime when examining the challenges inherent to maintaining global security. Identity theft enables other crimes, including acts of terrorism. In addition, jurisdictional issues hamper investigations. If a victim lives in one county and the perpetrator in another, it compounds the problems associated with investigating and prosecuting identity theft cases. The preceding chapters explored the repercussions of the crime in the United States. This chapter discusses the problem of identity theft as it relates to other countries. In order to address global concerns and find potential solutions, it is paramount that the research, laws, and policies of other countries be examined.

Canada

In the early 1990s, Canada was viewed as a sanctuary for international criminals who used identity fraud to facilitate transnational crimes such as drug trafficking, human trafficking, and terrorism (Ronderos 2000). This view stemmed from the fact that fraudulent or stolen Canadian passports were purported to be readily available and used regularly by transnational offenders. Canadian passports were said to be available to purchase for anywhere from US$500 to $25,000, or they could be rented for $5,000.

In addition, Canada's refugee policies were extremely liberal when compared to policies of many other countries (Ronderos 2000). Compounding the problem is the fact that those who were refused asylum ignored deportation orders and simply disappeared. Between 1995 and early 2000, nearly 20,000 people were ordered to be deported from Canada. Instead of honoring deportation orders, they chose to go underground in Canada or cross the border into the United States.

As mentioned earlier, identity theft is often used as a method to facilitate other crimes, including terrorism, as, by its very definition, it enables criminals to travel from one country to another and serves as cover as they plan their criminal activities. The case of the Millennium Bomber illustrates how perpetrators move around and plan their crimes. The 1999 arrest of Ahmed Ressam, known as the Millennium Bomber by U.S. authorities, brought many issues to the attention of countries around the world. One of these was the ease with which fraudulent or stolen identification documents could be obtained in most countries. Thus, terrorists could travel freely around the world, particularly between the United States and Canada, and they often financed their activities with credit card fraud and other financial crimes.

Ahmed Ressam left Algeria, his home country, in 1992 (Bernton et al. 2002). At that time, Algeria was in a state of economic depression and political unrest. Ressam went to France on a 30-day visa. When the visa expired, he fled to the island of Corsica. There, Ressam obtained a fraudulent French passport with his picture on it but in the name of Nasser Ressam. On November 8, 1993, he was arrested on immigration violations. A trial was set for March 1994 and he was released from custody.

In February 1994, Ressam boarded a plane to Canada instead of risking deportation back to Algeria, and he traveled using a stolen and altered passport (Bernton et al. 2002). The owner's picture had been removed and replaced with one of Ressam. When he deplaned in Montreal, Canadian authorities detected the fraud and arrested him. To avoid deportation, Ressam applied for political asylum. He was released and ordered to appear at a hearing on March 28th. In the meantime, he began collecting welfare from the Canadian government in the amount of $550 per month. When Ressam failed to show up for the hearing, he was arrested again, but released after being photographed, fingerprinted, and advised of a new court date.

When his welfare payments ran out, Ressam resorted to stealing (Bernton et al. 2002). He was arrested on January 30, 1995 for shoplifting a designer suit. After the court found him guilty, he was fined $100, sentenced to two years on probation, and ordered to leave Canada within six weeks—by July 23, 1995. In an effort to stall deportation, Ressam filed an appeal. As he waited for his court date, he continued stealing. He stole money by shoulder surfing at automatic teller machines. He also pilfered purses, wallets, and luggage. Ressam used the stolen cash, credit cards, travelers' checks, and account information to sustain his lifestyle.

Once again, Ressam did not go to his hearing (Bernton et al. 2002). By this time, he had a buyer for the identity documents he had stolen: Ressam sold them to Fateh Kamel, a naturalized citizen and fellow Algerian. He agreed to sell the documents for $60 to $200 each. In October 1996, he and a friend were arrested again for stealing. This time, they had stolen $300 from a guest at a Holiday Inn. Ressam was fined $500 and released.

Ressam had made many new friends in Canada (Bernton et al. 2002). Most of them were men from Algeria. One of his new friends, Abderraouf Hannachi, talked about training at Osama bin Laden's camp in Afghanistan. He professed to be a recruiter with close ties with Abu Zubaydah, coordinator of the recruits entering the training camps, and Hannachi encouraged the young men to join the holy war, or jihad. Hannachi spoke of his hatred for the West, especially the United States. Ressam and his friends started attending services at a mosque Hannachi recommended. Soon, the young men were planning their own jihad activities. However, the Canadian Security Intelligence Service (CSIS) had the men under surveillance based on tips the CSIS had received from the French and Italian authorities.

In 1996, Hannachi made arrangements with Zubaydah in Afghanistan to send Ahmed Ressam to a training camp (Bernton et al. 2002). To prepare for the trip, Ressam created a new identity for himself. This time, he chose to be a Canadian citizen in order to reduce the risk of being detected as he traveled to the camp. The process began with a stolen baptismal certificate, something referred to as a *breeder document*. Ressam combed through local parish records until he found the name of a priest who was there in 1970, the year Ressam adopted as his new year of birth. He filed out the baptismal certificate with his new name, Benni Antoine Noris, and forged the priest's signature. With the certificate, Ressam obtained a Canadian passport and purchased airline tickets.

Next, Ressam flew from Toronto to Frankfurt, Germany and then on to Pakistan (Bernton et al. 2002). From there, he was taken by automobile into the Khyber Pass of Afghanistan. The final portion of the trip involved Ressam and several hundred other recruits walking over rugged terrain into the Kalden training camp. Ressam completed training in self-defense, guerilla warfare, weapons, airport security, explosives, and many other subjects and was assigned an Al-Qaeda contact, a man named Abu Doha who was an Algerian residing in London. Ressam left the Kalden training camp and went to the Darunta camp for specialized training in making bombs. While at the Darunta camp, he and a group of fellow Algerians began planning an attack. Their target would be a U.S. airport, an embassy in Israel, or a military base. No matter the target, the bombing would correspond with the millennium. When Ressam left the camp, he took with him $12,000, a notebook containing instructions for building and detonating bombs, and an assignment. His assignment was to return to Canada and rent a safe house where he could stockpile passports and weapons. Ultimately, he was to build the bomb that would be detonated somewhere in the United States.

Ressam's return trip was uneventful (Bernton et al. 2002). Security personnel at Los Angeles International Airport (LAX) stopped him, but after asking a few questions and checking Benni Noris's passport against a watch list, they cleared him to board a plane bound for Canada. Security officials were unaware of the contents of Ressam's luggage (e.g., bomb recipes and a couple of bomb-making ingredients hidden in shampoo and Tylenol bottles). While waiting to board his flight, Ressam decided that LAX would be the target for the millennium bombing.

Ressam and other members of the training camp were supposed to meet in Vancouver, British Columbia (Bernton et al. 2002). When no one else arrived, Ressam went to Montreal and rented an apartment as instructed. There, he and some friends continued making plans for the bombing. They lived on stolen cash and credit cards, and when the group needed more money, Ressam applied for and received a Visa credit card under the name of Benni Noris. On August 31, 1999, he used the credit card to purchase bomb-making supplies at an electronics store. The next day, he used the Visa card to purchase alarm watches to be used as detonators. Ressam was undecided about whether to plant one or two bombs, so he asked Mourad Ikhlef, a former roommate, for advice. Ikhlef was experienced in these matters; he had fled Algeria in 1992 after being charged with detonating a bomb in the Algiers airport. Together, Ressam and Ikhlef decided that one bomb would be sufficient and that it should explode near a crowded checkpoint.

Although still living in Montreal, Ressam sometimes stayed overnight with friends who were renting his old apartment on Sherbrooke in Montreal (Bernton et al. 2002). He was at the Sherbrooke apartment on October 4, 1999, when the Royal Canadian Mounted Police raided it. Ressam, however, was able to escape without being apprehended. Among the items confiscated by police were nine stolen passports and a backpack containing Ressam's address book. The address for Evergro Products in British Columbia, an agricultural supply store, was on the first page of the book. Despite the raid, Ressam continued plotting the LAX bombing. He enlisted three fellow Algerians even though they had not trained in Afghanistan. One of the men was Ressam's old friend in Montreal, Abdelmajid Dahoumane, who could help make the bomb. The second member was a credit card thief, Mokhtar Haouari, whose role was to provide the money the mission required. Abdelghani Meskini, a con man living in Brooklyn, was the third man recruited to help deliver the bomb to LAX. Although Ressam had never met Meskini, he arranged by telephone to meet him in Seattle, Washington in December.

In the meantime, Ressam contacted Abu Jaffar, an Al-Qaeda member who was close to Osama bin Laden (Bernton et al. 2002). He requested that Jaffar obtain bin Laden's blessing for the LAX bombing and then Ressam called his designated contact, Abu Doha, in London and advised him to arrange for his return to Algeria after the bombing. Doha promised to provide Ressam with the money and identity documents he requested.

On November 17, 1999, Ressam and Dahoumane flew from Montreal to Vancouver, where they rented a car and a small cabin (Bernton et al. 2002). The two men built the bomb in the cabin and then Dahoumane returned to Montreal. On December 14, 1999, Ressam drove to Victoria, British Columbia to board a ferry to Port Angeles, Washington. The immigration officer inspected Ressam's passport, which had been issued in the name of Benni Noris. The officer checked his driver's license against a computer database, and after inspecting a suitcase in the truck of the car, he allowed Ressam to drive the rental car onto the ferry.

The ferry arrived in Port Angeles, where a customs inspector checked each vehicle as it drove off the ferry and onto American soil (Bernton et al. 2002). However, the inspector became suspicious of Ressam. He seemed nervous and was slow to comply with her requests. Soon, other inspectors joined in questioning him and examining his car. When an inspector removed the spare tire, he found bags of white powder and bottles of brown liquid hidden underneath it. Ressam took the first opportunity that came along to flee on foot. Eventually, he was apprehended and turned over to the Port Angeles police. After consulting with the Federal Bureau of Investigation (FBI) and customs officials, the police detained Ressam on suspicion of using false identification. Within a couple of days, it was determined that Benni Noris was really Ahmed Ressam, an Algerian with connections to suspected terrorists. The items found in the trunk of the rental car were the ingredients for a bomb.

While Ressam was in custody, one of his co-conspirators was waiting in Seattle (Bernton et al. 2002). The con man from Brooklyn, Abdelghani Meskini, thought he was meeting someone named Reda. He did not know Ressam's true identity or what their mission entailed. All he knew was that, in exchange for participating in the mission, he would receive a fraudulent visa so he could travel to an Al-Qaeda training camp in Afghanistan. Meskini waited for a few days for Ressam to arrive and made several cash withdrawals using a stolen credit card. Finally, Meskini flew back to New York. On December 30, 1999, FBI agents arrested him.

Ressam was tried and convicted of several felonies, including conspiring to commit an act of international terrorism (Bernton et al. 2002). He faced a prison sentence of 57 to 130 years. In exchange for a 27-year prison sentence, Ressam agreed to testify against his co-conspirators and to reveal everything he knew about Al-Qaeda.

This case sparked debates between Canada and the United States concerning immigration policies and border security and it also brought attention to the issue of identity fraud. The fact that this is a worldwide problem and used by terrorists to facilitate their activities is not arguable, but in the midst of the debates, a Canadian-based study showed there is also a connection between identity fraud and international organized crime (Ronderos 2000). The study, "Identity Fraud and Transnational Crime," was published in 2000 and indicates that identity fraud, the use of fraudulent identification documents, aids in organized criminal activities such human smuggling, drug trafficking, and weapons trafficking. As in the case of terrorism, fraudulent documents obtained in one country can have negative consequences in another country. The study also found that there is a lack of statistical data documenting the extent to which identity theft is utilized by organized crime. Thus, it is impossible to assess the problem accurately. However, subsequent research, publicized cases, and data released by PhoneBusters have shed new light on the scope and nature of identity fraud in Canada.

PhoneBusters is the central repository for collecting identity theft complaints from victims residing in Canada (Phonebusters n.d.). According to Canadian regulations, identity theft occurs when a person's identifying information is obtained and used, without their permission, to commit criminal acts (OPC 2008a). PhoneBusters is a collaboration between the Royal Canadian Mounted Police and the Ontario Provincial Police and was founded in 1993 to address the problem of mass marketing fraud such as telemarketing schemes and advanced fee scams. However, victims did not have a central agency for reporting identity theft. Since PhoneBusters already dealt with other types of consumer fraud complaints, the government designated it to be the central repository for identity theft cases as well.

PhoneBusters aids in investigations by distributing case information to appropriate law enforcement agencies. The United States and Canada cooperate in cross-border investigations. PhoneBusters is also a member of the U.S. Federal Trade Commission's Consumer Sentinel and works in conjunction with the Competition Bureau of Canada. The Competition Bureau promotes consumer awareness and a competitive marketplace for businesses.

Complaints received by PhoneBusters are analyzed and compiled into annual reports that help to identify fraud trends in Canada and offer solutions to the crime. The reports are also used for the development of public awareness programs. In 2006, PhoneBusters indicated that the number of victims reporting the theft of their identities had decreased from 8,204 in 2002 to 7,778. However, losses directly attributed to the crime increased from $11,832,166 in 2002 to $16,283,777 in 2006. PhoneBusters estimated that the figures represent only a fraction, perhaps five percent, of the actual losses (CBC News 2007). The Canadian Council of Better Business Bureaus agreed (Moore 2009). The organization estimated that identity theft costs consumers, retailers, financial institutions, and others over $2 billion annually.

The Strategic Council for the Competition Bureau of Canada has conducted three annual national surveys. The most recent study included 1,000 Canadians who took part in a telephone survey between April 5, 2007, and April 15, 2007 (The Strategic

Counsel 2007). One of the objectives of the survey was to measure public awareness and response to marketing fraud and identity theft. The results indicate that, in 2007, 20 percent of respondents age 18 and older had been victims of identity theft or that someone in their household had been victimized, compared to 17 percent in 2006 and 18 percent in 2005. College (26%) and university graduates (21%) most often reported being identity theft victims as compared to other education groups.

The 2007 survey asked the victims how they, or the victims residing in their household, reacted to the theft of their identities (The Strategic Counsel 2007). Most (23%) indicated they contacted the credit card companies, as compared to 33 percent in 2006. However, the percentage of respondents who notified their bank or credit union increased from 12 percent in 2006 to 20 percent in 2007. Thirteen percent stated they reported the incident to their local police department. Sixteen percent reported that they did nothing at all about the theft.

The survey also gauged the effectiveness of the public awareness program (The Strategic Counsel 2007). Over three quarters (80%) of the respondents stated that they remembered hearing, seeing, or reading messages regarding marketing fraud and identity theft. Of those, 63 percent acknowledged that awareness messages prompted them to alter their response, or that they would alter their response in the future, to an incident of marketing fraud or identity theft. However, only 22 percent of the respondents were aware of PhoneBusters. Once the surveyors provided information about PhoneBusters, 83 percent stated they would probably contact the organization should they suspect or fall victim to marketing fraud or identity theft. The survey concluded that public awareness could greatly influence how Canadians respond to marketing fraud and identity theft. In addition, over half of the respondents (59%) indicated that public education is the best method for fighting the crimes.

Despite efforts to assess the extent and nature of identity theft in Canada, it remains unclear for several reasons (Tibbetts 2007). First, PhoneBusters was originally founded to combat mass marketing fraud. When it became the national clearinghouse for identity theft complaints, the number of phone calls increased, which put a strain on their available resources. Reportedly, the center receives about 1,200 calls per day. Second, federal law addresses the offenses connected with the use of another person's identifying information, however it excludes other issues, such as trafficking in identities. Third, law enforcement agencies expend their time and personnel on investigating violent crimes. Thus, identity theft complaints are typically not investigated due to the lack of resources. Compounding the problem is the fact that identity thieves are difficult to apprehend. Whether committed online or offline, the crimes often cross jurisdictional boundaries, and the perpetrators rarely act alone. In some cases, organized criminal syndicates victimize individuals and businesses to finance illicit activities. Finally, even if identity thieves are arrested and convicted, the penalties are minimal. The following case illustrates how one man traveled around the world committing fraud and identity theft for more than 10 years. Throughout his career, he was arrested and convicted several times.

Michael Reid, a British national, attempted to cross the border from Canada into the United States in October 1992 (Asian Pacific Post 2004). U.S. officials tried to confiscate his vehicle and detain him on an immigration infraction, but Reid fled the scene and almost ran over a customs officer. In 1993, he was arrested and convicted on an assault charge connected with the incident. He served six months in jail.

In 1995, Reid and two accomplices were arrested in Canada on fraud charges (Asian Pacific Post 2004). One co-conspirator was a young woman with a passport issued in Fiji. The other was a U.S. citizen wanted by federal authorities on fraud charges. The three fraudsters used stolen identities to procure funds from financial institutions and credit card companies in Canada and the United States. Many of their victims were deceased. They found their victims by reading obituaries in newspapers published in both countries and in the Caribbean.

While searching Reid's residence, police discovered blank driver's licenses from countries around the world such as the United States and New Zealand (Asian Pacific Post 2004). They also found several fraudulent U.S. driver's licenses. In addition, authorities confiscated equipment and supplies for manufacturing fraudulent checks and driver's licenses. Reid served a short jail term and was released. In 1998, Interpol arrested him in Copenhagen for having a number of fake identification documents on his person.

In April 2001, Reid was arrested once more by Canadian authorities (Asian Pacific Post 2004). This time, authorities uncovered 50 files in his automobile, each containing a separate identity dossier such as a birth certificate, driver's license, and credit cards.

From his residence, police confiscated a computer and equipment for manufacturing bogus checks and driver's licenses. Reid admitted to police that he had not held a job in over a decade. In fact, he claimed that being a fraudster was his occupation. During court proceedings, it was revealed that he had stolen nearly $130,000 in credit card transactions and traveler's checks from American Express. Discover lost $23,000 to credit card fraud. Reid was found guilty and received a sentence of two years in prison, but was released on parole a short time later.

Reid left Canada and relocated to Thailand in 2003 (Asian Pacific Post 2004). Shortly thereafter he was arrested for credit card fraud. After posting bond, Reid fled to the Philippines, where he and two accomplices from the United States engaged in credit card and other financial fraud schemes. Authorities began investigating the trio. Reid's partners cooperated with police, so in retaliation Reid employed an assassin to kill the Americans. He did not know, however, that he had hired an undercover agent. Reid was arrested again in 2004.

This case clearly shows that identity theft enables criminals to travel the world committing crimes. Fraudulent passports, birth certificates, and driver's licenses are some of the tools most often used by identity thieves, but criminals also target other types of personal identifying information.

The Canadian Social Insurance Number (SIN) is another area of concern (Ghoreishi 2007). SINs are comparable to the Social Security Numbers (SSNs) issued in the United States. In 1964, the Canadian government began issuing SINs as an account number for administering the Canada Pension Plan and other employment insurance programs (OPC 2008b), and three years later it was adopted as a tax reporting number. Today, it is the most commonly used and accepted personal identifier in Canada, much like the SSN is in the United States. According to Auditor General Sheila Fraser, 2.4 million more SINs have been issued than there are citizens in Canada (Ghoreishi 2007). Although it is unknown why this happened, one expert suggests several reasons for the discrepancy: the SINs of the deceased may not have been withdrawn from the system, numbers belonging to those who have moved out of Canada may still be active in the system, or the problem may be attributed to organized crime rings who are known to commit SIN fraud.

Recent research published by The Office of Privacy Commissioner of Canada (OPC) indicates that SIN fraud is a major concern for citizens along with credit card fraud and identity theft (OPC 2007). The OPC is a unit of government that serves as privacy advocates on behalf of Canada's citizens. It has the authority to examine security concerns involving government and private entities entrusted with protecting personal information. As part of their ongoing research, OPC commissioned EKOS Research Associates to conduct a survey in March 2007. The purpose of the study was to ascertain how Canadian citizens perceived privacy matters, how their concerns have evolved over time, and to identify emerging privacy concerns.

The study found that half of all Canadians thought the Privacy Act, which was enacted in 1983, should be updated to reflect the threat posed by widespread use of technology in daily life (OPC 2007). As stated previously, respondents indicated that credit card fraud, identity theft, and SIN fraud were among their major concerns. When technology is factored into the equation, citizens are increasingly worried about their privacy and the measures they should take to protect their personal information. The majority of respondents believed that their personal information was better protected 10 years ago than it was at the time of the survey. Over half of the respondents were unaware of the existing privacy protection laws which govern the collection and disclosure of personal information (OPC 2007). They also had strong opinions about disclosure of security breaches. The majority of respondents indicated that, when an information breach occurs, individuals affected by it, along with the government, should be notified. If a government agency is responsible for a breach, nearly 8 out of 10 respondents thought that the agency should be fined. In addition, most stated that victims of such a breach should and could sue the government agency in federal court.

Nearly three out of four respondents thought that one of the most important problems Canada will encounter in the future is protecting citizens from identity theft (OPC 2007). Despite these concerns, the study found that most of those surveyed carried their SIN card on their person, yet the study also found that the respondents were reluctant to provide their SIN when asked for it as a routine part of doing business.

The substantial research conducted over the years reflects the many issues that must be addressed in order to decrease the incidents of identity theft and the impact the crime has upon the Canadian economy (CBC News 2007). The Privacy Act needs to be amended to coincide with modern technological advances.

Public and private entities should be placed under more stringent requirements for protecting the personal information they collect. Civil and criminal laws require revision to reflect harsher penalties for identity theft. Finally, it is essential to continue efforts to raise public awareness.

United Kingdom

The nucleus of the United Kingdom's government is the Cabinet Office and the Treasury (Cabinet Office 2008). The Cabinet Office makes sure that all governmental departments are aware of the Prime Minister's objectives and oversees their implementation. In 2002 it released a report, called "Identity Fraud: A Study" (Cabinet Office 2002). The purpose of the study was to assess the scope and nature of identity fraud in the United Kingdom.

The study found that incidents of identity fraud have steadily increased over the years and are expected to continue to rise in the future (Cabinet Office 2002). The crime cost the economy more than £1.3 billion (approximately US$1.9 billion) from 2000 to 2001. Victims included government agencies, businesses, and individuals. In addition to financial crimes, the study indicated that identity fraud is used by organized crime to facilitate other crimes, such as unlawful immigration, human trafficking, drug trafficking, and money laundering.

The study also identified many components that are believed to contribute to the increasing prevalence of identity theft (Cabinet Office 2002). To begin, the lack of standardized definitions of identity theft and identity fraud is a factor, as government definitions are different from those used by public entities, and the definitions vary from one government agency to another. Thus, it is almost impossible to get a true picture of the nature and extent of the crime. Authors of the study recommended standardizing the definitions of identity theft and identity fraud. They also recommended that the definitions be adopted as the criterion for reporting and measuring the effects of the crime.

The study suggested that identity fraud was defined as the use of a fictitious identity (also referred to as false identity) or the use of another person's identity (also referred to as hijacked identity) to obtain goods and services (Cabinet Office 2002). It is perpetrated for three primary purposes. First, it is used to conceal one's real identity. Undocumented immigrants use identity fraud to conceal their illegal status and avoid deportation. It is used to launder illicit funds through the financial system. Identity fraud enables ineligible drivers to get a driver's license and allows pedophiles to obtain jobs where they will be in direct contact with children. Identity fraud also helps consumers to hide poor credit histories from potential creditors. Offenders use identity fraud to avoid detection while perpetrating crimes. It permits wanted criminals to evade law enforcement. Identity fraud can even enable individuals to be married to more than one spouse at a time. It also facilitates acts of terrorism. On the other hand, the study found that identity fraud can serve a good purpose when it is used by law enforcement to conceal their identities while working undercover operations.

Second, identity fraud is used to commit other frauds for financial gain (Cabinet Office 2002). A person may commit identity fraud, for example, in order to defraud the welfare system. In other words, he may collect government benefits to which he is not entitled. Identity fraud is used to obtain all types of loans, including mortgages, and to procure employment. An applicant may claim another person's educational background as his own, or may provide a completely fictitious identity and false qualifications.

Third, identity fraud is used to avoid financial obligations (Cabinet Office 2002). It makes it possible for individuals to avoid repaying their outstanding debts. Identity fraud allows parents to dodge familial responsibilities such as paying child support. It can be used as a means for citizens and businesses to evade tax obligations.

The study further established the three basic elements of an identity: the biometric identity, attributed identity, and biographical identity (Cabinet Office 2002). A *biometric identity* is made up of physical qualities that distinguish one person from another, such as fingerprints, facial form, DNA makeup, and retinal characteristics. An *attributed identity* is comprised of official information associated with one's birth, such as complete name, birth date, birthplace, and the names and addresses of both parents. A *biographical identity* accumulates over a person's lifetime. It includes historical information regarding voting habits, employment, education, marriage, mortgages, insurance, and financial transactions.

The authors of the study acknowledged that identity fraud cannot be completely eradicated however they also suggested

AMERICAN RIVER COLLEGE LIBRARY

that the crime could be made more difficult to commit (Cabinet Office 2002). To that end, the study indicates that identity fraud flourishes because of flaws inherent in the procedures used to issue and verify the authenticity of identity documents. Government procedures were found to be less stringent than those of private entities. For example, the databases used by government agencies to verify identities often contain erroneous information. Furthermore, government agencies were less likely to verify identities than private entities. The study also noted that the private sector dedicates more resources to verification procedures than the government sector does. Private entities verify identities by checking government-issued identity documents and credit bureau databases. They also utilize databases containing information about known fraud schemes and offenders.

The British government's procedures for issuing identity documents were also found to be less stringent than those of many other countries (Cabinet Office 2002). The government-issued identity cards in some countries are relatively effective in deterring identity fraud. For example, Belgium requires all citizens to register their current address with the local police who physically go to the dwellings and confirm residency. Citizens must also carry their identity cards with them at all times, and the cards must be presented when authorities ask to see them. On the other hand, Spain requires all Spanish nationals to register with their local police when they reach the age of 14. Upon registration, they are issued identity cards containing a photograph, name, address, signature, birthplace, date of birth, nationality, and the cardholder's parents' names. Cardholders must renew their identification every 10 years. The cards can be scanned and read at computer terminals, and Spanish nationals are required to present their identity cards upon request by police, other government agencies, and businesses.

The study warned that, in conjunction with issuing procedures, identity cards are only as good as the security features built into them to guard against counterfeiting and to prevent the use of lost or stolen cards (Cabinet Office 2002). In addition, the study acknowledged that criminals find and exploit weaknesses inherent in the practices employed by both the public and private sector, yet these sectors do not work together in counteracting identity fraud. Many separate government and public entities are responsible for detecting identity fraud and prosecuting the offenders. Thus, most identity thieves are not likely to

AMERICAN RIVER COLLEGE LIBRARY

be prosecuted. In addition, penalties are minimal or nonexistent if a criminal fabricates or uses the personal identifying information of another person to commit crimes, particularly fraud such as applying for a passport, credit, government benefits, and so forth.

Based upon the findings of the study, many changes were instituted after it was published. One response to the study was the development of the Home Office Identity Fraud Steering Committee (IFSC)(Home Office 2009b). The Home Office is one of the largest branches of government in the United Kingdom. Its most important functions are to protect citizens from crime and terrorism, enforce immigration policies, secure the borders, ensure that the criminal justice system is fair, proficient, and professional, and guard against identity fraud. Under the auspices of the Home Office, the IFSC was formed to bring existing resources together in one place and to introduce new programs aimed at reducing identity theft and identity fraud (Identity Theft.org.uk 2009c). The IFSC is made up of representatives from the public and private sectors who are responsible for detecting, investigating, and prosecuting identity-related cases (Identity Theft.org.uk 2009b).

The committee issued a standard set of definitions highlighting the difference between identity theft and identity fraud (Identity Theft.org.uk 2009a). *Identity theft* comes about when enough of a victim's personal information is obtained, whether they are deceased or alive, to aid in the commission of identity fraud. *Identity fraud* occurs when a fabricated identity or another person's identifying information is used to commit a crime or is used to help someone avoid honoring obligations by pretending to be a victim of identity fraud. Identity theft, making up an identity, or committing identity fraud, are all defined as identity crimes.

Since businesses are also victims of identity crimes, the IFSC defined corporate identity theft and corporate identity fraud (Identity Theft.org.uk 2009a). *Corporate identity theft* occurs when enough of a corporation's identifying information is obtained to aid in the commission of identity fraud. *Corporate identity fraud* is when a fictitious or a real company's information is used to aid in the commission of a crime. *Corporate identity crime* includes identity theft, fabricating a corporate identity, or committing corporate identity fraud.

Once the standardized definitions were in place, the British Crime Survey was updated to gather more accurate statistics about personal and corporate identity-related crimes (Identity Theft.org.uk 2009a). In the future, the survey will provide data on the prevalence, nature, and impact of the crimes. The British Crime Survey is similar to the Uniform Crime Reporting system used in the United States; for example, local and county law enforcement agencies submit regional statistical reports to a state agency. The reports contain the number of incidents and types of crimes reported in their respective jurisdictions. At the state level, the reports are aggregated and submitted to a federal agency. National statistical data that reflects all types of crimes in the United States is then compiled and published.

Two of the most common types of identity crimes in the United Kingdom involve driver's licenses and passports (Identity Theft.org.uk 2009c). To address the problem, the Criminal Justice Act 2003 increased the penalties for driver's license fraud to match the penalties for passport fraud. Both crimes became offenses for which offenders could be arrested and sentenced to a maximum of two years in prison. In addition, a database of lost and stolen passports was established by the Identity and Passport Service (IPS). The purpose of this database is to help detect and prevent identity fraud whenever a passport is used for identification or travel purposes, and public and private sector organizations were given access to the database. To strengthen passport security further, individuals requesting a passport for the first time must appear in person.

In June 2003, the Home Office, UK Passport Service, Driver and Vehicle Licensing Agency, and private credit and financial groups introduced *Identity Fraud – The UK Manual* (Identity Theft. org.uk 2009c). The purpose of the manual is to help organizations, and particularly financial institutions, detect fraudulent or forged driver's licenses and passports. The manual contains pictorial illustrations of the security features incorporated into the documents and other pertinent information. This is similar to the *U.S. Identification Manual* used by law enforcement and other government and financial agencies in the United States.

In 2004, the Identity Fraud Steering Committee (IFSC) launched a Web site to help raise public awareness of the risks of identity fraud, to provide information on avoiding identity theft and fraud, and detailing procedures to follow if victimized (IdentityTheft.org.uk 2009c). The following year, the Single Points of Contact (SPOC) network was formed (Identity Theft.org.uk 2009c). It is made up of representatives from police departments in England

and Wales and other government and intelligence agencies. The network was established to facilitate the successful prosecution of offenders through cooperation and information sharing.

Many more changes were implemented in 2006. The Police and Justice Act 2006 addressed the problem of impersonation of the deceased, thereby giving access to death records to agencies that are involved in investigating and prosecuting identity fraud cases (Identity Theft.org.uk 2009c). Also in 2006, the IFSC released a follow-up report, "Updated Estimate of the Cost of Identity Fraud," that revised the data in the 2002 work, "Identity Fraud: A Study" (IFSC 2006).

The new 2006 report found that the cost to the economy due to identity fraud was £1.72 billion per year (approximately US$2.8 billion), a considerable increase from the statistics provided in 2002 of £1.3 billion (approximately US$1.9 billion) (IFSC 2006). The insurance industry accounted for annual losses estimated at £22 million (approximately US$38 million). Several factors motivate offenders to commit insurance fraud, facilitated by identity fraud (Cabinet Office 2002). It is a means for laundering proceeds from illegal activities. Those who are uninsurable can purchase coverage. Insurance fraud allows for the procurement of cheaper rates or hides an unfavorable claims record. It is sometimes used to defraud insurers by filing several claims relating to a single incident.

In the 2006 report, the Association of Payment Clearing Services (APACS) reported losses of approximately £504.8 million (approximately US$869 million) as a result of credit card fraud (IFSC 2006). Losses attributed to counterfeit cards amounted to £129.7 million (approximately US$223 million). Card not present transactions accounted for an additional £150.8 million (approximately US$259 million) in losses. The Building Societies' Association (BSA), made up of financial institutions similar to credit unions in the United States, reported losses during 2005 of £3.1 million (approximately US$5.3 million) due to identity fraud. Government benefit fraud resulted in £20 million (approximately US$34 million) of losses to the Department for Work and Pensions (DWP). In other words, claimants used identity fraud as a means for collecting benefits that they were not entitled to receive. The costs associated with implementing and maintaining detection and prevention programs were also included in the total expense of £1.72 billion (approximately US$2.96 billion) to the UK economy. For example, the Driver and Vehicle Licensing Agency spent £2.5 million (approximately US$4.3 million) on measures aimed at keeping drivers' licenses from being used in identity crimes. It cost the UK Passport Service (UKPS) £62.8 million (approximately US$108 million) to implement measures for screening passport applications for identity fraud.

Another change that took place in 2006 was the creation of the Identity and Passport Service, formerly the UKPS, under the auspices of the Home Office (Identity and Passport Service 2007a). In addition to issuing passports, the department is charged with developing and implementing the National Identity Scheme. This program is designed to protect citizens against identity theft and fraud, to ensure that public services are provided only to those who are eligible for benefits, to stop criminals and terrorists from using stolen identities to carry out criminal acts, to avoid issuing passports to ineligible applicants, and to prevent foreign nationals from abusing student and work visa privileges. As of April 1, 2008, the Identity and Passport Service assumed management of the General Register Office (GRO) (Identity and Passport Services 2007b). The GRO is responsible for keeping detailed vital records (such as those for births, deaths, and marriages) in England and Wales. The goal is to coordinate the agencies responsible for issuing passports, national identification cards, and maintaining vital records. In the end, the efforts are predicted to foster cooperation, information sharing, and efficiency among government agencies while also making them more cost-effective. One of the most important outcomes is the ability to generate more accurate identity records.

The National Identity Scheme is a compulsory national identification card system (Identity and Passport Services 2007a). Although introduced in 2006, it is not scheduled to be implemented until late in 2009 (Identity and Passport Services 2009). The goal of the program is to streamline the identification process (Identity and Passport Services 2007a). Many different documents were accepted as proof of identity before the National Identity Scheme was implemented. These documents covered everything from a driver's license to an electric bill. Thus, the new plan eliminates the reliance upon documents that can be stolen, faked, or forged.

When the system if fully implemented, British citizens that are over the age of 16 can apply for a National ID card (Identity and Passport Services 2007a). Biometric data, verified personal identifying information, and other characteristics unique to the cardholder will be recorded on a chip that is embedded in the card, and the information will be entered into the National Identity Register (NIR) database. When a person applies for a service, such government benefits, the National ID card must be presented as proof of identity and the information from the chip on the card will be scanned and compared to the database contents. The cardholder must be a physical match to the biometric data and able to recite the biographical data. In addition to government entities, the NIR will be available to other organizations, including financial institutions.

Mexico

Identity theft is rare in Mexico (Nevaer 2007). The vigorous process implemented to stop election fraud in the country has also served as a deterrent for identity theft. The Federal Elections Institute, or Instituto Federal Electoral (IFE), is charged with verifying and registering voters. Every Mexican citizen over 18 years old must obtain a national identification card, and an applicant must present her original birth certificate and photo identification to a local IFE field office for examination. Once these documents have been presented, the applicant is fingerprinted and photographed and all of the information is transmitted electronically to Mexico City where it is stored in a database. A few weeks later, the applicant must return to the IFE office to be fingerprinted again. An IFE card is issued if the applicant's identity is confirmed. This process is so effective in stopping identity theft and voter fraud that the European Union is considering implementing a similar system. However, a ruling by Mexico's Foreign Ministry may compromise the integrity of the IFE identification system.

Historically, Mexican consulates located in the United States have issued *matriculas consulares* to immigrants who do not have passports or visas (Nevaer 2007). According to an article written by Kevin O'Neil of the Migration Policy Institute, *matriculas consulares* have been in existence for over 130 years, but the events of September 11, 2001 triggered concern among the millions of Mexicans living illegally in the United States (O'Neil 2003). Many U.S. public and private agencies changed their policies for security reasons, and began to, for example, require that individuals have and show proper identification before entering buildings, gaining access to secure areas, or attending high-profile events. In addition, steps were taken to tighten the eligibility requirements for Social Security cards and driver's licenses. All of these changes made it harder for those without documentation to live in the United States.

While in existence for over a hundred years, Mexico began recognizing *matriculas consulares* as a legitimate form of identification in 2006 (Nevaer 2007). When an individual with a *matricula consular* moves back to Mexico from the United States, he can retain his U.S. address as his home address, in essence, putting him in two places at one time. Critics believe that this practice may facilitate identity theft and other crimes.

Additional criticism comes from Marti Dinerstein of The Center for Immigration Studies (Dinerstein 2003a). Dinerstein published the first in-depth examination of the program and its role in Mexico's attempt to shape U.S. immigration policy. She argues against the use of the *matricula consulares* for several reasons. The first is that the Mexican government does not authenticate the breeder documents used to obtain these cards. An original or certified copy of a Mexican birth certificate is required, as is another piece of photo identification, preferably one issued in Mexico. These documents include voter registration cards, military service cards, and passports. While the documents are required, Dinerstein's criticism stems from the fact that the documents are rarely authenticated. The authentication process is often simply a visual check. She argues that authentication needs to be more in-depth through the use of a computerized system. Furthermore, Dinerstein suggests that consular officials can use their discretion about the types of documents to accept if an individual does not have photo identification. In the past, employee ID cards, student ID cards, and department of motor vehicles cards have been accepted, but the inconsistent nature of the cards makes them difficult to authenticate. Dinerstein notes that *matricula consulares* are often issued on the same day as they are requested which allows for little time to authenticate the identity documents. This is especially true when large numbers of *matricula consulares* are issued over a short time period, as was the case in April 2003 when 1,500 *matricula consulares* were issued in only two days at a Mexican consulate in Chicago (Dinerstein 2003b). Another of Dinerstein's concerns is that security features are lacking to prevent the issuance of multiple *matricula consulares* to the same person. With no centralized computer database to compare information between consulates, a person could go from one consulate to another and obtain multiple cards that all possess the authentic security features.

Dinerstein argues that the possession of *matricula consulares* aids illegal immigrants in the commission of additional crimes (2003a). If an individual commits a misdemeanor or felony, he is required to show identification to law enforcement personnel. Without the *matricula consulare* as identification, the illegal immigrant is more likely to be arrested. As a result, that person would be fingerprinted and subject to a background check. However, many U.S. localities accept the *matricula consulares* as legitimate proof of identification. Thus, law enforcement personnel are simply issuing citations and releasing the perpetrators.

Dinerstein's final concern is that there is the potential for illegal immigrants in the United States to obtain a driver's license using their *matricula consulares* as proof of identity. Some states do not allow this practice, though others take the position that illegal immigrants are going to drive anyway, so they are required to pass a driver's exam before being issued a license, thus making the roads safer for other drivers.

As previously stated, identity theft is less of a problem in Mexico than most countries due to the IFE card system (Nevaer 2007). However, perpetrators have been known to come to the United States illegally and commit identity theft (Woo Yang 2006). The following case is an example of this phenomenon.

Fadi Kourani, of Lebanese origin, was a resident of Mexico (Woo Yang 2006). He came across the border into the United States without documentation. After arriving in California, Kourani became part of a fraud network acquiring the Social Security numbers of U.S. citizens. The stolen numbers were then used to commit over $1.7 million in credit card fraud. Kourani was arrested, and in June 2006 he pled guilty to conspiracy to commit credit card fraud and aggravated identity theft. He was sentenced to four years in prison. Upon his release, Kourani will be deported.

Russia

Identity theft in the form of bank and credit card fraud has been a problem in Russia for many years (Center for Strategic and International Studies 1997). There is a direct connection between Russian Organized Crime, fraud, and the use of technology to facilitate crimes. Nearly $4.35 million was stolen electronically in Russia in 1995. In Moscow alone, credit card fraud increased 150% between January and May 1995 and January and June 1996

(Center for Strategic and International Studies 1997). The following case illustrates how one man used his knowledge of technology to perpetrate credit card fraud.

Artur Lyakhov was well known in Russia as a government expert on reducing credit card fraud (Schreck 2005). At the same time that he was consulting with financial institutions, holding seminars, and granting media interviews, he was also the ringleader of a group of identity thieves.

In 2002, Lyakhov and his accomplices set up a credit and debit card fraud business (Schreck 2005). They obtained their victims' information by hacking into legitimate Visa, MasterCard, and American Express accounts and manufacturing replicas of at least 5,000 cards. About 2,500 of these cards were sold on the Internet for $100 to $500 each. Lyakhov also gave his customers real-time, online access to the stolen accounts they purchased. This account monitoring reduced the chances that the debit card accounts would be overdrawn or the credit card limits surpassed. Thus, the chances of being caught were greatly diminished. To further reduce risk, the cards were used to shop at retail establishments spread around the world. Eventually, Lyakhov and five of his accomplices were arrested. Authorities then discovered that Lyakhov was not a legitimate government employee, but rather that his career as an expert on reducing credit card fraud was built around fraudulent Interior Ministry identification documents. At least $1 million in losses has been attributed to Lyakhov and his associates.

A Russian government agency, the Ministry of Internal Affairs (MVD), tracks organized crime and also helps to demonstrate the impact that identity theft has on the Russian economy. In a report issued in 1997, the MVD found that the majority of the Russian economy was controlled by criminal organizations (Center for Strategic and International Studies 1997). Between 50 and 85 percent of financial institutions were saturated with crime. The report further indicates that nearly 8,000 Russian organized crime syndicates had been identified. Some of them operate internationally, including in 17 major U.S. cities. Shortly after the Soviet Union was dissolved, many individual syndicate members came to the United States once they were released from prison and entered the country with fraudulent credentials such as visas, passports, and resumes.

Technology also makes it possible for identity thieves to collaborate on crimes when the offenders are thousands of miles apart. The following case illustrates how technology facilitated identity theft when the principals resided in different countries.

Roman Karelov was granted a temporary work and student visa in May 2006 (United States Department of Justice 2007). Before leaving Russia, he met with Aleksey Chugaev and agreed to participate in an identity theft scheme. Karelov arrived in Baltimore, Maryland where he and a co-conspirator, Radik Nizamov, began defrauding U.S. businesses. Much of their criminal activity took place online. Chugaev had access to stolen identities, and, via the Internet, he used the information to purchase traveler's checks, electronic equipment, jewelry, and gift cards. The items were shipped to Karelov's and Nizamov's residences. The men repacked the merchandise and forwarded the packages to Chugaev in Russia. To facilitate the electronic transfer of cash between the United States and Russia, Chugaev opened accounts using stolen debit cards. All the while, the men communicated by instant messaging, e-mail, and cell phone.

Karelov and Nizamov were arrested, and Karelov admitted to stealing between $200,000 and $400,000. Both men received prison terms and face deportation after their release. Chugaev, on the other hand, was not apprehended. It is believed that he still lives in Russia (United States Department of Justice 2007).

Identity theft is sometimes committed for purposes other than immediate financial gain. It contributes to the trafficking of drugs, human beings, and weapons from Russia to countries around the globe and government corruption exacerbates the problems (Center for Strategic and International Studies 1997). Officials have been known to protect organized criminal syndicates, and some have even provided the fraudulent documents that allowed the illicit activities to be carried out outside of Russia in destinations across the globe. For example, one syndicate devised a scheme to launder money and export the funds out of Russia. They set up thousands of fake companies. Credit cards were issued to the companies, and the cards were used in Russia until the credit limits were reached. To get the money out of Russia, they recruited couriers by providing them with visas to the United States, Canada, and some Western European countries.

In summation, identity theft is rampant in Russia, and research indicates that there is a direct correlation between organized criminal enterprises and identity theft.

South Africa

Identity theft is a major problem in South Africa. One estimate states that identity theft cost South African businesses approximately 276 million rand (approximately $29 million USD) in the first three months of 2008 alone (CHARGED! 2009). Another estimate, made by a major credit bureau and a national insurance organization, found that identity theft costs South Africa more than 1 billion rand per year (approximately $106 million USD) (Joseph 2008).

The article, "Steep Rise in Identity Theft in South Africa," offers insight into the identity theft problem in South Africa; the article is based on information provided by the Managing Director of the Consumer Profile Bureau, Fred Steffers (CHARGED! 2009). Established in 1981, the Consumer Profile Bureau is considered the most comprehensive source of credit data in South Africa. Steffers believes that, since identity theft is so easy to commit, it is the crime of choice for many white collar criminals and he identifies several reasons for the increase in incidences of the crime. Corruption is one of the key reasons why identity theft is easy to commit. It is not difficult to obtain fraudulent identification. Furthermore, the Department of Home Affairs, the agency responsible for maintaining the ID book, is wrought with corruption. Steffers also points to increasingly sophisticated hackers who can access information online and via cell phones and predicts that, as advances are made in technology, hackers will be able to steal more and more information. Steffers also indicates that South Africans, in general, have not taken enough measures to protect themselves. Many citizens do not realize that they should guard their identification numbers. They are simply unaware of how to protect their personal information.

Mohamed Allie, a freelance journalist in Cape Town, has also commented on the need for South Africans to guard their identification numbers (Allie 2005). He states that many impoverished citizens are being enticed into marriages by people seeking residency in South Africa. While many enter into these unions fully aware of the marriage arrangements, others are unaware that they are getting married. These people are victims of identity theft, and they often first learn that their identities have been stolen when they check with the Department of Home Affairs and discover that their marital status is listed as "married."

According to Leslie Mashokwe, a spokesperson for the Department of Home Affairs, over 3,000 fraudulent marriages have been recorded. Some of these marriages have been expunged, but others remain on record. Women are usually victims of these *identity theft marriages*. Other women suffer identity theft when they are mugged or robbed of documents containing their identification numbers.

As of 2005, it was relatively easy to assume the identity of another person in South Africa because the national identity cards lacked security features; for example, they can easily be altered by cutting out the original photo and replacing it with another (Allie 2005). In response to the identity theft problem, the government has begun to examine information and communication technologies (ICTs) for potential solutions. More specifically, knowing that there is government corruption that causes some of the identity theft, South African officials are looking for ways to make information more accessible to the public and make it more difficult for government employees to hide their misdeeds. The basic philosophy behind ICTs is that the more information made available to the citizenry, the less likely it becomes for authorities to alter identity documents without being noticed by others. One way in which the Department of Home Affairs in South Africa has utilized ICTs to help fight identity theft was to create a campaign called "Know Your Status" to encourage women to use a government Web site to compare their identification number to their marital status.

Asia

Another region of the world where citizens are deeply concerned about identity theft is Asia. One study conducted in 2006, the "Unisys Security Index," assessed the degree of concern in Singapore related to national, financial, Internet, and personal security (Tan 2006). The study found that Singaporeans are more concerned about identity theft than they are about issues such as terrorism. At least eighty percent of the respondents indicated that the abuse of their personal information was their main security concern. The serious health epidemics occurring in Singapore at the time of the survey and the risk of terrorist attacks were considered less of a threat than identity fraud and identity theft issues (Tan 2006). These findings were similar to those of a study conducted in 2007.

Eighty-three percent of respondents then stated they were anxious about identity theft (Ho 2007).

Research indicates that Asia is a hotbed of phishing activity. A 2007 report by the Anti-Phishing Working Group (APWG) found that 4 of the top 10 phishing Web sites in the world are hosted in Asian countries (ID Theft Protect 2008).

During a 2008 seminar, Cyber Security in East Asia, Dr. Nicholas Thomas from the University of Hong Kong discussed current cyber security concerns and their relationship to identity theft (Thomas 2008). According to Thomas, cybercrime is one of the most serious problems faced by any nation. He stated that reports of cybercrime in Japan increased 52 percent between 2004 and 2005. In South Korea, cybercrimes increased from 121 reports in 1997 to 60,000 in 2002. Thomas noted that part of the increase is most likely due to new legislative and enforcement efforts to curb the crimes.

Thomas argues that there is need for greater focus on cyber security policies (Thomas 2008). In part, his concerns stem from the fact that those working toward improved policies do not understand the environment they are examining, and boundaries in cyberspace are not limited to the physical boundaries present in other crimes. In addition, it is difficult to determine what types of policies are best for combating this sort of crime. Some focus on individual state or government policies, while others incorporate a regional or even an international stance for combating cybercrime. Given the limitless physical boundaries of cybercrime, policymakers need to address the issue by first generating a greater understanding of the ramifications of limitless boundaries and then developing policies that address cybercrime on a global level.

Thomas notes that differences within Asian countries influences the development of cybercrime and cyber security policies (Thomas 2008). First, economic and political divides may influence technology. Governments in poorer, more repressed states are less likely to address issues of cyber security than the governments of more developed and politically open states. Furthermore, the ability for a state to develop its economy and become more modernized is influenced by its capacity to access, utilize, and integrate the global aspects of the Internet and computer technology into society. Second, there are cultural divides present in many Asian states. Given that the norms and values may vary greatly, addressing cyber security on a regional level would require a greater understanding of these cultures and the concerns associated with them.

Regional and international responses to security threats have been utilized in the past (Thomas 2008). For instance, the Association of South East Asian Nations (ASEAN) Regional Forum has worked to address regional insecurities since its inception in 1994. Other regional groups, such as Asia Pacific Economic Cooperation (APEC), also addressed security issues from a regional perspective. The 2001 European Convention on Cybercrime approached security from an international stance. It addressed cyber security issues throughout the world.

The Threat to International and Homeland Security

As demonstrated through Dr. Thomas's arguments, cybercrimes, including identity theft, pose a threat to countries' domestic security as well as global security. Understanding the nature of the crimes and the environment in which they are committed is essential for meeting the challenge of developing security measures. Once again, it is important to remember the attacks that took place on September 11, 2001 in the United States because some of the terrorists involved in this incident had also committed identity theft. One of them, for example, used the credit card of a deceased woman.

After September 11, the media, lawmakers, and researchers addressed the role of identity theft in the attacks. A report released in 2002 by the U.S. General Accounting Office (GAO) examined how identity theft aids in terrorism and other crimes (Stana 2002). In the study, identity fraud is distinguished from identity theft. *Identity fraud* is defined as the illegal use of another person's identifying information or the illegal use of fabricated identifying information to commit a wide array of crimes. *Identity theft* is a category of identity fraud involving stealing and using another person's identifying information to commit some type of financial fraud.

Identity fraud and identity theft are implicated in most, if not all, terrorist plots against the United States (Stana 2002). In 2002, the U.S. Attorney General described identity theft as the main component of worldwide terrorist activities. Dennis

Lormel of the FBI testified before Congress that terrorist groups finance their activities by all types of fraud, including identity theft. The report also addressed another category of identity fraud, called *identity document fraud* (Stana 2002). This is the use of fraudulent identity documents to illegally enter the United States. Examples of these documents include foreign and domestic passports, student and work visas, foreign and domestic citizenship papers, border crossing cards, green cards, refugee travel papers, immigrant visas, and reentry papers. In 1998, the Immigration and Naturalization Service seized 99,171 fraudulent identity documents. The number of seized documents rose to 114,023 in 2001.

Identity document fraud (e.g., passport fraud), allowed one of the planners of the 1993 World Trade Center bombing to enter the United States (Stana 2002). Six people were killed and another 1,000 were injured in that explosion. Stolen identities were also used in the foiled millennium plot to bomb Los Angeles International Airport. In addition, Rand Beers, Assistant Secretary of State for International Narcotics and Law Enforcement Affairs, notes that terrorists often work with organized criminal groups to raise funds through activities such as drug trafficking and weapons smuggling. These crimes are facilitated by fraudulent identity documents.

Once in the country, fraudulent or stolen U.S. identity documents can be purchased in the underground marketplace and used to avoid deportation. The most sought-after documents are driver's licenses, birth certificates, and Social Security cards. By using one of these identification documents, it is possible to obtain the other two, but the most important piece of identifying documentation in the United States is the SSN (Stana 2002). Patrick O'Carroll of the Social Security Administration (SSA) testified before the U.S. Senate Committee on Finance and stated that those wishing to do harm to the country often try to procure an SSN by stealing it from a living or deceased person, buying it through the online or offline black markets, fabricating it, or applying for it using fraudulent identity documents (O'Carroll 2003). During 2000, the SSA issued nearly 63,000 numbers to noncitizens who applied for SSNs using fraudulent identity documents. For all intents and purposes, an SSN allows an individual to integrate into American society (Stana 2002). Thus, securing SSNs is a key component to securing the United States against terrorist threats.

Identity theft in the form of credit card fraud is another security threat. In Indonesia, police claim that credit card fraud is more prevalent than anywhere else in the world (Sipress 2004). There is evidence that the 2002 bombing of a Bali nightclub, which killed 202 people, was financed by credit card fraud. Iman Samudra, a member of an extremist Muslim group with ties to Al-Qaeda, was convicted of the crime and sentenced to execution. While on death row, he wrote a book that was published in 2004. Most of the book is about his educational background as a computer programmer and the weapons training he received in Afghanistan; it also covers his views on U.S. foreign policy in the Middle East and rationalizes murdering Western civilians. However, one chapter in the book validated the concerns of Internet security professionals, security experts, and government officials (Sipress 2004).

The title of the chapter is "Hacking, Why Not?" It encourages extremists to wage an online holy war against the United States through computer hacking. Although it does not contain details, the chapter refers readers to sources on the Internet such as Web sites and chat rooms for tutorials on the subject. The chapter also stresses the importance of credit card fraud as a viable means for raising and laundering the funds that are needed to support a holy war. It even provides basic instructions for committing the crime.

The chapter was important for several reasons. First, it confirmed what experts had predicted: identity theft is a real and growing threat to national and international security (Sipress 2004). The chapter also gave insight into how cybercrime is used to fund terrorist activities. It raised concerns that networks of extremist fraudsters could raise a lot of money online in a very short amount of time. Lastly, it confirmed that extremists may enlist the help of skilled hackers to attack computers belonging to their perceived enemies.

It is evident that identity fraud poses a threat to both global security and countries' national security (Gordon and Willox 2003). The threat becomes more menacing when one considers the role of technology in the crime. It allows terrorists to remain anonymous while they communicate with each other, recruit members from around the world, and raise funds. Therefore, a two-pronged solution is needed in order to address the problem effectively. Comprehensive national strategies, and a global strategy, aimed at eradicating the crime should be implemented. For a plan to be effective, a global definition of identity theft must be adopted to aid in determining the scope and nature of the problem. The plan must include cooperation among law enforcement agencies across the nation and around the world, and successes and failures in policy making, both national and international, should be assessed regularly. Identity theft is a global problem for which global solutions are needed.

References

Allie, Mohamed. 2005. ICTs employed to fight identity theft. *Panos London*, April 4. http://www.panos.org.uk/?lid=19749. Accessed February 2, 2009.

Asian Pacific Post. 2004. Master forger wanted in Canada arrested in the Philippines, *The Asian Pacific Post*, October 7. http://www.asianpacificpost.com/portal2/402881910674ebab010674f4e8d11587.do.html. Accessed February 4, 2009.

Bernton, Hal, et al. 2002. The Terrorist Within: The story behind one man's holy war against America. *Seattle Times*, June 23–July 7, Special Report. http://seattletimes.nwsource.com/news/nation-world/terroristwithin/. Accessed February 1, 2009.

CBC News. 2007. Is that a SIN card in your pocket? Privacy Commissioner hopes not. *CBC News*, October 18. http://www.cbc.ca/consumer/story/2007/10/18/identity-theft.html. Accessed February 4, 2009.

Cabinet Office. 2002. Identity fraud: A study. http://www.identitycards.gov.uk/downloads/id_fraud-report.pdf. Accessed October 20, 2007.

Cabinet Office. 2008. About the Cabinet Office. http://www.cabinetoffice.gov.uk/about_the_cabinet_office.aspx. Accessed February 4, 2009.

Center for Strategic and International Studies. 1997. Russian Organized Crime: Global Organized Crime Project. CSIS Task Force Report. http://www.russianlaw.org/roc_csis.pdf. Accessed May 31, 2009.

CHARGED! 2009. Steep rise in identity theft in South Africa. *CHARGED!*, January 28. http://www.charged.co.za/frontpage/steep-rise-in-identity-theft-in-south-africa. Accessed January 30, 2009.

Dinerstein, Marti. 2003a. IDs for Illegals: The 'Matricula Consular' Advances Mexico's Immigration Agenda. http://www.cis.org/articles/2003/back303.html. Accessed February 2, 2009.

Dinerstein, Marti. 2003b. The Issuance, Acceptance and Reliability of Consular Identification Cards. Statement prepared for the U.S. House of Representatives Committee on the Judiciary, Subcommittee on Immigration, Border Security, and Claims. June 19. http://www.cis.org/articles/2003/martitestimony61903.html. Accessed January 9, 2009.

Ghoreishi, Omid. 2007. Identity Fraud Widespread, Costing Millions: Over 2 million more SINs than there are people, *The Epoch Times*, October 11. http://en.epochtimes.com/tools/printer.asp?id=60641. Accessed February 4, 2009.

Gordon, Gary R. and Norman A. Willox, Jr. 2003. Identity Fraud: A Critical National and Global Threat. http://www.lexisnexis.com/presscenter/hottopics/ ECIReportFINAL.pdf. Accessed February 10, 2009.

Ho, Victoria. 2007. Identity Theft Still Asia's Top Concern, *Business Week*, December. http://www.businessweek.com/globalbiz/content/dec2007/gb20071211 016169.htm?chan=top+news_top+news+index_global+business. Accessed February 3, 2009.

Home Office. 2009a. About Us: Home Office Structure. http://www.homeoffice.gov.uk/about-us/organisation/home-office-structure/?version=3. Accessed February 7, 2009.

Home Office. 2009b. About Us: Our Objectives and Values. http://www.homeoffice.gov.uk/about-us/purpose-and-aims/. Accessed February 7, 2009.

ID Theft Protect. 2008. "Global: BoxSentry and Internet Identity join forces to fight online fraud." *ID Theft Protect*, February 27. http://www.id-theftprotect.com/news.php?news_id=261&news_keyword=identity fraud. Accessed February 3, 2009.

Identity and Passport Services. 2007a. About Identity and Passport Services. http://www.ips.gov.uk/identity/about-us.asp. Accessed February 15, 2009.

Identity and Passport Services. 2007b. General Register Office to join Identity and Passport Service. http://www.ips.gov.uk/identity/press-2007–10–9.asp. Accessed February 15, 2009.

Identity and Passport Services. 2009. Identity cards: The Identity and Passport Service (IPS) is responsible for issuing identity cards to UK citizens. http://www.ips.gov.uk/cps/rde/xchg/ips_live/hs.xsl/53.htm. Accessed September 5, 2009.

Identity Fraud Steering Committee (IFSC). 2006. Updated Estimate of the Cost of Identity Fraud to the UK Economy. http://www.identity-theft.org.uk/ID%20fraud%fraud%20table.pdf. Accessed December 3, 2007.

Identity Theft.org.uk. 2006–2007. New Estimate of Cost of Identity Fraud to the UK Economy. http://www.identitytheft.org.uk/cms/

assets/cost_of_identity_fraud_to_ the_uk_economy_ 2006–07.pdf. Accessed February 15, 2009.

Identity Theft.org.uk. 2009a. Identity Crime Definitions. https://www. identitytheft.org.uk/definition.asp. Accessed February 7, 2009.

Identity Theft.org.uk. 2009b. Home Office Identity Fraud Steering Committee. http://www.identity-theft.org.uk/committee.asp. Accessed February 7, 2009.

Identity Theft.org.uk. 2009c. What is being done. http://www.identity-theft.org.uk/what-is-being-done.htm. Accessed February 7, 2009.

Joseph, Natasha. 2008. "Identity Theft 'costing SA millions.'" *The Mercury*, June 4. http://www.iol.co.za/index.php?set_id=1&click_id= 13&art_id=vn20080604060110244C665305. Accessed January 30, 2009.

Moore, Rob. 2009. Government Re-Introduces Legislation Targeting Identify Theft. http://www.robmooremp.com/033109.htm. Accessed May 25, 2009.

Nevaer, Louis. 2007. "For Mexico, 'Local Residence' Now Includes New York and Los Angeles." *New American Media*, July 17, http://news. newamericamedia.org/news/view_article.html?article_id=ddbb 298638ab34eeb371dbaa3e1f17ac. Accessed February 11, 2009.

O'Carroll, P. P. 2003. "The homeland security and terrorism threat from document fraud, identity theft and social security number misuse." Statement for the record before the U.S. Senate Committee on Finance by the Office of the Inspector General, Social Security Administration. http://finance.senate.gov/hearings/testimony/2003test/091003pctest. pdf. Accessed January 9, 2006.

O'Neil, Kevin. 2003. "Consular ID Cards: Mexico and Beyond." *Migration Information Source*, April, http://www.migrationinformation. org/feature/display.cfm?ID=115. Accessed January 28, 2009.

Office of the Privacy Commissioner of Canada. 2007. Canadians and the Privacy Landscape. http://www.priv.gc.ca/information/survey/2007/ ekos_2007_02_e.cfm. Accessed February 4, 2009.

Office of the Privacy Commissioner of Canada. 2008a. Identity theft: What is it and what you can do about it. http://www.privcom.gc.ca/fs-fi/02_05_d_10_e.asp. Accessed February 4, 2009.

Office of the Privacy Commission of Canada. 2008b. Social Insurance Numbers. http://www.privcom.gc.ca/fs-fi/02_05_d_02_e.asp. Accessed February 4, 2009.

PhoneBusters. About Us. www.phonebusters.com/english/aboutus. html. Accessed February 2, 2009.

Ronderos, Juan G. 2000. Identity Fraud and Transnational Crime. Paper presented at the Seventh Meeting of the CSCAP Working Group on

Transnational Crime, May 31-June 1, Manila, Philippines. http://www.ncjrs.gov/nathanson/id_fraud.html. Accessed February 10, 2009.

Schreck, Carl. 2005. "Credit Card Adviser Faces Trial for Fraud." *The Moscow Times*, October 19. http://www.moscowtimes.ru/article/882/49/209146.htm. Accessed January 29, 2009.

Sipress, Alan. 2004. "An Indonesian's Prison Memoir Takes Holy War Into Cyberspace." *Washington Post Foreign Service*, December 14. http://www.washingtonpost.com/ac2/wp-dyn/A62095-2004Dec13?language=printer. Accessed February 14, 2009.

Stana, Richard. 2002. "Identity Fraud Prevalence and Links to Alien Illegal Activities." Statement for the record before the Subcommittee on Crime, Terrorism and Homeland Security and the Subcommittee on Immigration, Border Security, and Claims, Committee on the Judiciary, House of Representatives. http://www.gao.gov/new.items/d02830t.pdf. Accessed February 1, 2009.

The Strategic Counsel. 2007. Final Report to The Competition Bureau—Findings from a Survey of Canadians: Post-Test of the Fraud Prevention Month Campaign—June 2007. http://www.ic.gc.ca/eic/site/ic1.nsf/eng/04321.html. Accessed February 5, 2009.

Tan, Aaron. 2006. "Identity theft bigger concern than terrorism." *ZDNet Asia*, October 6. http://www.zdnetasia.com/news/security/0,39044215,61957688,00.htm. Accessed February 3, 2009.

Thomas, Nicholas. 2008. "Cyber Security In East Asia, Asia Governing Anarchy." Paper presented at the Seminar for the Centre for Non-Traditional Security Studies, S. Rajaratnam School of International Studies, Singapore, December 4. http://www.rsis.edu.sg/NTS/Events/Nick%20Thomas.html. Accessed February 2, 2009.

Tibbetts, Janice. 2007. "Anti-fraud service swamped by victims of identity theft." *Ottawa Citizen*, July 5. http://www.canada.com/victoriatimescolonist/news/story.html?id=55818fc0- 15a0–4e82–8ab9-d50db3fbf46f. Accessed February 14, 2009.

United States Department of Justice. 2007. "Russian Man Pleads Guilty to Participating in Identity Theft and Fraud Ring." Press Release, September 24. http://www.usdoj.gov/usao/cae/press_releases/docs/2007/09–24- 07KarelovPlea.pdf. Accessed May 31, 2009.

Woo Yang, Debra. 2006. Lebanese Credit Card Fraudster Sentenced to Four Years in Prison, United States Department of Justice, September 26. Press release. http://www.usdoj.gov/usao/cac/pressroom/pr2006/127.html. Accessed February 2, 2009.

4

Chronology

1914   *Federal Trade Commission Act*

President Woodrow Wilson signed the Federal Trade Commission Act into law, which resulted in the creation of the Federal Trade Commission (FTC). The FTC is compromised of five commissioners. The President, with consent from the Senate, appoints these commissioners. One of the duties of the FTC is to help protect consumers from unfair business practices.

1935   *Social Security Act*

President Franklin D. Roosevelt enacted the Social Security Act to help restore economic security and ensure stability in the future. This Act led to the creation of the Social Security numbering system that is still in use today.

1968   *Truth in Lending Act, Public Law 90–321 (Title I § 104), 82 Stat. 147, May 29, 1968*

This early attempt to protect consumers requires creditor-grantors to disclose the terms of credit accounts. The Act requires the disclosure of information, such as annual percentage rate and maximum interest rate, to perspective account holders to allow consumers to compare the cost of credit offered by various institutions and to protect current customers from billing problems. The disclosure requirements set forth in the Act also apply to leases of personal property such as automobile leases.

1971   *Privacy Act of 1971, Public Law 93–579, 88 Stat. 1896, December 31, 1974*

The Privacy Act of 1971 limits access to the personal identifying information gathered by government agencies and restricts the agencies' ability to disclose that information to others. The Act requires federal government agencies to establish measures to inform individuals of why they are collecting personal information, give individuals access to their own information, and allow them to dispute any erroneous, incomplete, outdated, and irrelevant information. In addition, the disclosure of personal information is prohibited except for reasons specified in the Act. Agencies must notify individuals in writing of the intent to disclose and receive written permission to do so. Furthermore, the Act establishes the Privacy Protection Agency, to make sure that agencies comply with all the requirements.

1974   *Family Educational Rights and Privacy Act of 1974*

This law protects individuals' educational records that are maintained by any school receiving federal funding. It limits the disclosure of information, requires the correction of inaccurate information, and permits parents, guardians, or the adult student to review all information that is in the educational record. The Act grants this protection to a student's parents or legal guardians until he or she turns 18, at which time it transfers to the student.

1978   *Electronic Funds Transfer Act*

The Electronic Funds Transfer Act is a 1978 federal law that provides specific protections for electronic fund transfers into and from a consumer's bank account. The financial institution must inform customers of the fees for making transfers, the procedures for disputing unauthorized transactions or errors, and the situations that warrant disclosing account information to third parties.

1982   *False Identification Crime Control Act of 1982*

The False Identification Crime Control Act of 1982 amended federal level criminal code and established penalties for a variety of false identification scenarios. The Act allows for penalties to be imposed upon anyone who knowingly creates or transfers identification documents. Furthermore, the Act allows for imposing penalties on those who are found to have in their possession five or more false identification documents. Penalties may also be assessed for the possession of false identification documents with the intent to defraud the country or for possession of stolen U.S. documents. Under this Act, the definition of identification document includes all documents issued by any level of government.

1986   *Fair Credit Billing Act*

The Fair Credit Billing Act amends the Truth in Lending Act. The Fair Credit Billing Act assists consumers by creating procedures to resolve billing errors on open-end credit accounts (i.e., credit cards). This Act protects consumers from fraudulent charges by limiting their liability to $50. It also protects consumers from charges for services or products not received or received in a manner that was not agreed upon. The Act defines what is considered a billing error and establishes procedures for consumers to follow for disputing billing errors or fraudulent charges.

1990   *Federal Elections Institute—Mexico (Instituto Federal Electoral [IFE])*

In response to the Constitution changes of 1989, the Mexican government created the Instituto Federal Electoral (IFE), the Federal Elections Institute, in October 1990. The purpose of this agency is to register and verify voters. It contributes to removing a political culture shrouded with suspicion, distrust, and illegalities. The IFE is considered one of the most reliable institutions in Mexico.

1992   *Privacy Rights Clearinghouse (PRC)*

The Privacy Rights Clearinghouse was founded in 1992. Some of the goals of the organization are to increase awareness of issues surrounding technology and its impact on privacy, educate consumers on how to take charge of the flow of their own personal information, respond to

1992 consumer complaints, keep records of complaints and
(*cont.*) provide them to interested parties, and serve as consumer advocates at all levels of government.

1993 *Phone Busters*

In January 1993 the Canadian government established a
national antifraud call center. Operated by the Ontario
Provincial Police and the Royal Canadian Mounted Police, this call center initially assisted in the prosecution of
telemarketing cases under the Criminal Code of Canada
in Ontario and Quebec, but has been expanded to include
assisting U.S.- and UK-based agencies through extradition. Phone Busters makes statistical information and
case evidence available to law enforcement agencies to
aid in prosecuting fraudsters. To help prevent telemarketing crimes, Phone Busters also provides up-to-date public
awareness programs.

1994 *Driver's Privacy Protection Act of 1994*

Congress passed the Driver's Privacy Protection Act as an
amendment to the Omnibus Crime Act of 1994. The Driver's Privacy Protection Act is a response to the unnecessary
disclosure of personal information by various states' Departments of Motor Vehicles (DMV). The concern stemmed
from cases in which stalkers bought information about their
victims through DMV offices. One of the most publicized
cases was that of actress Rebecca Schaeffer, who was mur-
dered in 1989 after a private investigator obtained information about her for an obsessed fan. Based on information
from the California motor vehicle records, the stalker located Ms. Schaeffer's place of residence and killed her. The
Driver's Privacy Protection Act restricts the disclosure of
personal information contained in DMV records. Government employees working within the scope of their jobs may
have access to the records. The records may be disclosed to
conduct a motor vehicle recall in order to protect the drivers' safety. DMV records can be released to government
officials to assist in proceedings involving a certain motor
vehicle. Individuals may have access to their own records.
Lastly, private investigators have access to DMV records.
The Act provides for criminal fines should a DMV fail to

comply with the law and it also gives victims the right to sue the DMV for punitive damages and attorneys fees.

1996   *The Health Information Portability and Accountability Act of 1996 (HIPAA)*

The purpose of this Act is to improve the efficiency of the healthcare system. Among other benefits, the Act sets national standards for the security, protection, and confidentiality of individuals' health-related information, known as the Privacy Rule. While HIPPA became effective on April 14, 2001, health insurers, healthcare providers, and clearinghouses were given until April 2003 to meet the terms of the Privacy Rule.

Fair Debt Collection Practices Act

Congressional findings of abuse, deception, and unfair debt collection practices led to the creation of the Fair Debt Collection Practices Act. The goal of this Act is to protect consumers from the unscrupulous methods used by some debt collectors. The Act also encourages States to take actions to protect consumers. In addition, the Act protects agencies who abide by the regulations from being placed at a competitive disadvantage within the industry.

1997   *Identification Act, No. 68 of 1997—South Africa*

The government of the Republic of South Africa enacted the Identification Act of 1997 to describe the policies and procedures regarding who must obtain a national identification card and what must be done in order to obtain one. This Act also allows for the creation and maintenance of a national population registry.

1998   *The Identity Theft and Assumption Deterrence Act*

Congress passed the Identity Theft and Assumption Deterrence Act in October 1998. The Act is an amendment to 18 U.S.C. §1028, and defines identity theft as a federal crime.

1999   *Identity Theft Data Clearinghouse*

The Federal Trade Commission, as a result of a mandate by the Identity Theft and Assumption and Deterrence

1999 Act, launched the Identity Theft Data Clearinghouse in
(*cont.*) November 1999 to collect identity theft complaints directly from victims.

Gramm-Leach Bliley Act

The Gramm-Leach Bliley Act (GLB Act) requires financial institutions to provide their customers with annual privacy notices. The notice explains the circumstances under which account holders' personal information will be shared with or sold to nonaffiliated third parties. Before the information can be disclosed, customers are given the opportunity to opt out or limit the disclosure to affiliates. The GLB Act requires financial institutions to establish and enforce customer information security policies; it also prohibits pretexting. The GLB Act of 1999 is also known as the Financial Services Modernization Act of 1999.

Victims of Crimes Extended Services (VOICES)/Identity Theft Resource Center (ITRC)

Linda and Jay Foley established the Victims of Crimes Extended Services (VOICES) under the auspices of the Privacy Rights Clearinghouse in 1999. It later became the Identity Theft Resource Center (ITRC), a stand-alone nonprofit organization. The ITRC is dedicated to victim advocacy and providing educational services for consumers as well as public and private entities.

Identity Theft Program

Dr. Judith Collins established the Identity Theft Program, formerly called the Identity Theft Partnerships in Prevention, at the School of Criminal Justice, Michigan State University, East Lansing, Michigan. An outreach initiative, the main focus of the program is to conduct research, provide victim advocacy, and assist in identity theft investigations. Training is also available in many areas such as public and workplace awareness program development.

2000 *California Identity Theft Registry*

The Identity Theft Data Base was established by California Penal Code Section 530.7 (Assembly Bill 1862-Torlakson; Chapter 631, Stats. of 2000). The purpose of the bill is to assist victims of criminal identity theft. This type of identity theft occurs when an individual's personal identifying information is used by another person, without permission, to aid or abet in the commission of a felony or misdemeanor. The bill allows victims, whose identities have been connected with criminal records, to register for inclusion into the Identity Theft Data Base that is maintained by the California Department of Justice. First, victims must submit a registration application and provide all required documentation. The information is verified and entered into the database. Then, a personal identification number (PIN) is issued to the victim. Information in the database is available 365 days a year by calling a toll-free number. The database is accessible to law enforcement officials, victims, and others who have obtained permission from the victims.

Social Security Number Confidentiality Act of 2000

The Social Security Number Confidentiality Act was signed into law by President Bill Clinton on November 6, 2000. The purpose of the bill is to protect Social Security numbers (SSNs) from theft due to unopened government mailings, including checks. It prohibits full or partial SSNs from being printed on the outside of all government mailings. The Act also prohibits mailings that allow SSNs to be visible through the envelopes of sealed mail.

Internet False Identification Act of 2000

The Internet False Identification Act of 2000 is an amendment to the Crime Control Act of 1982. The Internet False Identification Act makes it illegal for false identity documents to be transferred electronically. It was passed to address the abundance of counterfeit identification documents, templates, and files being distributed over the Internet or downloaded and distributed from storage devises. The Act mandated that a committee be formed to make sure that existing resources, such as task forces, are used to aggressively investigate and prosecute violators.

Internet Crime Complaint Center

The Internet Crime Complaint Center (IC3), formerly known as the Internet Fraud Complaint Center (IFCC),

2000 was founded. The IC3 is a joint venture between the Fed
(cont.) eral Bureau of Investigation (FBI) and the National White
Collar Crime Center (NW3C). It collects complaints from
victims of online fraud or the parties that were defrauded
and refers them to federal, state, or local law enforcement
agencies for investigation. The complaints are included in
the Federal Trade Commission's database and reflected in
their annual statistical reports. The IC3 complaint form is
available on their Web site at http://www.ic3.gov/com
plaint.

2001 *FTC's Annual Reports*

The Federal Trade Commission released its first annual
statistical report based on the complaints filed by victims
of identity theft from January to December 2000. The report consisted of 12 pages of charts and graphs.

2002 *Military Sentinel*

The Federal Trade Commission established the Military
Sentinel database to collect identity theft and fraud-
related complaints directly from members of the armed
forces, military civilian employees, and their families.

2003 *Fair and Accurate Credit Transaction Act (FACTA)*

This Act added new provisions to the Fair Credit Reporting Act (FCRA). The purpose of the legislation is help
consumers detect and prevent identity theft. The major
provision of the Act requires the three major credit bureaus (TransUnion, Equifax, and Experian) to provide
consumers with one free credit report every 12 months
upon the consumer's request. It resulted in the formation
of a centralized source for requesting credit reports. The
Act also created procedures whereby consumers can correct inaccurate, erroneous, or fraudulent information contained in their credit bureau reports.

Identity Theft Consumer Notification Act, 108th Congress,
H.R. 818, Pending

Congress introduced the Identity Theft Consumer Notification Act on February 13, 2003. It was referred to the

Subcommittee on Financial Institutions and Consumer Credit and has yet to be signed into law. The Act is an attempt to require financial institutions to notify customers immediately upon discovering that their records have succumbed to a security breach. The Act contains one exception to the disclosure requirement, that is, financial institutions may delay notifying customers if requested by the law enforcement agencies that are conducting an investigation into the incident.

2004   *Identity Theft Penalty Enhancement Act*

President George W. Bush signed the Identity Theft Penalty Enhancement Act into law. The Act created the offense of "aggravated identity theft" and set forth mandatory sentences for the crime. In addition, the Act directs the U.S. Sentencing Commission to increase the penalties when a person uses their position, such as an employee or officer of a company, as a means to steal personal identifying information or to launder stolen identities.

Check Clearing for the 21st Century Act (Check 21)

Although the Check Clearing for the 21st Century Act, also known as the Check 21 Act, was enacted in 2003, it went into effect on October 28, 2004. It allows banks to process checks electronically, which is more cost-efficient and less time-consuming than the traditional method of moving the original paper checks from one bank to another.

Shadowcrew Web Site Taken Down

In October 2004, the United States Secret Service (USSS) busted one of the largest international crime rings, known as Shadowcrew. The worldwide organization consisted of more than 4,000 participants and operated entirely online for two years. Members, owners, operators, and moderators participated in buying and selling personal information, identity documents, Social Security numbers, credit card numbers, and debit card numbers. At the time the Shadowcrew Web site was taken down by the USSS, group members had compromised approximately 1.7 million credit card numbers, leading to more than $4 million in losses to financial institutions.

2004
(*cont.*)

Ohio's Identity Theft Verification Passport Program

Ohio Attorney General Jim Petro received funding from the U.S. Department of Justice to establish the Identity Theft Verification Passport Program. In 2004 law enforcement officials began learning to use the program. Its purpose is to help protect victims of identity theft against future problems. Current victims, or those who became victims within a retroactive seven-year time period beginning December 14, 2004, may be eligible to participate in the program. Consumers may call 1-888-MY-ID-4ME (1-888-694-3463) for information.

2005

ChoicePoint Data Breach

ChoicePoint, a company that collects, stores, compiles, and resells consumer information, announced a large data security breach. The dossiers of over 160,000 individuals had been inadvertently sold to a group of identity thieves. Each file, compiled from a variety of pubic and private sources, contained personal identifying information such as Social Security number and date of birth. The thieves set up at least 50 fake business accounts in order to gain access to the ChoicePoint files.

2006

Identity Cards Act 2006

The Identity Cards Act 2006 was signed into law in March. The Act set forth the legal structure required to establish a national, personal identification card program in the United Kingdom. The purpose of the program is to address the problems created by identity theft, immigration fraud, and government benefit abuse. The Act also makes it a crime for a person to have an identity document in his or her possession that belongs to someone else or equipment and/or supplies needed to make fake identity documents.

United States of America (for the Federal Trade Commission) v. ChoicePoint Inc.

On January 26, 2006, the Federal Trade Commission (FTC) announced that a settlement had been reached with ChoicePoint on charges stemming from a 2005 data breach. The company, which collects and sells personal information to subscribers, sold personal information to a ring of identity thieves. ChoicePoint agreed to pay $10 million in civil fines and $5 million in consumer reparations. This was the highest civil penalty ever assessed by the FTC. ChoicePoint was charged with several violations of the Fair Credit Reporting Act (FCRA) and the FTC Act, including failure to properly screen subscribers. In addition to the monetary settlement, the company agreed to an independent audit of their security measures every two years for the next 20 years.

Estep v. Blackwell

In March 2006, Darrell Estep prompted the filing of a class-action lawsuit in the U.S. District Court in Cincinnati. The complaint alleged that Ohio Secretary of State, Kenneth Blackwell, posted documents containing Social Security numbers (SSNs) on the office's Web site, which exposed thousands of Ohioans to identity theft. The Ohio attorney general issued an opinion stating that SSNs must not appear on documents accessible to the public because it violates an individual's right to privacy. According to the complaint, Blackwell did not stop the practice despite the attorney general's opinion. The case was settled when Blackwell agreed to remove the SSNs from any financial documents posted on the secretary of state's Web site and agreed to take steps to prevent it in the future.

Ohio Secretary of State's Office Data Breach

In April 2006 the Ohio secretary of state's office acknowledged a data security breach that put registered voters at risk of identity theft. In accordance with the Freedom of Information Act, political groups may request and be granted access to voter registration lists for use in their campaign projects. In this case, the secretary of state's office mailed CDs containing voter information, such as names, addresses, and past voting histories, to 20 political groups. It was discovered, however, that the Social Security numbers (SSNs) belonging to some Ohio voters were accidently included on the CDs. The CDs were recalled and replaced with new ones that lacked that information.

2006
(cont.)

ID Safety (www.IDSafety.org)

In 2006 a partnership between the International Association of Chiefs of Police and Bank of America was formed to address identity theft prevention, investigations, and victim assistance. This is the first time that law enforcement and the banking industry made a large-scale cooperative effort to combat the crime of identity theft.

2007

The President's Identity Theft Task Force

On May 10, 2006, President George W. Bush signed Executive Order 13402, which established The President's Identity Theft Task Force. The task force, made up of representatives from several federal agencies, was chaired by the attorney general of the United States and co-chaired by the chairman of the Federal Trade Commission. As set forth by the Order, the purpose of the task force was to address identity theft from many perspectives and prepare a comprehensive plan for fighting the crime. The resulting report, *Combating Identity Theft: A Strategic Plan*, was introduced on April 23, 2007.

United States Department of Veterans Affairs, VA Medical Center Data Breach

The U.S. Department of Veteran's Affairs reported that a portable hard drive was discovered missing in January from a VA hospital in Alabama. The hard drive contained the patients' personal information and the doctors' billing information.

Fidelity National Information Services Data Breach

Fidelity National Information Services announced the theft of customer records in July 2007. The firm stated that an employee of a subsidiary company, Certegy Check Services, was responsible for accessing and selling at least 2.3 million records containing personal identity information. Certegy later revised the number of records breached to 8.5 million.

Luciano Pisciotti and Daniel Mills v. Old National Bancorp

On August 23, 2007, the U.S. Court of Appeals, Seventh Circuit, upheld the decision of the U.S. District Court,

Southern District of Indiana, to dismiss a class action lawsuit filed on the behalf of Old National Bancorp customers. In 2005 the bank's Web site was hacked and the lawsuit sought damages for emotional distress and reimbursement for the cost of credit monitoring services. The Court of Appeals ruled that the costs incurred by the bank's customers for credit monitoring services are not considered compensable damages under Indiana's security breach notification law. Additionally, the Court stated that none of the plaintiffs claimed to have become victims of identity theft due to the breach, thus, they did not suffer any actual damages.

The Clean Credit and Identity Theft Protection Act: Model State Laws

The Consumers Union and the U.S. Public Interest Research Groups (U.S. PIRG) introduced the Model in 2004 and updated it in 2007. The purpose of the Model is to aid those states seeking to enact tougher consumer-protection laws as provided under the Fair and Accurate Credit Transactions Act (FACTA). The Model addresses six key issues: Social Security number protection, security freeze, the prevention of and protection from security breaches, right to file a police report regarding identity theft, adequate destruction of personal records, and a severability clause.

2008   *Data Protection Day/Data Privacy Day*

January 28, 2008 was designated Data Privacy Day in the United States and Canada. The international initiative began in 2007 when the day was declared Data Protection Day in Europe. The goals of the program are to encourage a global dialogue regarding privacy issues and increase awareness among businesses and consumers of the importance of security-sensitive information.

Texas Attorney General Reaches Settlement with Radio Shack

In July 2008 Attorney General Abbott announced that an agreement had been reached with Radio Shack. The retailer was charged with violating Texas law governing the disposal of documents containing personal identifying

2008 information. Charges were filed by the attorney general
(cont.) after customer records containing Social Security numbers, credit card information, debit card information,
names, addresses, and telephone numbers were discovered in a dumpster at a store located in Portland, Texas.
Radio Shack agreed to pay $630,000 to the state as well as
implement security procedures to protect their customers'
sensitive information.

The Identity Theft Enforcement and Restitution Act of 2008

In September 2008 President George W. Bush signed the
Identity Theft Enforcement and Restitution Act into law.
The bill was designed to provide financial recourse for
victims of cybercrimes, including identity theft, and to
help in the investigation and prosecution of the crimes.
The Act also calls for the U.S. Sentencing Commission to
consider harsher penalties for identity theft, hacking, and
computer-related fraud offenses.

2009 *United States Department of Veterans Affairs Data Breach
Settlement*

In January 2009 the U.S. Department of Veterans Affairs
(VA) agreed to settle the class action suits brought by veterans groups as a result of a data breach that occurred
in 2006. A laptop computer and external hard drive containing the personal information of nearly 26.5 million
veterans and active military personnel were stolen from
the home of a VA employee. According to the settlement,
a $20 million fund was set up to reimburse the veterans
who could prove that they incurred damages. Claims
were limited to a maximum of $1,500 per person.

Flores-Figueroa v. United States

On May 4, 2009, the U.S. Supreme Court of Appeals,
Eighth Circuit, ruled that prosecutors must show that a
person knowingly used someone else's identifying information in order to be charged and convicted of aggravated identity theft. Ignacio Flores Figueroa, a citizen
of Mexico, gave documents to his Illinois employer that
contained counterfeit identification numbers. Figueroa
was arrested and charged with immigration offenses and

aggravated identity theft. During proceedings in District Court, Figueroa asked for dismissal of the aggravated identity theft charge because the government could not prove that he knew that the identification numbers were assigned to other people. Figueroa was originally found guilty but appealed the case and won.

United States of America v. Albert Gonzalez, a/k/a cumbajohny, a/k/a cj, a/k/a UIN 201679996, a/k/a UIN 476747, a/k/a soupnazi, a/k/a segvec, a/k/a kingchilli, a/k/a stanozololz

In September 2009 the leader of a credit and debit card fraud ring, Albert Gonzalez, was sentenced to 25 years in prison in a case that was dubbed "the largest known case of identity theft in history." Gonzalez, who had 10 accomplices, is responsible for stealing the information from millions of credit and debit cards by hacking into the computer networks belonging to BJ's Wholesale Club, OfficeMax, TJX Companies, Boston Market, Barnes & Noble, and Sports Authority between 2003 and 2006. Several other defendants are scheduled to appear in federal court in late 2009 and during 2010.

5

Biographical Sketches

While identity theft in some form may have been around since the earliest of civilizations, it is clear that it has taken a more prominent role in today's society. As the crime has become more prevalent and technology has spawned new ways for it to be committed, it is evident that there is a need for reform in how this crime is addressed. This chapter focuses on some of the key persons who have helped to teach society about what identity theft is and how to prevent it. Many of those profiled in this chapter are politicians who introduced new ideas and concepts about the crime through legislation. These individuals fought for tougher penalties, more inclusive laws, and a greater level of accountability by government and other private entities who commonly handle consumers' personal information. In addition to those who hold political office, many other people have worked to gain a greater understanding of identity theft in order to provide information that helped to direct and reform policies. Some of these individuals were victims themselves who took their own experiences and offered insight to others about ways to address the issue. While reading through the list of people involved in combating identity theft, it is important to note that some of the legislation discussed herein did not become law in its original format; however, the introduction of that legislation led to other pieces of legislation being introduced and passed into law. The ideas that were generated by the list of people below have helped to shape the way in which the United States handles identity theft cases today.

Abagnale, Frank, Jr. (1948–)

Frank Abagnale was born in New York in 1948. His childhood has been described as normal and uneventful. However, when he was 13, his mother and father separated and this seems to have paved the way for the future life he would live. In recent years, his name has become well known as a result of the movie *Catch Me If You Can*, in which Leonardo DiCaprio portrayed him. The movie is based on Abagnale's book by the same title and depicts his life as a confidence man. Throughout his life, Abagnale has taken on many roles. He was an airline pilot, a doctor, a lawyer, a college professor, and a businessman, at least on paper. He never had any formal education or training for most of the positions he held, but instead read about the positions and observed people working in those positions so that he might pass himself off as one of them. In order to do this, Abagnale had to learn how to create documents that could pass for being authentic. He was able to fabricate fraudulent transcripts, name badges, checks, a Federal Aviation Administration license, and other documents that helped to hide his true identity. He lived his life as a man for approximately five years. At 21 years of age, Abagnale was apprehended in France, and he served time in France, Sweden, and the United States for his crimes. Upon his release, U.S. officials realized what a wealth of knowledge Abagnale had and, under the terms of his release, he was required to teach federal law enforcement agencies about security and fraud schemes. He is now recognized as one of the leading authorities on fraud, document security, and embezzlement. He runs his own security business, and continues to work with law enforcement. Today, he also works with corporations and financial institutions to help them develop policies and procedures to address and prevent fraud. Abagnale is the author of *Stealing Your Life*, *The Art of the Steal*, and the *Real U Guide to Identity Theft*.

Ashcroft, John (1942–)
U.S. Attorney General

John Ashcroft was born in Chicago, Illinois. He graduated from Yale University in 1964, and in 1967 he was awarded a Juris

Doctorate degree from the University of Chicago. That same year, he married his wife, Janet, who now teaches at Howard University. They have three children.

Ashcroft began his political career shortly after graduating from the University of Chicago. In 1972, he ran for office in Missouri, but he lost in the primary. In 1973, the Missouri governor appointed him as state auditor. He remained the state auditor until 1975. At that time, he was hired by Missouri Attorney General Jack Danforth to serve as an Assistant Attorney General. In 1976, when Danforth was elected to the U.S. Senate, Ashcroft was elected to replace him. Ashcroft was re-elected as Attorney General in 1980. He went on from the Attorney General's office to serve two consecutive terms as Missouri governor, and in 1994, he moved into the federal arena and was elected to the U.S. Senate. In 2000, President George W. Bush appointed Ashcroft to the position of United States Attorney General.

Though Ashcroft is a Republican, he crossed party lines when it came to working on the problem of identity theft. In 2005 he worked with California's senior Senator Dianne Feinstein and held press conferences to encourage the passage of stiffer penalties for identity thieves. The significance of these press conferences was that they demonstrated the federal government's interest in fighting identity theft and enacting harsher punishments for those who commit the crime. In addition, Ashcroft and Feinstein focused on making it easier for prosecutors to obtain convictions for identity theft cases and sought to expand the definition of identity theft to include the possession of false identity documents, in addition to the use of those documents.

Bliley, Thomas Jerome, Jr. (1932–)
U.S. Representative (R-Va.)

Thomas "Tom" Bliley was born in 1932 in Chesterfield County, Virginia. At the age of, 16 he graduated from Benedictine High School in Richmond, Virginia. He earned his undergraduate degree from Georgetown University in 1952 and then served in the U.S. Navy from 1952 to 1955. Bliley's political career began when he was elected vice-mayor of Richmond in 1968. He was elected mayor of Richmond in 1970, and held that position until

1977. In 1980, Bliley was elected to the U.S. House of Representatives, and he served as a representative from January 1981 until January 2001.

Bliley co-sponsored the Gramm-Leach-Bliley Act of 1999. The Act gives eight federal agencies the authority to enforce the Financial Privacy Rule and the Safeguards Rule and protects consumers from individuals and companies who might try to obtain personal financial information under false pretenses. This technique, known as pretexting, allowed criminals to obtain information for the purpose of identity theft. The Act also required that financial institutions create policies and safeguards to protect their customers' personal information.

Bowen, Debra (1955–)
California Secretary of State

Debra Bowen was born in 1955 in Illinois. She attended Michigan State University and received her Bachelor's degree in 1976. Bowen then earned a Juris Doctorate degree from the University of Virginia School of Law in 1979. She moved to California and started her own law firm in 1984. Bowen served on the California State Assembly from 1992–1998 and then in the California State Senate from 1998–2007. She is currently the California Secretary of State.

Bowen's record shows that she is concerned about identity theft and privacy protection. She is the author of California Senate Bill 168 (SB 168) which was passed and became law. In authoring this bill, Bowen helped to create a law that protects Social Security numbers, allows consumers to place a credit freeze on their credit reports, and also clarifies how fraud alerts should work. In general, this bill allows for greater security for California citizens' credit records. She also authored California Senate Bill 1279 in hopes of trying to encompass all types of personal data in the requirements for disclosure to consumers in the event of security breaches. The California Senate passed the bill, but the California State Assembly did not; hence the bill did not become law. Although this piece of legislation did not pass, it demonstrates Bowen's comittment to protecting personal information.

Calderon, Charles (1950–)
State Senator (D-Calif.)

Charles Calderon was born in 1950 in Montebello, California. He holds a degree in Political Science from California State University–Los Angeles and a Juris Doctorate degree from the University of California at Davis. He began his political career by winning a seat on the Montebello School Board. Calderon was first elected to the California State Assembly in 1982; he was the first Latino lawyer to win a seat in the Assembly. In 1990, he ran for the California State Senate and won.

During his time in office, Calderon introduced Assembly Bill 424 (AB 424) in 2005. The purpose of the bill was to revise the definition of the word "person" in the current law. Understanding that identity theft happens not only to people but also to companies, organizations, and the like, and that there are many pieces of information that can be considered personally identifying, Calderon proposed that the definition be broadened to include a wider range of entities, including but not limited to firms, associations, organizations, and partnerships. The bill also stated that, just as the definition of identity theft needed to be broadened to incorporate these other entities, the list of what constitutes a piece of identifying information also needed to be expanded to include identifiers that are specific to these entities.

Also in 2005, Calderon sponsored Assembly Bill 1566, which was created to help protect members of the armed forces who are deployed to a location outside of the state of California. This Bill was specifically designed emphasize the importance of protecting those who are serving in the armed forces.

Cantwell, Maria (1958–)
U.S. Senator (D-Wash.)

Maria Cantwell was born in 1958 in Indianapolis, Indiana. She earned her Bachelor of Arts degree in Public Administration from Miami University (Ohio) in 1981, and later moved to Seattle, Washington, in 1983. In 1986, Cantwell was elected to the

Washington State House of Representatives. In 1992, she was elected to the U.S. House of Representatives, where she served one term. After she was defeated in the House race in 1994, Cantwell returned to work in the private sector and became the vice president of marketing for RealNetworks.

During her time with RealNetworks, there were questions pertaining to the privacy policy of the company. Cantwell's experience in the computer software industry helped to shape her views on privacy issues and demonstrated her concern for protecting the privacy of Internet users. This further aided her when she ran for a seat on the U.S. Senate in 2000, as privacy was an early issue in that campaign.

Since becoming a U.S. Senator in 2001, Cantwell has demonstrated her concern about identity theft and the victims of this crime. She has proposed several bills, including the Reclaim Your Identity Act of 2001 and the Identity Theft Victims Assistance Act of 2002. These acts were designed to help victims face the challenges that accompany having their identities compromised. Knowing that identity theft is often not discovered for some time and that victims often struggle to obtain information pertaining to their case, the bills offered victims more control over their situation. Although the bills did not pass, they have helped to make legislators and others more aware of the impact of identity theft and have helped to shape future legislation. In 2007, Cantwell continued to demonstrate her desire to better understand the identity theft problem and how it correlates to other crimes and problems within society when she proposed a national study to determine the relationship between identity theft and methamphetamine labs. As the number of methamphetamine labs continues to grow within the United States, signs were beginning to emerge that many of the lab operators are using stolen identities to obtain the products needed to manufacture the drug.

Carter, Steve (1954–)
Indiana Attorney General

Steve Carter received his Juris Doctorate degree from the Indiana University School of Law, and served as the Chief of Staff to Indiana Lieutenant Governor John M. Mutz. He was the Attorney

General for Indiana from 2000–2008. During his time as Attorney General, he gained a strong reputation for working to protect the state's citizens. He enforced one of the nation's strongest Do Not Call Laws to help protect constituents from unwanted telemarketing calls. In 2008, he launched an Identity Theft Unit for the state of Indiana to help residents who have been victims of identity theft and to educate the public on ways to protect their personal identifying information. The Identity Theft Unit is part of the Consumer Protection Division, which is a division of the Attorney General's Office. The Identity Theft Unit is also responsible for investigating alleged fraud and serves as a resource for local law enforcement and prosecutors. During his time as Attorney General, Carter's office worked to pass the Security Breach Disclosure Law, which requires businesses in the state to notify customers of security breaches that may have made their personal information vulnerable to theft. Furthermore, companies that do not properly disclose security breaches to their customers risk fines of up to $150,000.

Cogdill, David (1950–)
State Assembly (R-Calif.)

Dave Cogdill was born in 1950 in Long Beach, California. He moved to Modesto in 1979 and built a real estate appraisal business. He began his career in politics in 1975 when he was elected to the Board of Directors of the Bridgeport Fire Protection District in Mono County. He also served two terms on the Modesto City Council. In 2006, Cogdill was elected to his current position as a California State Senator. From April 2008 until February 2009, he also served as the Senate Republican Leader. Prior to working for the California State Senate, Cogdill served on the California State Assembly. During his years as a public servant, Cogdill has received numerous awards, including Legislator of the Year by Crime Victims United of California in 2007, the Mickey Conroy Legislator of the Year by the California State Commanders Veterans Council in 2007, Outstanding Legislator by the Chief Probation Officers of California in 2008, and Special Recognition as an Outstanding Legislator by the California Sheriffs' Association also in 2008. Cogdill also sponsored Assembly Bill 618 (AB 618), which was designed to assist law enforcement and prosecutors' offices in investigating and prosecuting cases of identity theft and other fraud offences. The bill allows law enforcement to request, in addition to account statements and a copy of the signature, surveillance photos or video recordings of persons accessing the victim's financial account at a financial institution or at an automated teller machine.

Cuccinelli, Ken (1968–)
State Senator (R-Va.)

Ken Cuccinelli was born in 1968 in Edison, New Jersey. He received his Bachelor of Science degree in Mechanical Engineering from the University of Virginia, a Juris Doctorate from George Mason University School of Law, and a Master of Arts degree in International Commerce and Policy from George Mason University. His career in politics began in 2002 when he was elected to his current position in the Virginia State Senate. In 2006, Cuccinelli proposed legislation that would give consumers greater control over their personal information by permitting them to put a credit freeze on their credit reports. While a credit report freeze in the state of Virginia was not put into place until 2008, Cuccinelli demonstrated progressive thinking in the fight against identity theft.

Feinstein, Dianne (1933–)
U.S. Senator (D-Calif.)

Born Dianne Emiel Goldman in San Francisco, California, Dianne Feinstein is a name commonly recognized in politics. She is currently the senior U.S. Senator from California. In 1991, Pete Wilson's Senate seat became vacant when he resigned to become Governor of California, and Feinstein won a special election in November 1992 that allowed her to fill the vacant seat. Feinstein became the first woman from California to serve in the U.S. Senate. She has been re-elected three times since her initial election in 1992.

Feinstein's political career covers a 40-year span. Prior to joining the U.S. Senate, she held numerous other political offices. She was elected to the San Francisco County Board of Supervisors in 1969, and went on to become the first female mayor of San Francisco, where she served from 1978 to 1988. During her tenure as mayor, she was named the nation's "Most Effective Mayor" by *City and State* magazine. Throughout her political career she has received numerous awards and honors for her hard work and dedication to her constituents.

Feinstein's political career can be described as one that has been filled with bi-partisan cooperation to help protect the nation and its citizens. She has focused her attention on matters of national security and on fighting crime and violence. She has worked border security and visa entry reforms that resulted in laws making it a crime to tunnel beneath a U.S. border. Furthermore, she has focused her attention on the rights of crime victims, helped to protect children through the support of the AMBER Alert Network, and worked to combat the nation's methamphetamine problem.

As times have changed, so has Feinstein. She has looked at the problems of society and offered insight into how to address them, including identity theft. In line with her focus on protecting U.S. citizens and helping crime victims, she has sponsored legislation pertaining to identity theft, including the Identity Theft Prevention Act of 2001. The Act gave prosecutors more tools for combating the crime by mandating that criminal intent is sufficient proof for conviction. She also cosponsored the Identity Theft Penalty Enhancement Act, which focused on determining penalties for aggravated identity theft charges.

Foley, Linda

Linda Foley's work on identity theft issues came about as a result of her own identity being stolen by her employer. Foley had been hired as an independent contractor (as a writer/advertiser) for the San Diego-based magazine *Essentially You*. Within months of filling out her employment paperwork, Citibank notified Foley that they had a new mailing address on file for her. Foley contacted law enforcement and immediately began the process of trying to correct her credit reports. After being a victim of identity theft, Foley became a volunteer for the Privacy Rights Clearinghouse, and then she and her husband, Jay Foley, founded the Identity Theft Resource Center in 1999.

Foley conducts seminars for a variety of audiences. She has testified at state and federal legislative hearings on the issues surrounding identity theft, and offers assistance to victims of the crime. She also works to educate the public about ways to protect themselves from identity theft. Foley has received numerous awards and has been featured on television in programs such as *The Montel Williams Show*, as well as in print, including in *Reader's Digest* and *Time*. Today, Foley is considered one of the leading experts on identity theft. Her passion for assisting victims has led her to make fighting identity theft her life's work.

Frank, Mari

Like many who become passionate about the fight against identity theft, Mari Frank was also a victim of the crime. In 1996, Frank learned that her identity had been stolen when she received a phone call from a bank requesting payment on an $11,000 debt she purportedly owed them.

Based on her experience as a victim, Frank used her legal expertise to create the Identity Theft Survival Kit. The kit is an all-encompassing tool for victims of the crime. She compiled expert information, a step-by-step manual on what to do if you are a victim, and how to stop being a victim. In addition, the kit includes samples of the legal documents and paperwork that victims may need. Frank is an attorney and a private consultant, and has also coauthored and authored books such as *Privacy Piracy* and *From Victim to Victor: A Step by Step Guide for Ending the Nightmare of Identity Theft*. She hosts a weekly radio show based at the University of California that addresses issues pertaining to privacy in today's society. Frank's desire to see changes in identity theft laws is evident in her testimonies before both the California legislature and the U.S. Congress. She has also appeared on television shows such as *"Dateline"* and *"48 Hours"*. CNN and PBS Television have aired a 90-minute special on identity theft featuring Frank. She serves on numerous advisory boards and is also the leader of a task force on identity theft in Los Angeles and Orange Counties, California.

Givens, Beth

Consumer advocate Beth Givens is a former librarian who specialized in resource sharing and library network development. In 1992, Givens established the Privacy Rights Clearinghouse, of which she is currently the director. The Clearinghouse's purpose is to help protect consumers' privacy and to educate the public about potential attacks against their privacy. In addition to being the director of the Clearinghouse, Givens is the author of encyclopedia entries on identity theft in the *Encyclopedia of Privacy,* the *World Book Encyclopedia,* and the *Encyclopedia of Crime and Punishment.* She is also the author of *The Privacy Rights Handbook: How to Take Control of Your Personal Information* and the coauthor of *Privacy Piracy: A Guide to Protecting Yourself from Identity Theft.* Not only is Givens an established author, but she speaks on behalf of consumers' interests at state and federal legislative hearings and participates in task forces and commissions aimed at identifying threats to personal information and developing methods to protect it. Given her expertise, she is often interviewed by the media.

Gramm, William Philip (1942–)
U.S. Senator (R-Tex.)

William Philip Gramm was born in 1942 in Fort Benning, Georgia. He graduated from the University of Georgia in 1964 with his undergraduate degree in business administration, and continued his education there, receiving a doctorate degree in economics in 1967. He taught economics at Texas A&M University from 1967 to 1978, and in 1978 launched his political career when he was elected to the U.S. House of Representatives as a representative from Texas. He served in the House as a Democrat from 1978 until he resigned in January 1983. Next, he ran in the special election that was required to fill his now-vacant seat, this time as a Republican. He won the election and continued to serve in the House from 1983–1985. At that time, he decided to run for the U.S. Senate, continuing on as a Republican. Gramm was elected to the Senate and served there from 1985–2002.

Gramm was one of the authors of the Financial Modernization Act of 1999, more commonly referred to as the Gramm-Leach-Bliley Act. While some claim that the Act does not do enough to protect consumers, others argue about whether or not it is a state or the federal government's responsibility to handle issues of privacy. Regardless of these concerns, the Act has significant features that protect the personal financial information of consumers. The main components of the Act that relate to privacy include the financial privacy rule, the safeguards rule, and the pretexting provision.

Kaine, Timothy M. (1958–)
Governor (D-Va.)

Timothy Kaine was born in 1958 in St. Paul, Minnesota. In 1979, he graduated from the University of Missouri. He then attended Harvard Law School, from which he graduated in 1983. Kaine has also served as a missionary in Honduras. In his professional career as an attorney, he gained recognition for his fair housing advocacy, as he often represented people who were discriminated against in the housing market. Kaine began his political career as a city council member for Richmond in 1994, where he was elected to four terms, and he also served two terms as the mayor of Richmond. While mayor, he had a tough on crime approach and received national accolades for his reduction in the city's violent crime rate. In 2001, Kaine was elected lieutenant governor of Virginia, and was elected governor of Virginia in 2005.

While governor of Virginia, Kaine worked to protect the private information of the citizens of his state. In January 2007, he signed Executive Order 43 assigning responsibility for protecting the private information of citizens to the secretary of technology, a position charged with ensuring that the privacy protection policies and procedures pertaining to and created by the state of Virginia are followed accordingly. Kaine also recommended that the state initiate credit report freezes for consumers who are interested. The credit report freeze for Virginia went into effect in July 2008 and is currently free to victims of identity theft and offered for $10.00 to all others. Kaine has also demonstrated his dedication to fighting identity theft by pushing for the disclosure of security breaches when they occur.

Kyl, Jon (1942–)
U.S. Senator (R-Ariz.)

Jon Kyl was born in Nebraska and currently resides in Arizona. He holds a Bachelor's degree and a law degree from the University of Arizona. His legislative career has included serving in both the U.S. House of Representatives and in the U.S. Senate, where he currently serves as the Republican Whip. This position gives him the opportunity to build support on key issues that face the country. Senator Kyl also serves on several committees, including the Senate Finance and the Judiciary Committees, and the Subcommittee on Terrorism, Technology, and Homeland Security.

Kyl's legislative career has allowed him the opportunity to address many key issues, such as concerns about the rights of victims, stronger border security, immigration enforcement, implementing antiterrorism tools, and focusing on the country's safety and security. With the increasing concerns about identity theft in the United States, Kyl has also focused his efforts on developing and supporting new ways to protect personal identifying information. He supported the passage of the 2003 Fair and Accurate Credit Transactions Act. In addition, he co-sponsored the Identity Theft Penalty Enhancement Act. In 2007, Kyl co-sponsored the Personal Data Protection Act, which, in part, set standards for notifying consumers when data breaches occur.

Leach, James Albert Smith (1942–)
U.S. Representative (R-Iowa)

James Albert Smith Leach was born in Davenport, Iowa in 1942. He earned an undergraduate degree from Princeton University in 1964, and a Master of Arts degree from John Hopkins University in 1966. From 1965–1970 Leach worked for Donald Rumsfeld. First, he worked on the staff of then U.S. Representative Donald Rumsfeld, and from 1969 to 1970 he served as the special assistant to Rumsfeld, who was then Director of the Office of Economic Opportunity. In 1976, Leach decided to run for office himself. He ran for and was elected to the U.S. House of Representatives as a representative from Iowa. Leach served in the House from 1977 to 2007.

During Leach's time in office he worked on many commit-tees and also helped to write the Gramm-Leach-Bliley Act with William Gramm and Thomas Bliley. There were three main com-ponents related to information privacy included in the Act: the financial privacy rule, the safeguards rule, and the pretexting provision. The Financial privacy rule established the require-ment that financial institutions must provide customers with a copy of the institution's privacy notice explaining the methods employed for collecting information and sharing it with oth-ers. Furthermore, the rule allows customers to limit some of the sharing of their information. The safeguards rule requires that financial institutions, including credit reporting agencies, create and maintain procedures for protecting customer information. The pretexting provision was designed to prevent organizations from trying to obtain consumers' personal information under false pretenses. The combination of these rules helps to protect the personal financial information of consumers.

Leahy, Patrick (1940–)
U.S. Senator (D-Vt.)

Patrick Leahy was born in Montpelier, Vermont in 1940. He grad-uated from Saint Michael's College in 1961, and received his Juris Doctorate degree from Georgetown University Law School in 1964. His career in politics began in 1966 when he was elected as the State's Attorney for Chittenden County. He remained in the position until 1974, when he was elected to the U.S. Senate. Leahy took his seat in the Senate in January 1975 and remains an active Senator today. Throughout his career in the Senate, he has been concerned with the issue of privacy and is considered one of the leading advocates for privacy policy.

In October 2007, Leahy introduced a bill that focused on increasing the ability for prosecutors to fight identity theft and other cyber crimes that are becoming increasingly common. Fur-thermore, the legislation was designed to allow victims greater access to restitution from the perpetrator. This piece of legisla-tion, known as the Identity Theft Enforcement and Restitution Act, passed in both the U.S. House of Representatives and the U.S. Senate, was sent to the President, and signed into law in September 2008.

Madigan, Lisa (1966–)
Illinois Attorney General

Lisa Madigan was born in 1966 in Chicago, Illinois. Her background demonstrates her concern for people. She worked as a teacher and in developing after-school programs aimed at keeping students in school and out of trouble. She served as Illinois State Senator from 1998 until 2002, and in 2002 was elected Attorney General of the State of Illinois. She won re-election in 2006 and currently holds that position. Madigan is the first woman elected to serve as Illinois' Attorney General.

During her tenure as Attorney General, one item on her agenda has been to protect residents from scams and other fraudulent practices. She works hard to stop fraud, recover losses, and educate the community about common fraud schemes. In order to help victims of identity theft, Madigan also initiated the Illinois Identity Theft Hotline in 2005, the nation's first hotline of this type. The purpose of the hotline is to assist residents who are victims of identity theft. Hotline counselors lead victims through the process of filing a police report, dealing with credit reporting agencies, repairing their credit, and preventing further problems from occurring.

May, Johnny

Johnny May attended the University of Detroit-Mercy and holds two degrees, a Bachelor of Science degree in Criminal Justice and a Master of Science degree in Security Administration. He is a Certified Protection Professional (CPP) by the American Society for Industrial Security (ASIS). ASIS requirements for a CPP include either nine years work experience, or a Bachelor's degree and seven years work experience, plus the applicant must pass an examination. In 2007, May also became a Certified Identity Theft Risk Management Specialist with the Institute of Consumer Finance Education. He works as a security consultant and trainer whose focus is on protecting not only individuals, but also businesses and organizations from identity theft. He is well known for his work in the security profession and is the author of *Johnny May's Guide to Preventing Identity Theft* and is the expert featured in the video *Identity Theft: How to Protect Your Credit, Your Money and Your Good Name*. His expertise has led to numerous appearances on both television and radio programs, including *NBC Nightly News* with Tom Brokaw, and he has been featured in many national publications, such as *Entrepreneur* magazine and *Consumers Digest*.

May serves as an adjunct professor at the University of Detroit-Mercy, Madonna University, and Henry Ford Community College. In conjunction with his teaching endeavors, May created the first college-level identity theft prevention course in the nation, which is offered at Madonna University and Henry Ford Community College.

Oller, Thomas (1958–)
State Assemblyman (R-Calif.)

Thomas Oller was born in 1958 in Fresno, California. He graduated from California State University, Stanislaus in 1980. Oller was a member of the California State Assembly from 1996–2000, and held a seat in the California State Senate from 2000–2004. In 2004, he was defeated in his bid for Congress, and in 2008 he dropped out of the Congressional race when California State Senator Tom McClintock announced that he would also be running for the vacant seat. Oller currently works in the private sector. But as a member of the California State Assembly, Oller sponsored Assembly Bill 2232 (AB 2232) in 2000, which was designed to create tougher penalties for computer hackers. The bill is aimed at those who hack into computer networks to intentionally spread computer viruses. Under this new law, the fines for first offenses were increased to $5,000 from $250. In addition, if the virus causes more than $10,000 in damages, then the perpetrator may face up to three years in a state facility. The bill also expands the definition of injury or damages to make it a crime to deny access to a system's legitimate users (as in denial of service attacks). California Governor Gray Davis signed the bill into law in 2000.

Ostergren, Betty "B. J."

Virginia-based identity theft activist Betty Ostergren received a Bachelor of Science degree in 1972 and worked as an insurance claims supervisor for many years. Today, however, she is known because of her work in reducing the incidents of identity theft. Ostergren is the founder, editor, and publisher of *The Virginia Watchdog* (www.thevirginiawatchdog.com). She is outspoken about the ways in which the government releases citizens' personal information on the Internet. Ostergren began her battle against the government publication of personal information in 2002 after finding out that the Circuit Court Clerk for the county in which she lived was going to put records online that contained her signature. Ostergren fought against this because she believes that there are certain types of information that should never be posted, such as a person's Social Security number, mother's maiden name, signature, account numbers, date of birth, and the names of minors. While able to stop her own county's Circuit Court Clerk, she has not been successful in stopping all other counties and local governments from posting personal information. Ostergren developed *The Virginia Watchdog,* in part, as a way to form a collective group of people who are willing to fight to keep records containing sensitive information off the Internet. The *Watchdog* was also developed as a means to educate the public about the types of information being placed online. Ostergren's work has brought her much attention and she has been featured on national television programs including the *CBS Evening News, CNN's Daybreak,* and *Fox News Channel's Weekend Live.*

Paterson, David A. (1954–)
Governor (D-N.Y.)

David A. Paterson was born in Brooklyn, New York in 1954. In 1977, he earned a Bachelor's degree in History from Columbia University and in 1982 he earned his Juris Doctorate degree from Hofstra Law School. Paterson has served the state of New York for over 20 years, as a New York State Senator, Lieutenant Governor, and Governor. He is also known for being the first African American to serve as Lieutenant Governor and Governor.

Throughout his political career, Paterson has taken the initiative to combat crime, including identity theft. As Governor of New York, he signed into law legislation that made it easier for consumers to freeze their credit reports. In addition, he has taken measures to further reduce the use of Social Security numbers as identifiers, in order to protect residents from identity theft.

In 2008 Paterson proposed a comprehensive bill that would allow for the creation of the New York State Consumer Protection Board's Identity Theft Prevention and Mitigation Program, which went into effect in early 2009. He also has taken an interest in making the citizens of New York aware of other common areas of fraud. Most recently, he promoted the use of public service announcements to raise awareness of lottery scams. Paterson promotes educating the public in order for them to better protect themselves from becoming victims of identity theft and other fraud-related crimes.

Petro, James (1948–)
Ohio Attorney General

James M. Petro was born in 1948 in Brooklyn, Ohio. He received a Bachelor of Arts degree from Denison University in Ohio and his Juris Doctorate degree from Case Western Reserve University School of Law in Ohio. He began his political career as a city council member in Rocky River, Ohio in 1977, and also served four years as a member of the Ohio House of Representatives. In 1991, Petro began a four-year term as Cuyahoga County Commissioner. Three years later, he was elected as the Ohio Auditor. From 2003–2007, Petro served as the state's Attorney General. During his tenure as Attorney General, Petro implemented a pilot program, the Identity Theft Verification Passport program, with funding from the U.S. Department of Justice and support from the Buckeye State Sheriffs' Association, Ohio Association of Chiefs of Police, Ohio Department of Public Safety, the Federal Trade Commission, and the National Notary Association. This program was designed to help protect victims of identity theft by giving them a means to demonstrate that they have been victims of the crime. The Passport program offers a centralized database that is maintained by the Attorney General's office and allows law enforcement to enter information into it about identity theft cases. The program also offers an identification card to victims that they can show, as needed, to prove that they are victims. This program serves as a model for other states, demonstrating what can be done to help protect victims of identity theft from the continued victimization.

Poochigian, Charles (1949–)
State Senator (R-Calif.)

Charles S. Poochigian was born in 1949 in Fresno, California. He graduated from California State University, Fresno in 1972 and received a Juris Doctorate degree from Santa Clara University in 1975. Since then, he has served as a California State Assemblyman, from 1994–1998, and as a Senator from 1998–2006. While in the Senate, Poochigian realized the importance of gaining a greater understanding about identity theft and being tougher on the criminals who commit the crime. As a result, in 2006 he sponsored Senate Bill 1390, which requires the collection of arrest data pertaining to identity thieves. By collecting this data, law enforcement can detect potential trends in the cases of identity theft being reported. By using this data to detect trends, law enforcement can focus their attention, time, and resources more effectively on apprehending perpetrators and, potentially, preventing additional crimes. Governor Arnold Schwarzenegger signed the bill into effect in 2006.

Simitian, Joe (1953–)
State Senator (D-Calif.)

Joe Simitian was born in 1953 in Palo Alto, California. He holds two Masters degrees, a Master of Arts in International Policy Studies from Stanford University and a Master of City Planning from the University of California, Berkeley. He also obtained his Juris Doctorate degree from the University of California, Berkeley. He served in many political positions prior to being elected to the state senate, including mayor of Palo Alto, a Supervisor for Santa Clara County, and as a member of the California State Assembly. In 2004, Simitian was elected to the California State Senate.

Throughout his time in politics, Joe Simitian has worked to help protect victims of identity theft and to prevent people from becoming victims of the crime. He has sponsored various pieces of legislation to address issues associated with identity theft, and in 2009, the California State Senate approved Senate Bill 20 (SB 20), which he proposed. The bill addresses some of the concerns associated with security breach notification laws in California. It calls for standardizing the breach notification process. Furthermore, SB 20 attempts to make the notifications easier for consumers to understand by requiring that details about the breach, as well as what needs to be done as a result, be written in easy to understand terminology. SB 20 also requires that any individual security breach that impacts 500 or more California residents must be reported to the state's Attorney General, thus allowing him or her to examine larger security breaches, investigate them, and also try to understand how to prevent them from occurring in the future.

In 2008, Governor Arnold Schwarzenegger signed into law another piece of legislation sponsored by Simitian. California State Senate Bill 31 (SB 31) was written to outlaw skimming, help protect personal information, and make it a criminal offense to remotely read, or attempt to read, personal identifying information by using radio frequency identification (RFID), also known as a skimmer. This legislation allows for punishment that may consist of jail time, a fine, or both. Simitian also sponsored California State Senate Bill 612 (SB 612), which was signed into law by Governor Schwarzenegger in 2008. This law is an attempt to assist in the prosecution of the crime of identity theft. Knowing that identity theft can take place anywhere and that the crime is often not committed in the same county where the victim resides, SB 612 was designed to make it easier for the victim to seek justice by allowing for the prosecution of an identity theft case to take place in the county where the victim resides, regardless of where the crime actually took place.

Simitian also received the 2007 Award for Excellence in Public Policy for his legislation on privacy protection and its role in preventing identity theft. This award came in response to Assembly Bill 700 (AB 700)/Senate Bill 1386 (SB 1386), which requires businesses to notify consumers of security breaches in which personal identifying information may have been compromised.

Specter, Arlen (1930–)
U.S. Senator (R-Pa.)

Arlen Specter was born in Wichita, Kansas in 1930. At age four, Arlen Specter was named Deputy Sheriff of Sedgwick

County, Kansas, giving him the distinction as being the youngest Deputy Sheriff in history according to *Ripley's Believe It or Not*. He graduated from the University of Pennsylvania in 1951 and then from Yale Law School in 1956. Specter also served in the U.S. Air Force from 1951–1953. Upon graduating from law school, Specter worked as an attorney and began his political career. From 1963–1964, he served on the Warren Commission investigating the assassination of John F. Kennedy. Specter won the 1965 race for District Attorney in Philadelphia, and served in that position until 1974. After a couple of unsuccessful campaigns for U.S. Senate and Governor of Pennsylvania, Specter was elected to the U.S. Senate in 1980 and took office in January 1981. He is now the senior Senator from Pennsylvania and holds the distinction of being Pennsylvania's longest serving senator. Partially in response to an identity theft case in which an employee of a car dealership used customer information to take out $4 million in loans, Specter proposed the PITFALL (Prevent Identity Theft from Affecting Lives and Livelihoods) legislation in 2003. Though the bill did not become law, Specter was not dissuaded. Specter continued to fight for consumer rights and the protection of personal identifying information. In 2007, Specter coauthored the Identity Theft Enforcement and Restitution Act, which was signed into law by President George W. Bush in 2008. Specter and Leahy also coauthored The Leahy-Specter Personal Data Privacy and Security Act of 2007, which did not pass.

Torlakson, Tom (1949–)
State Assemblyman (D-Calif.)

Tom Torlakson was born in San Francisco, California in 1949. He worked as a Merchant Marine during the Vietnam War. He earned his Bachelor and Master of Arts degrees in 1971 and 1977, respectively, from the University of California, Berkeley. Before entering politics, he was a science teacher in the San Francisco area. He was elected to the city council in Antioch in 1978, and since then has held seats in both the California State Assembly, from 1996 through 2000, and the California State Senate, from 2000–2008. At that time, he was not able to run for State Senate again because of term limit rules. In 2008, he once more ran for

State Assembly and regained his old seat. He will be able to serve one final term in the Assembly, but cannot run for reelection, as he will have reached the maximum Assembly term limit as well.

During his time in office, Torlakson has focused on many issues. From fitness, to education, to consumer protection, Torlakson has made an impact on the people of California. He was responsible for proposed Assembly Bill 1862 in 2000 that called for the creation of a statewide database of identity theft victims. The bill was signed by Governor Gray Davis in 2000. It required the Department of Justice to establish and maintain the database of identity theft victims. The database is designed to help victims clear their names and, due to its centralized nature, allows for easier access to records of identity theft victims, thus allowing for easier verification that a person has, indeed, been a victim of identity theft.

Wyland, Mark (1946–)
State Senator (R-Calif.)

Mark Wyland was born in Escondido, California in 1946. He earned a Bachelor of Arts degree from Pomona College and a Master of Arts degree from Columbia University. He began his government career as a member of the Escondido Union School District Board, where he served from 1997 until 2000. He then ran for the California State Assembly and was elected in 2000. He remained a member of the State Assembly until 2006, when he was elected to the California State Senate.

As a member of the California state legislature, Wyland has sought to protect the rights of consumers and to protect them from identity theft. Wyland introduced Assembly Bill 245 (AB 245) in 2001. The Act, approved by the governor in October 2001, was created to give law enforcement and prosecutors more leeway regarding the arrest and prosecution of those suspected of identity theft. Wyland realized that identity theft may not be committed by a stranger to the victim. The previous wording of the penal code required that, in order to be charged with identity theft, the perpetrator must have used the personal information of the victim for unlawful purposes and must have received the information without the victim's consent. The new law allows for prosecution to take place even when the information was obtained with the victim's consent. Thus, the act of using that information for unlawful purposes is enough to constitute the crime of identity theft. Wyland also proposed Assembly Bill 946 (AB 946), which called for tougher penalties and fines for those convicted of identity theft. Although this bill did not pass, it demonstrates Wyland's continued commitment to the fight against identity theft.

6

Data and Documents

This chapter was designed to allow readers to access some of the key documents pertaining to identity theft; it presents pertinent information regarding the Federal Trade Commission and legislation that has been passed relating to identity theft.

Executive Summary Consumer Fraud and Identity Theft Complaint Data January–December 2008

The Federal Trade Commission collects identity theft complaints from victims and compiles annual statistical reports of that data. Following is an executive summary of the data collected by the Federal Trade Commission during 2008.

- The Consumer Sentinel Network (CSN) now contains over 7.2 million complaints, and over 5.8 million do-not-call complaints.
- The CSN received over 1.2 million complaints during calendar year 2008: 52% fraud complaints; 26% identity theft complaints; and 22% other types of complaints. This year's report is the first to include the other types of complaints.
- Identity theft was the number one complaint category in the CSN for calendar year 2008 with 26% of the overall complaints, followed by Third Party and Creditor Debt Collection (9%); Shop-at-Home and Catalog Sales (4%); Internet Services (4%);

Foreign Money Offers and Counterfeit Check Scams (3%); Credit Bureaus, Information Furnishers and Report Users (3%); Prizes, Sweepstakes and Lotteries (3%); Television and Electronic Media (2%); Banks and Lenders (2%); and Telecom Equipment and Mobile Services (2%). The complete ranking of all thirty complaint categories is listed on page six of this report.

Fraud

- A total of 643,195 CSN 2008 complaints are fraud-related. Consumers reported paying over $1.8 billion in those fraud complaints; the median amount paid was $440. Eighty-four percent of the consumers reporting fraud also reported an amount paid.
- Fifty-eight percent of all fraud complaints reported the method of initial contact. Of those complaints, 52% said email, while another 11% said an Internet website. Only 7% of those consumers reported the phone as the initial point of contact.
- Colorado is the state with the highest per capita rate of reported fraud and other types of complaints, followed by Maryland and Nevada.

Identity Theft

- Credit card fraud (20%) was the most common form of reported identity theft followed by government documents/benefits fraud (15%), employment fraud (15%), and phone or utilities fraud (13%).Other significant categories of identity theft reported by victims were bank fraud (11%) and loan fraud (4%).
- Government documents/benefits fraud is now the second most common reported type of identity theft after credit card fraud. Fraudulent tax return-related identity theft, a subtype of government documents/benefits fraud, has increased nearly six percentage points since calendar year 2006.
- Electronic fund transfer-related identity theft continues to be the most frequently reported type of identity theft bank fraud during calendar year 2008, despite declining since calendar year 2006.
- Arizona is the state with the highest per capita rate of reported identity theft complaints, followed by California and Florida.

Federal Trade Commission. 2009. *Consumer sentinel network data book for January–December 2008.* http://www.ftc.gov/sentinel/reports/sentinel-annual-reports/sentinel-cy2008.pdf. Accessed April 3, 2009.

President's Identity Theft Task Force

The following are the recommendations made by the President's Identity Theft Task Force in April 2007. Based on the recommendations listed below, many changes have taken place within the government concerning how personal information is handled, the assistance and protection victims receive, and the investigation of incidents of identity theft.

President's Identity Theft Task Force Summary of Interim Recommendations Prevention

Improving Government Handling of Sensitive Personal Data

Recommendation 1: The Task Force recommends that the Office of Management and Budget (OMB) issue to all federal agencies the attached Task Force guidance that covers (a) the factors that should govern whether and how to give notice to affected individuals in the event of a government agency data breach that poses a risk of identity theft, and (b) the factors that should be considered in deciding whether to offer services such as free credit monitoring.

Recommendation 2: To ensure that government agencies improve their data security programs, the Task Force recommends that OMB and the Department of Homeland Security (DHS), through the interagency effort already underway to identify ways to strengthen the ability of all agencies to identify and defend against threats, correct vulnerabilities, and manage risks: (a) outline best practices in the areas of automated tools, training, processes, and standards that would enable agencies to improve their security and privacy programs, and (b) develop a list of the top 10 or 20 "mistakes" to avoid in order to protect government information.

Recommendation 3: To limit the unnecessary use in the public sector of Social Security numbers (SSNs), the most valuable consumer information for identity thieves, the Task Force recommends the following:

- The Office of Personnel Management (OPM), in conjunction with other agencies, should accelerate its review of the use of SSNs in its collection of human resource data from agencies and on OPM-issued papers and electronic forms, and take steps to eliminate, restrict, or conceal their use (including the assignment of employee identification numbers, where practicable).
- OPM should develop and issue policy guidance to the federal human capital management community on the appropriate and inappropriate use of an employee's SSN in employee records, including the proper way to restrict, conceal, or mask SSNs in employee records and human resource management information systems.

- OMB should require all federal agencies to review their use of SSNs to determine where such use can be eliminated, restricted, or concealed in agency business processes, systems, and paper and electronic forms.

Recommendation 4: To allow agencies to respond quickly to data breaches, including by sharing information about potentially affected individuals with other agencies and entities that can assist in the response, the Task Force recommends that all federal agencies, to the extent consistent with applicable law, publish a new "routine use" for their systems of records under the Privacy Act, modeled after the attached "routine use" recently drafted by the Department of Justice, that would facilitate the disclosure of information in the course of responding to a breach of federal data.

Improved Authentication Methods

Recommendation 5: Because developing reliable methods of authenticating the identities of individuals would make it harder for identity thieves to access existing accounts and open new accounts using other individuals' information, the Task Force should hold a workshop or series of workshops, involving academics, industry, and entrepreneurs, focused on developing and promoting improved means of authenticating the identities of individuals.

Victim Assistance

Recommendation 6: To allow identity theft victims to recover for the value of time they spend in attempting to remediate the harms suffered, the Task Force recommends that Congress amend the criminal restitution statutes to allow for restitution from a criminal defendant to an identity theft victim, in an amount equal to the value of time reasonably spent by the victim attempting to remediate the intended or actual harm incurred from the identity theft offense.

Law Enforcement

Recommendation 7: To ensure that victims can readily obtain the police reports that they need to take steps to prevent the misuse of their personal information by identity thieves, and to ensure that their complaint data is entered in a standardized format that will allow complaints to flow into a central complaint database and that thereby would assist law enforcement officers in responding to such complaints, the FTC, with support from the Task Force, will develop a universal police report, which an identity theft victim can complete, print, and take to any local law enforcement agency for verification and incorporation into the police department's report system.

Improving Government Handling of Sensitive Personal Data

1. Establishing a Data Breach Policy for the Public Sector

Identity theft and related harms are a consequence of sensitive information about consumers that criminals obtain through theft or other improper means. In many cases, providing notice to the affected individuals can help prevent or mitigate the harms to consumers. Notice permits consumers to take protective actions, while also allowing relevant private sector entities to assist the consumers. Appropriate notice can also enable law enforcement to investigate, punish, and deter crime. At the same time, however, unnecessary or excessive breach notification can overwhelm the public and impose undue burdens and costs on consumers, as well as on government agencies. Several federal government agencies have suffered high-profile security breaches involving sensitive consumer data over the past several months. These and other agencies have faced difficult decisions about when and how to notify the public of such incidents, and whether the agencies should offer free credit monitoring or other services to those who may be affected. Federal agencies need guidance in how to make these important decisions.

Recommendation 1: The Task Force recommends that the Office of Management and Budget (OMB) issue the attached guidance memorandum, advising federal agencies on steps to take in the event of a compromise of data. The Task Force has developed and formally approved a set of guidelines, produced in Attachment A, that provides the factors that should be considered in deciding whether, how, and when to inform affected individuals of the loss of personal data that can contribute to identity theft, and whether to offer services such as free credit monitoring to the persons affected.

2. Improving Data Security in the Public Sector

The high-profile data breaches suffered by several federal agencies have focused attention on whether the government is doing enough to secure the massive amounts of data held by federal agencies as part of their core missions. The President's Management Agenda (PMA) Scorecard, OMB reports to Congress, Congress' annual security report card, Government Accountability Office reports, and many agency Inspector General (IG) reports show that agency performance in both information privacy and security is uneven. Common findings are that agencies would benefit from increased sharing of best practices, group purchases of automated tools and training courses, and development of a more effective common curriculum for training. OMB and the Department of Homeland Security (DHS) are already leading an interagency Information Systems Security Line of Business (ISS LOB) effort to explore ways to address these issues, including to identify and defend against threats, correct vulnerabilities, and manage risks. The ISS LOB can be a useful forum for developing best practices and a list of practices that should be avoided in order to protect government information.

Recommendation 2: To ensure that government agencies improve their data security programs, the Task Force recommends that OMB and DHS enhance the activities of the ISS LOB. Specifically, the Task Force recommends that the ISS LOB should (a) outline best practices in the area of automated tools, training, processes, and standards that would enable agencies to improve their security and privacy programs, and (b) develop a list of the top 10 or 20 "mistakes" to avoid in order to protect information held by the government.

3. Decreasing the Use of Social Security Numbers by the Public Sector

One way to reduce the incidence of identity theft is to make it more difficult for criminals to obtain consumer information. Currently, the most valuable consumer information identity thieves can find is the Social Security Number (SSN). SSNs are key to assuming another's identity because they are used to match consumers with their credit histories and many government benefits.

Consequently, if federal agencies were to eliminate unnecessary uses of SSNs, they could reduce the opportunities for unauthorized use by identity thieves. The Office of Personnel Management (OPM), which issues or approves many of the federal forms and procedures using the SSN, and OMB, which oversees the management and administrative practices of federal agencies, can play pivotal roles in restricting the unnecessary use of SSNs, offering guidance on potential substitutes that would be of equal use to the agencies but of no use to identity thieves, and establishing greater consistency when the use of SSNs is unavoidable.

Recommendation 3: To limit the unnecessary use in the public sector of SSNs, the most valuable consumer information for identity thieves, the Task Force recommends the following:

Recommendation 3a: OPM should accelerate its review of the use of SSNs in its collection of human resource data from agencies and on OPM-based papers and electronic forms, and take steps to eliminate, restrict, or conceal their use (including the assignment of employee identification numbers, where practicable). If necessary to implement this recommendation, Executive Order 9397, effective 11/23/1943, which requires federal agencies to use SSNs in "any system of permanent account numbers pertaining to individuals," should be partially rescinded. It should also be noted that steps are already being taken to facilitate implementation of this recommendation. This month, each OPM program office designated staff to review the use of SSNs in that office, and OPM is prepared to complete its inventory of forms, procedures, and systems that currently display SSNs by October 13, 2006. This new inventory will be the basis for OPM's actions to change, eliminate, or mask the use of SSNs on OPM approved/authorized forms.

Recommendation 3b: OPM should develop and issue policy guidance to the federal human capital management community on the appropriate and inappropriate use of an employee's SSN in employee records, including the appropriate way to restrict, conceal, or mask SSNs in employee records and human resource management information systems. OPM already has begun work to implement this recommendation, such as by working to establish a unique employee identifier that can be used in human resource and payroll systems rather than SSNs. Pursuant to the Task Force's recommendation, OPM is also prepared in September 2006 to begin consulting with a working group of agencies to develop a new OPM policy regarding the use of a unique employee identifier and limitations on the use of SSNs. The policy would include instructions on when SSNs can be displayed, when SSNs must be masked in employee records, and when SSNs must be masked on human resource and payroll system computer screens. The policy could be drafted by November 1, 2006 and would be issued by May 2007, following internal coordination and comment by agencies. OPM would then be prepared to work with the various human resource and payroll systems to implement the changes required by any new policy, with a phased-in implementation expected to take up to 18 months to complete.

Recommendation 3c: OMB should require all federal agencies to review their use of SSNs to determine the circumstances under which such use can be eliminated, restricted, or concealed in agency business processes, systems, and paper and electronic forms, other than those authorized or approved by OPM. Already, OMB has developed a survey instrument to be in a position to implement this recommendation, which OMB could issue to all agencies this year. To add to this effort, and to ensure consistency, the Task Force will identify factors that agencies should take into consideration in determining whether the use of the SSN is essential to the agency's mission and necessary to ensure program integrity or to maintain national security. The Task Force will also evaluate the availability of practical alternatives to use of the SSN.

4. Publication of a "Routine Use" for Disclosure of Information Following a Breach

A federal agency's ability to respond quickly and effectively in the event of a breach of sensitive personal data is critical to its efforts to prevent or minimize any consequent harms. An effective response may include disclosure of information regarding the breach to those individuals affected by it. Similarly, expeditiously notifying persons and entities in a position to cooperate (either by assisting in informing affected individuals or by actively preventing or minimizing harms from the breach) will help mitigate consequences of a breach. However, the very information that may be most necessary to disclose to such persons and entities will often be information maintained by federal agencies that is subject to the Privacy Act of 1974, 5 U.S.C. § 552a. Critically, the Privacy

Act prohibits the disclosure of any record in a system of records, by any means of communication to any person or agency, unless the subject individual has given written consent or unless the disclosure falls within one of twelve statutory exceptions. See 5 U.S.C. §§ 552a(b)(1)-(12).

To address this issue, federal agencies could, in accordance with the Privacy Act exception set forth in subsection § 552a(b)(3), publish a "routine use" that specifically permits the disclosure of information in connection with response and remedial efforts in the event of a data breach. Such a "routine use" would serve to protect the interests of the people whole information is at risk by allowing agencies to take appropriate steps to facilitate a timely and effective response, thereby improving their ability to prevent, minimize, or remedy any harms that may result from a compromise of data maintained in their systems of records. For example, such a routine use would permit an agency that has lost data such as bank account numbers to quickly share that information with the appropriate financial institutions, which could assist in monitoring for bank fraud and in identifying the account holders, thereby facilitating the agency's ability promptly to notify the affected individuals. The Department of Justice recently drafted such a "routine use," which is reproduced in Attachment B, and which the Task Force offers as a model for other federal agencies to use in developing and publishing their own "routine uses" as soon as practicable.

Recommendation 4: To allow agencies to respond quickly to data breaches, including by sharing information about potentially affected individuals with other agencies and entities that can assist in the response, the Task Force recommends that all federal agencies, to the extent consistent with applicable law, publish a new "routine use" for their systems of records under the Privacy Act, modeled after the attached "routine use" recently drafted by the Department of Justice, that would facilitate the disclosure of information to other agencies, entities, and persons in the course of responding to a breach of federal data.

Improved Authentication Methods
5. Developing Alternate Means of Authenticating Identities
In addition to its widespread use by government, the SSN is used throughout the private sector. In particular, the SSN often is used for the dual purposes of identification (to match individuals to records of their information) and authentication (to prove that individuals are who they say they are). Two factors combine to heighten the risk of identity theft: the ready availability of SSNs to identity thieves as a result of their ubiquitous use, and the SSN's use as a sole or primary means of authenticating individuals to open new accounts or obtain other benefits.

Both the private and public sectors have made strides in developing improved means of verification and authentication. For example, the Customer Identification Program already requires financial institutions regulated by the federal banking agencies and the SEC to develop and implement procedures for verifying customers' identities when opening new accounts. Technology also can substantially improve the authentication process by, for example, the use of biometrics to authenticate the consumer's identity, making it less likely that a criminal can gain access to another's account. However, many questions remain about emerging technologies, consumer acceptance, and system implementation.

One way to sharpen the focus on improving the means for authenticating the identities of individuals would be to hold public workshops that bring together academics, industry, and entrepreneurs who are developing better authentication systems. These experts can discuss the existing problem, examine the limitations of current processes of authentication, and probe viable solutions that will reduce identity fraud. As an initial step, the FTC and other Task Force member agencies are prepared to announce in the fall of 2006 that they will host such a workshop in the early part of 2007.

Recommendation 5: Because developing reliable methods of authenticating the identities of individuals would make it harder for identity thieves to open new accounts or access existing accounts using other individuals' information, the Task Force should hold a workshop or series of workshops, involving academics, industry, and entrepreneurs, focused on developing and promoting improved means of authenticating the identities of individuals.

Victim Assistance

6. Restitution for Identity Theft Victims

One reason that identity theft can be so destructive to its victims is the sheer amount of time and energy often required to remediate the consequences of the offense. This may be time spent clearing credit reports with credit-reporting agencies, disputing charges with individual creditors, or monitoring credit reports for additional impacts of the theft. The FTC estimated in 2003, based on the results of its Identity Theft Survey Report, that the average identity theft victim spends 30 hours resolving the problems created by identity theft. Those individuals who were victimized most seriously (from both the false opening of new accounts in their names *and* the unauthorized use of their validly-issued credit cards) spent an average of 60 hours resolving the problems. Overall, according to the survey, approximately 297 million hours were expended in one year by consumers attempting to resolve identity theft-related problems.

While restitution is available for direct pecuniary costs of identity theft offenses, the federal restitution statutes, 18 U.S.C. § § 3663(b) and 3663A(b), do not provide for compensation for this time spent by consumers rectifying accounts and avoiding more harm. Moreover, courts have interpreted the restitution statutes in such a way that would likely preclude the recovery of such amounts from criminal defendants, absent explicit statutory authorization.

In order to better remediate the harm caused by identity theft, the Department of Justice has drafted amendments to the restitution statutes, reproduced in Attachment C, that would allow a victim to obtain restitution from a criminal defendant for the time reasonably spent trying to rectify the consequences of the offense. Under these proposed amendments, the district court judge would determine the amount of time reasonably spent and the value of the victim's time. The Department of Justice can propose that Congress adopt these amendments immediately.

Recommendation 6: The Task Force recommends that Congress amend the criminal restitution statutes, 18 U.S.C. §§ 3663(b) and 3663A(b), based on the attached proposal developed by the Department of Justice, to allow for restitution from a criminal defendant to an identity theft victim, in an amount equal to the value of time reasonably spent by the victim attempting to remediate the intended or actual harm incurred from the identity theft offense.

Law Enforcement

7. Development of a Universal Police Report

Victims of identity theft often need police reports documenting the misuse of their information in order to recover fully from the effects of the crime. For example, identity theft victims can use a detailed police report as an "identity theft report" under the Fair and Accurate Credit Transactions Act to request that fraudulent information on their credit report be blocked, or to obtain a seven-year fraud alert on their credit file. Further, identity theft victims also must have a police report to obtain documents relating to fraudulent applications and transactions, and creditors may require a police report before establishing the victim's *bona fides* in challenging a fraudulent account or purchase. Filing a police report also makes it more likely that law enforcement will pursue an investigation of the identity theft.

Some victims report, however, that they are unable to get a police report. FTC complaint data show that during the last three years, about 25% of victims of new-account fraud who sought police reports were not able to obtain them, in part because of overtaxed local police departments and the time involved in preparing what often can be a highly detailed document. Simplifying the process of writing and receiving a police report would both relieve the burden on local law enforcement and allow victims to more easily repair the damage to their credit from the crime. A universal law enforcement report that the victim could complete online and take to the local police department would help achieve this goal. Additionally, the data from such standardized reports would be in a format that is used by the FTC's Identity Theft Data Clearinghouse, increasing the ability of law enforcement to effectively spot significant patterns of criminal activity.

At present, the FTC has an online complaint form that is used to enter data into its Identity Theft Data Clearinghouse, which is in turn made available to law enforcement nationwide through Consumer Sentinel. The FTC is also prepared to develop a revised online complaint form at www.ftc.gov/idtheft that victims can complete, print, and take to a local law enforcement agency for verification and incorporation into the police department's report system. The victim will then have a valid, detailed police report; the police department will have a record of the crime; and the victim's complaint information will have been entered into the FTC's Identity Theft Data Clearinghouse. The Public Sector Liaison Committee of the International Association of Chiefs of Police supports and has been involved in this effort.

Recommendation 7: To ensure that victims can readily file the police reports necessary to allow them to prevent the continued misuse of their personal information, and to assist law enforcement in analyzing significant patterns of criminal activity in investigating identity theft complaints, the FTC, with support from Task Force members, should develop a universal police report, which an identity theft victim can complete, print, and take to any local law enforcement agency for verification and incorporation into the police department's report system.

President's Identity Theft Task Force. 2007. *Summary of interim recommendations: Prevention.* www.ftc.gov/os/2006/09/060916interimre commend.pdf. Accessed May 3, 2007.

Identity Theft and Assumption Deterrence Act

This legislation established identity theft as a felony and set forth penalties associated with it. Additionally, the Identity Theft and Assumption Deterrence Act required the Federal Trade Commission to collect complaints directly from victims and share that information with law enforcement agencies and other specified organizations.

Identity Theft and Assumption Deterrence Act As amended by Public Law 105–318, 112 Stat. 3007 (Oct. 30, 1998) An Act

To amend chapter 47 of title 18, United States Code, relating to identity fraud, and for other purposes. [NOTE: Oct. 30, 1998—[H.R. 4151]

Be it enacted by the Senate and House of Representatives of the United States of America in Congress assembled, [NOTE: Identity Theft and Assumption Deterrence Act of 1998.]

Sec.
001. Short Title
002. Constitutional Authority to Enact this Legislation.
003. Identity Theft
004. Amendment of Federal Sentencing Guidelines for Offenses Under Section 1028
005. Centralized Complaint and Consumer Education Service for Victims of Identity Theft
006. Technical Amendments to Title 18, United States Code
007. Redaction of Ethics Reports Filed by Judicial Officers and Employees

§ 001. Short Title. [NOTE: 18 USC 1001 note.]
This Act may be cited as the "Identity Theft and Assumption Deterrence Act of 1998".

§ 002. Constitutional Authority to Enact this Legislation. [NOTE: 18 USC 1028 note.]
The constitutional authority upon which this Act rests is the power of Congress to regulate commerce with foreign nations and among the several States, and the authority to make all laws which shall be necessary and proper for carrying into execution the powers vested by the Constitution in the Government of the United States or in any department or officer thereof, as set forth in article I, section 8 of the United States Constitution.

§ 003. Identity Theft.
    (a) Establishment of Offense.—Section 1028(a) of title 18, United States Code, is amended—
    (b) in paragraph (5), by striking "or" at the end;

        (2) in paragraph (6), by adding "or" at the end;
        (3) in the flush matter following paragraph (6), by striking "or attempts to do so,"; and
        (4) by inserting after paragraph (6) the following:
    "(7) knowingly transfers or uses, without lawful authority, a means of identification of another person with the intent to commit, or to aid or abet, any unlawful activity that constitutes a violation of Federal law, or that constitutes a felony under any applicable State or local law;".

(b) Penalties.—Section 1028(b) of title 18, United States Code, is amended—

    (b) in paragraph (1)—

        (A) in subparagraph (B), by striking "or" at the end;

        (B) in subparagraph (C), by adding "or" at the end; and

        (C) by adding at the end the following:

      "(D) an offense under paragraph (7) of such subsection that involves the transfer or use of 1 or more means of identification if, as a result of the offense, any individual committing the offense obtains anything of value aggregating $1,000 or more during any 1-year period;";

    (2) in paragraph (2)—

        (A) in subparagraph (A), by striking "or transfer of an identification document or" and inserting ", transfer, or use of a means of identification, an identification document, or a"; and

        (B) in subparagraph (B), by inserting "or (7)" after "(3)";

    (3) by amending paragraph (3) to read as follows:

    "(3) a f2ine under this title or imprisonment for not more than 20 years, or both, if the offense is committed—

      "(A) to facilitate a drug trafficking crime (as defined in section 929(a)(2));

      "(B) in connection with a crime of violence (as defined in section 924(c)(3)); or

      "(C) after a prior conviction under this section becomes final;";

    (4) in paragraph (4), by striking "and" at the end;

    (5) by redesignating paragraph (5) as paragraph (6); and

    (6) by inserting after paragraph (4) the following:

      "(5) in the case of any offense under subsection (a), forfeiture to the United States of any personal property used or intended to be used to commit the offense; and".

    I Circumstances.—Section 1028I of title 18, United States Code, is amended by striking paragraph (3) and inserting the following:

"(3) either—

      "(A) the production, transfer, possession, or use prohibited by this section is in or affects interstate or foreign commerce; or

      "(B) the means of identification, identification document, false identification document, or document- making implement is transported in the mail in the course of the production, transfer, possession, or use prohibited by this section.".

(d) Definitions.—Subsection (d) of section 1028 of title 18, United States Code, is amended to read as follows:

"(d) In this section—

"(1) the term 'document-making implement' means any implement, impression, electronic device, or computer hardware or software, that is specifically configured or primarily used for making an identification document, a false identification document, or another document-making implement;

"(2) the term 'identification document' means a document made or issued by or under the authority of the United States Government, a State, political subdivision of a State, a foreign government, political subdivision of a foreign government, an international governmental or an international quasi-governmental organization which, when completed with information concerning a particular individual, is of a type intended or commonly accepted for the purpose of identification of individuals;

"(3) the term 'means of identification' means any name or number that may be used, alone or in conjunction with any other information, to identify a specific individual, including any—

"(A) name, social security number, date of birth, official State or government issued driver's license or identification number, alien registration number, government passport number, employer or taxpayer identification number;

"(B) unique biometric data, such as fingerprint, voice print, retina or iris image, or other unique physical representation;

"(C) unique electronic identification number, address, or routing code; or

"(D) telecommunication identifying information or access device (as defined in section 1029(e));

"(4) the term 'personal identification card' means an identification document issued by a State or local government solely for the purpose of identification;

"(5) the term 'produce' includes alter, authenticate, or assemble; and

"(6) the term 'State' includes any State of the United States, the District of Columbia, the Commonwealth of Puerto Rico, and any other commonwealth, possession, or territory of the United States.".

(e) Attempt and Conspiracy.—Section 1028 of title 18, United States Code, is amended by adding at the end the following:

"(f) Attempt and Conspiracy.—Any person who attempts or conspires to commit any offense under this section shall be subject to the same penalties as those prescribed for the offense, the commission of which was the object of the attempt or conspiracy.".

(f) Forfeiture Procedures.—Section 1028 of title 18, United States Code, is amended by adding at the end the following:
"(g) Forfeiture Procedures.—The forfeiture of property under this section, including any seizure and disposition of the property and any related judicial or administrative proceeding, shall be governed by the provisions of section 413 (other than subsection (d) of that section) of the Comprehensive Drug Abuse Prevention and Control Act of 1970 (21 U.S.C. 853)."

(g) Rule of Construction.—Section 1028 of title 18, United States Code, is amended by adding at the end the following:
"(h) Rule of Construction.—For purpose of subsection (a)(7), a single identification document or false identification document that contains 1 or more means of identification shall be construed to be 1 means of identification."

(h) Conforming Amendments.—Chapter 47 of title 18, United States Code, is amended—
(1) in the heading for section 1028, by adding "**and information**" at the end; and
(2) in the table of sections at the beginning of the chapter, in the item relating to section 1028, by adding "and information" at the end.

§ 004. Amendment of Federal Sentencing Guidelines for Offenses Under Section 1028. [NOTE: 28 USC 994 note.]

(a) In General.—Pursuant to its authority under section 994(p) of title 28, United States Code, the United States Sentencing Commission shall review and amend the Federal sentencing guidelines and the policy statements of the Commission, as appropriate, to provide an appropriate penalty for each offense under section 1028 of title 18, United States Code, as amended by this Act.
(b) Factors for Consideration.—In carrying out subsection (a), the United States Sentencing Commission shall consider, with respect to each offense described in subsection (a)—
(1) the extent to which the number of victims (as defined in section 3663A(a) of title 18, United States Code) involved in the offense, including harm to reputation, inconvenience,

and other difficulties resulting from the offense, is an adequate measure for establishing penalties under the Federal sentencing guidelines;

(2) the number of means of identification, identification documents, or false identification documents (as those terms are defined in section 1028(d) of title 18, United States Code, as amended by this Act) involved in the offense, is an adequate measure for establishing penalties under the Federal sentencing guidelines;

(3) the extent to which the value of the loss to any individual caused by the offense is an adequate measure for establishing penalties under the Federal sentencing guidelines;

(4) the range of conduct covered by the offense;

(5) the extent to which sentencing enhancements within the Federal sentencing guidelines and the court's authority to sentence above the applicable guideline range are adequate to ensure punishment at or near the maximum penalty for the most egregious conduct covered by the offense;

(6) the extent to which Federal sentencing guidelines sentences for the offense have been constrained by statutory maximum penalties;

(7) the extent to which Federal sentencing guidelines for the offense adequately achieve the purposes of sentencing set forth in section 3553(a)(2) of title 18, United States Code; and

(8) any other factor that the United States Sentencing Commission considers to be appropriate.

§ 005. Centralized Complaint and Consumer Education Service for Victims of Identity Theft. [NOTE: 18 USC 1028 note.]

(a) In <<NOTE: Deadline.>> General.—Not later than 1 year after the date of enactment of this Act, the Federal Trade Commission shall establish procedures to—

(1) log and acknowledge the receipt of complaints by individuals who certify that they have a reasonable belief that 1 or more of their means of identification (as defined in section 1028 of title 18, United States Code, as amended by this Act) have been assumed, stolen, or otherwise unlawfully acquired in violation of section 1028 of title 18, United States Code, as amended by this Act;

(2) provide informational materials to individuals described in paragraph (1); and

(3) refer complaints described in paragraph (1) to appropriate entities, which may include referral to—

(A) the 3 major national consumer reporting agencies; and
(B) appropriate law enforcement agencies for potential law
enforcement action.

(b) Authorization of Appropriations.—There are authorized to be
appropriated such sums as may be necessary to carry out this
section.

§ 006. Technical Amendments to Title 18, United States Code.

(a) Technical Correction Relating to Criminal Forfeiture
Procedures.—Section 982(b)(1) of title 18, United States Code,
is amended to read as follows: "(1) The forfeiture of property
under this section, including any seizure and disposition
of the property and any related judicial or administrative
proceeding, shall be governed by the provisions of section
413 (other than subsection (d) of that section) of the
Comprehensive Drug Abuse Prevention and Control Act of
1970 (21 U.S.C. 853)."

(b) Economic Espionage and Theft of Trade Secrets as Predicate
Offenses for Wire Interception.—Section 2516(1)(a) of title
18, United States Code, is amended by inserting "chapter 90
(relating to protection of trade secrets)," after "to espionage."

§ 007. Redaction of Ethics Reports Filed by
Judicial Officers and Employees.

Section 105(b) of the Ethics in Government Act of 1978 (5 U.S.C. App.) is
amended by adding at the end the following new paragraph:

"(3) (A) This section does not require the immediate and uncondi-
tional availability of reports filed by an individual described in
section 109(8) or 109(10) of this Act if a finding is made by the
Judicial Conference, in consultation with United States Mar-
shall Service, that revealing personal and sensitive information
could endanger that individual.

"(B) A report may be redacted pursuant to this paragraph only—
"(i) to the extent necessary to protect the individual who filed
the report; and
"(ii) for as long as the danger to such individual exists.

"I The Administrative Office of the United States Courts shall
submit to the Committees on the Judiciary of the House of
Representatives and of the Senate an annual report with respect
to the operation of this paragraph including—
"(i) the total number of reports redacted pursuant to this
paragraph;

"(ii) the total number of individuals whose reports have been
redacted pursuant to this paragraph; and
"(iii) the types of threats against individuals whose reports are
redacted, if appropriate.
"(D) The Judicial Conference, in consultation with the Department
of Justice, shall issue regulations setting forth the circumstances under which redaction is appropriate under this
paragraph and the procedures for redaction. [NOTE:
Regulations.]
"(E) This paragraph shall expire on December 31, 2001, and apply
to filings through calendar year 2001." [NOTE: Expiration
date.]

Identity Theft and Assumption Deterrence Act of 1998, as amended by
Public Law 105-318, 112 Stat. 3007, 105th Cong., 2d sess. (October 30,
1998). http://thomas.loc.gov/cgi-bin/query/D?c105:4:./temp/
~c105UybEJU::. Accessed April 9, 2009.

Title V of the Gramm-Leach-Bliley Act, 1999

*The purpose of this federal legislation is to ensure that financial institu-
tions protect the privacy and sensitive information of their customers. To
that end, Title V of the Gramm-Leach-Bliley Act mandates the financial
industry to develop safeguards. The Act also provides customers with
the ability to opt-out of having their information shared with third parties other than those directly affiliated with the institution with which
they do business.*

Title V—Privacy Subtitle A—Disclosure of Nonpublic Personal Information

Sec. 501. Protection of Nonpublic Personal Information.

(a) PRIVACY OBLIGATION POLICY.—It is the policy of the
Congress that each financial institution has an affirmative and
continuing obligation to respect the privacy of its customers and
to protect the security and confidentiality of those customers'
nonpublic personal information.
(b) FINANCIAL INSTITUTIONS SAFEGUARDS.—In furtherance
of the policy in subsection (a), each agency or authority
described in section 505(a) shall establish appropriate standards

for the financial institutions subject to their jurisdiction relating to administrative, technical, and physical safeguards—

(1) to insure the security and confidentiality of customer records and information;

(2) to protect against any anticipated threats or hazards to the security or integrity of such records; and

(3) to protect against unauthorized access to or use of such records or information which could result in substantial harm or inconvenience to any customer.

Sec. 502. Obligations with Respect to Disclosures of Personal Information.

(a) NOTICE REQUIREMENTS.—Except as otherwise provided in this subtitle, a financial institution may not, directly or through any affiliate, disclose to a nonaffiliated third party any nonpublic personal information, unless such financial institution provides or has provided to the consumer a notice that complies with section 503.

(b) OPT OUT.—

(1) IN GENERAL.—A financial institution may not disclose nonpublic personal information to a nonaffiliated third party unless—

(A) such financial institution clearly and conspicuously discloses to the consumer, in writing or in electronic form or other form permitted by the regulations prescribed under section 504, that such information may be disclosed to such third party;

(B) the consumer is given the opportunity, before the time that such information is initially disclosed, to direct that such information not be disclosed to such third party; and

(C) the consumer is given an explanation of how the consumer can exercise that nondisclosure option.

(2) EXCEPTION.—This subsection shall not prevent a financial institution from providing nonpublic personal information to a nonaffiliated third party to perform services for or functions on behalf of the financial institution, including marketing of the financial institution's own products or services, or financial products or services offered pursuant to joint agreements between two or more financial institutions that comply with the requirements imposed by the regulations prescribed under section 504, if the financial institution fully discloses the providing of such information

and enters into a contractual agreement with the third party that requires the third party to maintain the confidentiality of such information.

(c) LIMITS ON REUSE OF INFORMATION.—Except as otherwise provided in this subtitle, a nonaffiliated third party that receives from a financial institution nonpublic personal information under this section shall not, directly or through an affiliate of such receiving third party, disclose such information to any other person that is a non-affiliated third party of both the financial institution and such receiving third party, unless such disclosure would be lawful if made directly to such other person by the financial institution.

(d) LIMITATIONS ON THE SHARING OF ACCOUNT NUMBER INFORMATION FOR MARKETING PURPOSES.—A financial institution shall not disclose, other than to a consumer reporting agency, an account number or similar form of access number or access code for a credit card account, deposit account, or transaction account of a consumer to any nonaffiliated third party for use in telemarketing, direct mail marketing, or other marketing through electronic mail to the consumer.

(e) GENERAL EXCEPTIONS.—Subsections (a) and (b) shall not prohibit the disclosure of nonpublic personal information—

(1) as necessary to effect, administer, or enforce a transaction requested or authorized by the consumer, or in connection with—

(A) servicing or processing a financial product or service requested or authorized by the consumer;

(B) maintaining or servicing the consumer's account with the financial institution, or with another entity as part of a private label credit card program or other extension of credit on behalf of such entity; or

(C) a proposed or actual securitization, secondary market sale (including sales of servicing rights), or similar transaction related to a transaction of the consumer;

(2) with the consent or at the direction of the consumer;

(3) (A) to protect the confidentiality or security of the financial institution's records pertaining to the consumer, the service or product, or the transaction therein; (B) to protect against or prevent actual or potential fraud, unauthorized transactions, claims, or other liability; (C) for required institutional risk control, or for resolving customer disputes or inquiries; (D) to persons holding a legal or beneficial interest relating to the consumer; or (E) to persons acting in a fiduciary or representative capacity on behalf of the consumer;

(4) to provide information to insurance rate advisory organizations, guaranty funds or agencies, applicable rating agencies of the financial institution, persons assessing the institution's compliance with industry standards, and the institution's attorneys, accountants, and auditors;

(5) to the extent specifically permitted or required under other provisions of law and in accordance with the Right to Financial Privacy Act of 1978, to law enforcement agencies (including a Federal functional regulator, the Secretary of the Treasury with respect to subchapter II of chapter 53 of title 31, United States Code, and chapter 2 of title I of Public Law 91–508 (12 U.S.C. 1951–1959), a State insurance authority, or the Federal Trade Commission), self-regulatory organizations, or for an investigation on a matter related to public safety;

(6) (A) to a consumer reporting agency in accordance with the Fair Credit Reporting Act, or (B) from a consumer report reported by a consumer reporting agency;

(7) in connection with a proposed or actual sale, merger, transfer, or exchange of all or a portion of a business or operating unit if the disclosure of nonpublic personal information concerns solely consumers of such business or unit; or

(8) to comply with Federal, State, or local laws, rules, and other applicable legal requirements; to comply with a properly authorized civil, criminal, or regulatory investigation or subpoena or summons by Federal, State, or local authorities; or to respond to judicial process or government regulatory authorities having jurisdiction over the financial institution for examination, compliance, or other purposes as authorized by law.

Sec. 503. Disclosure of Institution Privacy Policy.

(a) DISCLOSURE REQUIRED.—At the time of establishing a customer relationship with a consumer and not less than annually during the continuation of such relationship, a financial institution shall provide a clear and conspicuous disclosure to such consumer, in writing or in electronic form or other form permitted by the regulations prescribed under section 504, of such financial institution's policies and practices with respect to—

(1) disclosing nonpublic personal information to affiliates and nonaffiliated third parties, consistent with section 502, including the categories of information that may be disclosed;

(2) disclosing nonpublic personal information of persons who have ceased to be customers of the financial institution; and

(3) protecting the nonpublic personal information of consumers. Such disclosures shall be made in accordance with the regulations prescribed under section 504.

(b) INFORMATION TO BE INCLUDED.—The disclosure required by subsection (a) shall include—

(1) the policies and practices of the institution with respect to disclosing nonpublic personal information to nonaffiliated third parties, other than agents of the institution, consistent with section 502 of this subtitle, and including—

(A) the categories of persons to whom the information is or may be disclosed, other than the persons to whom the information may be provided pursuant to section 502(e); and

(B) the policies and practices of the institution with respect to disclosing of nonpublic personal information of persons who have ceased to be customers of the financial institution;

(2) the categories of nonpublic personal information that are collected by the financial institution;

(3) the policies that the institution maintains to protect the confidentiality and security of nonpublic personal information in accordance with section 501; and

(4) the disclosures required, if any, under section 603(d)(2)(A)(iii) of the Fair Credit Reporting Act.

Sec. 504. Rulemaking.

(a) REGULATORY AUTHORITY.—

(1) RULEMAKING.—The Federal banking agencies, the National Credit Union Administration, the Secretary of the Treasury, the Securities and Exchange Commission, and the Federal Trade Commission shall each prescribe, after consultation as appropriate with representatives of State insurance authorities designated by the National Association of Insurance Commissioners, such regulations as may be necessary to carry out the purposes of this subtitle with respect to the financial institutions subject to their jurisdiction under section 505.

(2) COORDINATION, CONSISTENCY, AND COMPARABILITY.—Each of the agencies and authorities required under paragraph (1) to prescribe regulations shall consult and coordinate with the other such agencies

and authorities for the purposes of assuring, to the extent possible, that the regulations prescribed by each such agency and authority are consistent and comparable with the regulations prescribed by the other such agencies and authorities.

(3) PROCEDURES AND DEADLINE.—Such regulations shall be prescribed in accordance with applicable requirements of title 5, United States Code, and shall be issued in final form not later than 6 months after the date of the enactment of this Act.

(b) AUTHORITY TO GRANT EXCEPTIONS.—The regulations prescribed under subsection (a) may include such additional exceptions to subsections (a) through (d) of section 502 as are deemed consistent with the purposes of this subtitle.

Sec. 505. Enforcement.

(a) IN GENERAL.—This subtitle and the regulations prescribed thereunder shall be enforced by the Federal functional regulators, the State insurance authorities, and the Federal Trade Commission with respect to financial institutions and other persons subject to their jurisdiction under applicable law, as follows:

(1) Under section 8 of the Federal Deposit Insurance Act, in the case of—

(A) national banks, Federal branches and Federal agencies of foreign banks, and any subsidiaries of such entities (except brokers, dealers, persons providing insurance, investment companies, and investment advisers), by the Office of the Comptroller of the Currency;

(B) member banks of the Federal Reserve System (other than national banks), branches and agencies of foreign banks (other than Federal branches, Federal agencies, and insured State branches of foreign banks), commercial lending companies owned or controlled by foreign banks, organizations operating under section 25 or 25A of the Federal Reserve Act, and bank holding companies and their nonbank subsidiaries or affiliates (except brokers, dealers, persons providing insurance, investment companies, and investment advisers), by the Board of Governors of the Federal Reserve System;

(C) banks insured by the Federal Deposit Insurance Corporation (other than members of the Federal Reserve System), insured State branches of foreign banks, and any subsidiaries of such entities (except brokers, dealers, persons providing insurance, investment companies, and investment advisers), by the Board of Directors of the Federal Deposit Insurance Corporation; and (D) savings associations the deposits of which are insured by the Federal Deposit Insurance Corporation, and any subsidiaries of such savings associations (except brokers, dealers, persons providing insurance, investment companies, and investment advisers), by the Director of the Office of Thrift Supervision.

(2) Under the Federal Credit Union Act, by the Board of the National Credit Union Administration with respect to any federally insured credit union, and any subsidiaries of such an entity.

(3) Under the Securities Exchange Act of 1934, by the Securities and Exchange Commission with respect to any broker or dealer.

(4) Under the Investment Company Act of 1940, by the Securities and Exchange Commission with respect to investment companies.

(5) Under the Investment Advisers Act of 1940, by the Securities and Exchange Commission with respect to investment advisers registered with the Commission under such Act.

(6) Under State insurance law, in the case of any person engaged in providing insurance, by the applicable State insurance authority of the State in which the person is domiciled, subject to section 104 of this Act.

(7) Under the Federal Trade Commission Act, by the Federal Trade Commission for any other financial institution or other person that is not subject to the jurisdiction of any agency or authority under paragraphs (1) through (6) of this subsection.

(b) ENFORCEMENT OF SECTION 501.—

(1) IN GENERAL.—Except as provided in paragraph (2), the agencies and authorities described in subsection (a) shall implement the standards prescribed under section 501(b) in the same manner, to the extent practicable, as standards prescribed pursuant to section 39(a) of the Federal Deposit Insurance Act are implemented pursuant to such section.

(2) EXCEPTION.—The agencies and authorities described in paragraphs (3), (4), (5), (6), and (7) of subsection (a) shall implement the standards prescribed under section 501(b) by rule with respect to the financial institutions and other persons subject to their respective jurisdictions under subsection (a).

(c) ABSENCE OF STATE ACTION.—If a State insurance authority fails to adopt regulations to carry out this subtitle, such State shall not be eligible to override, pursuant to section 45(g)(2)(B)

(iii) of the Federal Deposit Insurance Act, the insurance customer protection regulations prescribed by a Federal banking agency under section 45(a) of such Act.

(d) DEFINITIONS.—The terms used in subsection (a)(1) that are not defined in this subtitle or otherwise defined in section 3(s) of the Federal Deposit Insurance Act shall have the same meaning as given in section 1(b) of the International Banking Act of 1978.

Sec. 506. Protection of Fair Credit Reporting Act.

(a) AMENDMENT.—Section 621 of the Fair Credit Reporting Act (15 U.S.C. 1681s) is amended—

(1) in subsection (d), by striking everything following the end of the second sentence; and

(2) by striking subsection (e) and inserting the following:

"(e) REGULATORY AUTHORITY.—

"(1) The Federal banking agencies referred to in paragraphs (1) and (2) of subsection (b) shall jointly prescribe such regulations as necessary to carry out the purposes of this Act with respect to any persons identified under paragraphs (1) and (2) of subsection (b), and the Board of Governors of the Federal Reserve System shall have authority to prescribe regulations consistent with such joint regulations with respect to bank holding companies and affiliates (other than depository institutions and consumer reporting agencies) of such holding companies.

"(2) The Board of the National Credit Union Administration shall prescribe such regulations as necessary to carry out the purposes of this Act with respect to any persons identified under paragraph (3) of subsection (b)."

(b) CONFORMING AMENDMENT.—Section 621(a) of the Fair Credit Reporting Act (15 U.S.C. 1681s(a)) is amended by striking paragraph (4).

(c) RELATION TO OTHER PROVISIONS.—Except for the amendments made by subsections (a) and (b), nothing in this title shall be construed to modify, limit, or supersede the operation of the Fair Credit Reporting Act, and no inference shall be drawn on the basis of the provisions of this title regarding whether information is transaction or experience information under section 603 of such Act.

Sec. 507. Relation to State Laws.

(a) IN GENERAL.—This subtitle and the amendments made by this subtitle shall not be construed as superseding, altering, or affecting any statute, regulation, order, or interpretation in effect in any State, except to the extent that such statute, regulation,

order, or interpretation is inconsistent with the provisions of this
subtitle, and then only to the extent of the inconsistency.
(b) GREATER PROTECTION UNDER STATE LAW.—
For purposes of this section, a State statute, regulation, order,
or interpretation is not inconsistent with the provisions of
this subtitle if the protection such statute, regulation, order, or
interpretation affords any person is greater than the protection
provided under this subtitle and the amendments made by
this subtitle, as determined by the Federal Trade Commission,
after consultation with the agency or authority with jurisdiction
under section 505(a) of either the person that initiated the
complaint or that is the subject of the complaint, on its own
motion or upon the petition of any interested party.

Sec. 508. Study of Information Sharing among Financial Affiliates.

(a) IN GENERAL.—The Secretary of the Treasury, in conjunction
with the Federal functional regulators and the Federal Trade
Commission, shall conduct a study of information sharing
practices among financial institutions and their affiliates. Such
study shall include—
(1) the purposes for the sharing of confidential customer
information with affiliates or with non-affiliated third
parties;
(2) the extent and adequacy of security protections for such
information;
(3) the potential risks for customer privacy of such sharing of
information;
(4) the potential benefits for financial institutions and affiliates
of such sharing of information;
(5) the potential benefits for customers of such sharing of
information;
(6) the adequacy of existing laws to protect customer privacy;
(7) the adequacy of financial institution privacy policy and
privacy rights disclosure under existing law;
(8) the feasibility of different approaches, including opt-out
and opt-in, to permit customers to direct that confidential
information not be shared with affiliates and nonaffiliated
third parties; and
(9) the feasibility of restricting sharing of information for
specific uses or of permitting customers to direct the uses for
which information may be shared.

(b) CONSULTATION.—The Secretary shall consult with
representatives of State insurance authorities designated by the
National Association of Insurance Commissioners, and also with

financial services industry, consumer organizations and privacy groups, and other representatives of the general public, in formulating and conducting the study required by subsection (a).

(c) REPORT.—On or before January 1, 2002, the Secretary shall submit a report to the Congress containing the findings and conclusions of the study required under subsection (a), together with such recommendations for legislative or administrative action as may be appropriate.

Sec. 509. Definitions.

As used in this subtitle:

(1) FEDERAL BANKING AGENCY.—The term "Federal banking agency" has the same meaning as given in section 3 of the Federal Deposit Insurance Act.

(2) FEDERAL FUNCTIONAL REGULATOR.—The term "Federal functional regulator" means—

  (A) the Board of Governors of the Federal Reserve System;

  (B) the Office of the Comptroller of the Currency;

  (C) the Board of Directors of the Federal Deposit Insurance Corporation;

  (D) the Director of the Office of Thrift Supervision;

  (E) the National Credit Union Administration Board; and

  (F) the Securities and Exchange Commission.

(3) FINANCIAL INSTITUTION.—

  (A) IN GENERAL.—The term "financial institution" means any institution the business of which is engaging in financial activities as described in section 4(k) of the Bank Holding Company Act of 1956.

  (B) PERSONS SUBJECT TO CFTC REGULATION.—Notwithstanding subparagraph (A), the term "financial institution" does not include any person or entity with respect to any financial activity that is subject to the jurisdiction of the Commodity Futures Trading Commission under the Commodity Exchange Act.

  (C) FARM CREDIT INSTITUTIONS.—Notwithstanding subparagraph (A), the term "financial institution" does not include the Federal Agricultural Mortgage Corporation or any entity chartered and operating under the Farm Credit Act of 1971.

  (D) OTHER SECONDARY MARKET INSTITUTIONS.—Notwithstanding subparagraph (A), the term "financial institution" does not include institutions chartered by Congress specifically to engage in transactions described in section 502(e)(1)(C), as long as such institutions do not sell or transfer nonpublic personal information to a nonaffiliated third party.

(4) NONPUBLIC PERSONAL INFORMATION.—
    (A) The term "nonpublic personal information" means personally identifiable financial information—
        (i) provided by a consumer to a financial institution;
        (ii) resulting from any transaction with the consumer or any service performed for the consumer; or
        (iii) otherwise obtained by the financial institution.
    (B) Such term does not include publicly available information, as such term is defined by the regulations prescribed under section 504.
    (C) Notwithstanding subparagraph (B), such term—
        (i) shall include any list, description, or other grouping of consumers (and publicly available information pertaining to them) that is derived using any nonpublic personal information other than publicly available information; but
        (ii) shall not include any list, description, or other grouping of consumers (and publicly available information pertaining to them) that is derived without using any nonpublic personal information.

(5) NONAFFILIATED THIRD PARTY.—The term "nonaffiliated third party" means any entity that is not an affiliate of, or related by common ownership or affiliated by corporate control with, the financial institution, but does not include a joint employee of such institution.
(6) AFFILIATE.—The term "affiliate" means any company that controls, is controlled by, or is under common control with another company.
(7) NECESSARY TO EFFECT, ADMINISTER, OR ENFORCE.—
The term "as necessary to effect, administer, or enforce the transaction" means—
    (A) the disclosure is required, or is a usual, appropriate, or acceptable method, to carry out the transaction or the product or service business of which the transaction is a part, and record or service or maintain the consumer's account in the ordinary course of providing the financial service or financial product, or to administer or service benefits or claims relating to the transaction or the product or service business of which it is a part, and includes—
        (i) providing the consumer or the consumer's agent or broker with a confirmation, statement, or other record of

the transaction, or information on the status or value of the financial service or financial product; and

(ii) the accrual or recognition of incentives or bonuses associated with the transaction that are provided by the financial institution or any other party;

(B) the disclosure is required, or is one of the lawful or appropriate methods, to enforce the rights of the financial institution or of other persons engaged in carrying out the financial transaction, or providing the product or service;

(C) the disclosure is required, or is a usual, appropriate, or acceptable method, for insurance underwriting at the consumer's request or for reinsurance purposes, or for any of the following purposes as they relate to a consumer's insurance: account administration, reporting, investigating, or preventing fraud or material misrepresentation, processing premium payments, processing insurance claims, administering insurance benefits (including utilization review activities), participating in research projects, or as otherwise required or specifically permitted by Federal or State law; or

(D) the disclosure is required, or is a usual, appropriate or acceptable method, in connection with—

(i) the authorization, settlement, billing, processing, clearing, transferring, reconciling, or collection of amounts charged, debited, or otherwise paid using a debit, credit or other payment card, check, or account number, or by other payment means;

(ii) the transfer of receivables, accounts or interests therein; or

(iii) the audit of debit, credit or other payment information.

(8) STATE INSURANCE AUTHORITY.—The term "State insurance authority" means, in the case of any person engaged in providing insurance, the State insurance authority of the State in which the person is domiciled.

(9) CONSUMER.—The term "consumer" means an individual who obtains, from a financial institution, financial products or services which are to be used primarily for personal, family, or household purposes, and also means the legal representative of such an individual.

(10) JOINT AGREEMENT.—The term "joint agreement" means a formal written contract pursuant to which two or more financial institutions jointly offer, endorse, or sponsor a financial product or service, and as may be further defined in the regulations prescribed under section 504.

(11) CUSTOMER RELATIONSHIP.—The term "time of establishing a customer relationship" shall be defined by the regulations prescribed under section 504, and shall, in the case of a financial

institution engaged in extending credit directly to consumers to finance purchases of goods or services, mean the time of establishing the credit relationship with the consumer.

Sec. 510. Effective Date.

This subtitle shall take effect 6 months after the date on which rules are required to be prescribed under section 504(a)(3), except—

(1) to the extent that a later date is specified in the rules prescribed under section 504; and
(2) that sections 504 and 506 shall be effective upon enactment.

Subtitle B—Fraudulent Access to Financial Information

Sec. 521. Privacy Protection for Customer Information of Financial Institutions.

(a) PROHIBITION ON OBTAINING CUSTOMER INFORMATION BY FALSE PRETENSES.—It shall be a violation of this subtitle for any person to obtain or attempt to obtain, or cause to be disclosed or attempt to cause to be disclosed to any person, customer information of a financial institution relating to another person—

(1) by making a false, fictitious, or fraudulent statement or representation to an officer, employee, or agent of a financial institution;
(2) by making a false, fictitious, or fraudulent statement or representation to a customer of a financial institution; or
(3) by providing any document to an officer, employee, or agent of a financial institution, knowing that the document is forged, counterfeit, lost, or stolen, was fraudulently obtained, or contains a false, fictitious, or fraudulent statement or representation.

(b) PROHIBITION ON SOLICITATION OF A PERSON TO OBTAIN CUSTOMER INFORMATION FROM FINANCIAL INSTITUTION UNDER FALSE PRETENSES.—It shall be a violation of this subtitle to request a person to obtain customer information of a financial institution, knowing that the person will obtain, or attempt to obtain, the information from the institution in any manner described in subsection (a).

(c) NONAPPLICABILITY TO LAW ENFORCEMENT AGENCIES.—No provision of this section shall be construed so as to prevent any action by a law enforcement agency, or any officer, employee, or agent of such agency, to obtain customer information of a financial institution in connection with the performance of the official duties of the agency.

(d) NONAPPLICABILITY TO FINANCIAL INSTITUTIONS
IN CERTAIN CASES.—No provision of this section shall be
construed so as to prevent any financial institution, or any
officer, employee, or agent of a financial institution, from
obtaining customer information of such financial institution in
the course of—
  (1) testing the security procedures or systems of such institution
      for maintaining the confidentiality of customer information;
  (2) investigating allegations of misconduct or negligence on
      the part of any officer, employee, or agent of the financial
      institution; or
  (3) recovering customer information of the financial institution
      which was obtained or received by another person in any
      manner described in subsection (a) or (b).

(e) NONAPPLICABILITY TO INSURANCE INSTITUTIONS
FOR INVESTIGATION OF INSURANCE FRAUD.—No
provision of this section shall be construed so as to prevent any
insurance institution, or any officer, employee, or agency of an
insurance institution, from obtaining information as part of an
insurance investigation into criminal activity, fraud, material
misrepresentation, or material nondisclosure that is authorized for
such institution under State law, regulation, interpretation, or order.
(f) NONAPPLICABILITY TO CERTAIN TYPES OF CUSTOMER
INFORMATION OF FINANCIAL INSTITUTIONS.—No
provision of this section shall be construed so as to prevent
any person from obtaining customer information of a financial
institution that otherwise is available as a public record filed
pursuant to the securities laws (as defined in section 3(a)(47) of
the Securities Exchange Act of 1934).
(g) NONAPPLICABILITY TO COLLECTION OF CHILD SUPPORT
JUDGMENTS.—No provision of this section shall be construed
to prevent any State-licensed private investigator, or any officer,
employee, or agent of such private investigator, from obtaining
customer information of a financial institution, to the extent
reasonably necessary to collect child support from a person
adjudged to have been delinquent in his or her obligations by
a Federal or State court, and to the extent that such action by a
State-licensed private investigator is not unlawful under any
other Federal or State law or regulation, and has been authorized
by an order or judgment of a court of competent jurisdiction.

Sec. 522. Administrative Enforcement.
(a) ENFORCEMENT BY FEDERAL TRADE COMMISSION.—
Except as provided in subsection (b), compliance with this

subtitle shall be enforced by the Federal Trade Commission in
the same manner and with the same power and authority as the
Commission has under the Fair Debt Collection Practices Act to
enforce compliance with such Act.
(b) ENFORCEMENT BY OTHER AGENCIES IN CERTAIN
CASES.—
(1) IN GENERAL.—Compliance with this subtitle shall be
enforced under—
(A) section 8 of the Federal Deposit Insurance Act, in the
case of—
(i) national banks, and Federal branches and Federal
agencies of foreign banks, by the Office of the
Comptroller of the Currency;
(ii) member banks of the Federal Reserve System (other
than national banks), branches and agencies of
foreign banks (other than Federal branches, Federal
agencies, and insured State branches of foreign banks),
commercial lending companies owned or controlled
by foreign banks, and organizations operating under
section 25 or 25A of the Federal Reserve Act, by the
Board;
(iii) banks insured by the Federal Deposit Insurance
Corporation (other than members of the Federal
Reserve System and national nonmember banks) and
insured State branches of foreign banks, by the Board of
Directors of the Federal Deposit Insurance Corporation;
and
(iv) savings associations the deposits of which are insured
by the Federal Deposit Insurance Corporation, by the
Director of the Office of Thrift Supervision; and (B) the
Federal Credit Union Act, by the Administrator of the
National Credit Union Administration with respect to
any Federal credit union.

(2) VIOLATIONS OF THIS SUBTITLE TREATED AS
VIOLATIONS OF OTHER LAWS.—For the purpose of
the exercise by any agency referred to in paragraph (1) of
its powers under any Act referred to in that paragraph, a
violation of this subtitle shall be deemed to be a violation
of a requirement imposed under that Act. In addition to its
powers under any provision of law specifically referred to in
paragraph
(1), each of the agencies referred to in that paragraph may
exercise, for the purpose of enforcing compliance with this
subtitle, any other authority conferred on such agency by
law.

Sec. 523. Criminal Penalty.

(a) IN GENERAL.—Whoever knowingly and intentionally violates, or knowingly and intentionally attempts to violate, section 521 shall be fined in accordance with title 18, United States Code, or imprisoned for not more than 5 years, or both.

(b) ENHANCED PENALTY FOR AGGRAVATED CASES.— Whoever violates, or attempts to violate, section 521 while violating another law of the United States or as part of a pattern of any illegal activity involving more than $100,000 in a 12-month period shall be fined twice the amount provided in subsection (b)(3) or (c)(3) (as the case may be) of section 3571 of title 18, United States Code, imprisoned for not more than 10 years, or both.

Sec. 524. Relation to State Laws.

(a) IN GENERAL.—This subtitle shall not be construed as superseding, altering, or affecting the statutes, regulations, orders, or interpretations in effect in any State, except to the extent that such statutes, regulations, orders, or interpretations are inconsistent with the provisions of this subtitle, and then only to the extent of the inconsistency.

(b) GREATER PROTECTION UNDER STATE LAW.—For purposes of this section, a State statute, regulation, order, or interpretation is not inconsistent with the provisions of this subtitle if the protection such statute, regulation, order, or interpretation affords any person is greater than the protection provided under this subtitle as determined by the Federal Trade Commission, after consultation with the agency or authority with jurisdiction under section 522 of either the person that initiated the complaint or that is the subject of the complaint, on its own motion or upon the petition of any interested party.

Sec. 525. Agency Guidance.

In furtherance of the objectives of this subtitle, each Federal banking agency (as defined in section 3(z) of the Federal Deposit Insurance Act), the National Credit Union Administration, and the Securities and Exchange Commission or self-regulatory organizations, as appropriate, shall review regulations and guidelines applicable to financial institutions under their respective jurisdictions and shall prescribe such revisions to such regulations and guidelines as may be necessary to ensure that such financial institutions have policies, procedures, and controls in place to prevent the unauthorized disclosure of customer financial information and to deter and detect activities proscribed under section 521.

Sec. 526. Reports.

(a) REPORT TO THE CONGRESS.—Before the end of the 18-month period beginning on the date of the enactment of this Act, the Comptroller General, in consultation with the Federal Trade Commission, Federal banking agencies, the National Credit Union Administration, the Securities and Exchange Commission, appropriate Federal law enforcement agencies, and appropriate State insurance regulators, shall submit to the Congress a report on the following:

(1) The efficacy and adequacy of the remedies provided in this subtitle in addressing attempts to obtain financial information by fraudulent means or by false pretenses.

(2) Any recommendations for additional legislative or regulatory action to address threats to the privacy of financial information created by attempts to obtain information by fraudulent means or false pretenses.

(b) ANNUAL REPORT BY ADMINISTERING AGENCIES.—The Federal Trade Commission and the Attorney General shall submit to Congress an annual report on number and disposition of all enforcement actions taken pursuant to this subtitle.

Sec. 527. Definitions.

For purposes of this subtitle, the following definitions shall apply:

(1) CUSTOMER.—The term "customer" means, with respect to a financial institution, any person (or authorized representative of a person) to whom the financial institution provides a product or service, including that of acting as a fiduciary.

(2) CUSTOMER INFORMATION OF A FINANCIAL INSTITUTION.—The term "customer information of a financial institution" means any information maintained by or for a financial institution which is derived from the relationship between the financial institution and a customer of the financial institution and is identified with the customer.

(3) DOCUMENT.—The term "document" means any information in any form.

(4) FINANCIAL INSTITUTION.—

(A) IN GENERAL.—The term "financial institution" means any institution engaged in the business of providing financial services to customers who maintain a credit, deposit, trust, or other financial account or relationship with the institution.

(B) CERTAIN FINANCIAL INSTITUTIONS SPECIFICALLY INCLUDED.—The term "financial institution" includes any depository institution (as defined in section 19(b)(1)

(A) of the Federal Reserve Act), any broker or dealer, any investment adviser or investment company, any insurance company, any loan or finance company, any credit card issuer or operator of a credit card system, and any consumer reporting agency that compiles and maintains files on consumers on a nationwide basis (as defined in section 603(p) of the Consumer Credit Protection Act).

(C) SECURITIES INSTITUTIONS.—For purposes of subparagraph (B)—

   (i) the terms "broker" and "dealer" have the same meanings as given in section 3 of the Securities Exchange Act of 1934 (15 U.S.C. 78c);

   (ii) the term "investment adviser" has the same meaning as given in section 202(a)(11) of the Investment Advisers Act of 1940 (15 U.S.C. 80b–2(a)); and

   (iii) the term "investment company" has the same meaning as given in section 3 of the Investment Company Act of 1940 (15 U.S.C. 80a–3).

(D) CERTAIN PERSONS AND ENTITIES SPECIFICALLY EXCLUDED.—The term "financial institution" does not include any person or entity with respect to any financial activity that is subject to the jurisdiction of the Commodity Futures Trading Commission under the Commodity Exchange Act and does not include the Federal Agricultural Mortgage Corporation or any entity chartered and operating under the Farm Credit Act of 1971.

(E) FURTHER DEFINITION BY REGULATION.—The Federal Trade Commission, after consultation with Federal banking agencies and the Securities and Exchange Commission, may prescribe regulations clarifying or describing the types of institutions which shall be treated as financial institutions for purposes of this subtitle.
F:\FSA99\REPORT\S900CRPT.005
F:\V6\102899\102899.0H6

Gramm-Leach-Bliley Act of 1999, Public Law 106-102, 106th Cong., 1t sess. (October 28, 1999). http://frwebgate.access.gpo.gov/cgi-bin/getdoc. cgi?dbname=106_cong_public_laws&docid=f:publ102.106. Accessed April 9, 2009.

7

Directory of Organizations, Associations, and Agencies

This chapter offers readers a list of organizations and government agencies that are routinely involved in identity theft issues. They focus on many types of fraud, security breaches, identity theft, computer crimes, and/or privacy violations. The information included here profiles the origins of the organizations, their focus, and their Web site (if available).

Anti-Phishing Working Group (APWG)
www.antiphishing.org

Tumbleweed Communications is one of the leading providers of computer security products. Their focus is on making certain that computer communications are conducted in a safe and secure manner by providing the highest level products available and developing new products. In 2003 Tumbleweed Communications and others in the banking, finance, and e-commerce industries founded the Anti-Phishing Working Group (APWG). The APWG first met in November 2003 in San Francisco, California. Since that time it has become an independent corporation controlled and operated by its own board of directors and officers. The APWG has over 3,000 members who represent more than 1,700 companies throughout the world. Membership is open to those who are involved with financial institutions, online retailers, Internet service providers, law enforcement communities, research institutions, and those who provide security solutions and products. Those who join the APWG are dedicated to eliminating identity theft and fraud. This group focuses on examining fraud that originates with phishing and e-mail spoofing and allows its members an arena to explore these issues to determine the nature of the problem and develop policies that can help to reduce or eliminate them.

Electronic Crimes Task Forces and Working Groups
http://www.ustreas.gov/usss/ectf.shtml

Under the USA Patriot Act, signed into law by President George W. Bush in October 2001, the United States Secret Service was directed to create a nationwide network of Electronic Crimes Task Forces (ECTF). The idea behind the ECTF was to get the public and private sectors working together and focused on ways to protect the nation's financial and other critical infrastructures. ECTF network participants include law enforcement personnel, prosecutors, and representatives from private businesses, colleges, and universities.

The Secret Service was made responsible for the establishment of the ECTF and Working Group because these duties fall under the general responsibilities assigned to the service upon its founding in 1865; the Secret Service is responsible for protecting the integrity of the financial payment system in this country. This responsibility typically involves the detection and control of counterfeit money; however, as new payment methods evolved, the Secret Service's responsibilities changed in order to protect the United States' financial payment system. Given that computers and other technological devices are commonly used in criminal activities that impact the United States' financial structure, the Secret Service also focuses on deterring cyber crime.

The Secret Service's ECTF and Electronic Crimes Working Group prioritize cases that involve electronic crime, then they provide support and resources to aid in the investigations of these cases. Typically, investigations that have a significant economic impact or involve domestic or transnational organized criminal rings are within the realm of the ECTF. Currently the Secret Service maintains ECTFs in the following U.S. cities and states: Atlanta, Baltimore, Birmingham, Boston, Buffalo, Charlotte, Chicago, Cleveland, Dallas, Houston, Las Vegas, Los Angeles, Louisville, Miami, Minneapolis, New York/New Jersey, Oklahoma, Orlando, Philadelphia, Pittsburgh, San Francisco, Seattle, South Carolina, and Washington, D.C.

Federal Trade Commission
www.ftc.gov

The Federal Trade Commission (FTC) was created in 1914 through the Federal Trade Commission Act. It was designed to be staffed by five commissioners who were appointed by the President of the United States with the consent of the Senate. While the first commissioners were to be appointed for terms that varied in length, today all serve a seven-year term. Only three members of the commission may be of the same political party. The president is also responsible for selecting a commissioner to serve as the FTC chairperson. As of this writing, the members of the Commission are: Chairman John Leibowitz, Pamela Jones Harbour, William E. Kovacic, and J. Thomas Rosch. Currently, there is one vacant seat on the Commission.

The FTC was created to help prevent unfair competition amongst businesses. As time has progressed, the FTC was given authority to create policies for protecting consumers.

The FTC consists of several offices. The Office of Public Affairs provides information to the public through various media outlets. The Office of Congressional Relations updates commissioners and other FTC staff members of pertinent Congressional legislation. The Office of the Executive Director is responsible for managing finances, personnel, technology, programs, and policies. The Office of the General Counsel acts as the Commission's legal advisors and also represents the FTC in court. The Office of International Affairs brings a global component to the FTC as it works with other consumer protection agencies around the world to address international issues of consumer protection. The Office of the Secretary is responsible for documenting decisions and for coordinating responses to inquiries by congressional constituents. The Office of the Inspector General is the policing arm of the Commission and is charged with preventing waste, fraud, and abuse within FTC. The Office of the Inspector General also investigates instances of staff misconduct. The Bureau of Competition is considered the antitrust component of the Commission. The Bureau of Economics analyses the economic impact of the actions taken by the FTC. The Bureau of Consumer Protection is designed specifically to protect consumers from fraud. The FTC has over 1,000 people on its staff and they all hold positions that are designed to protect U.S. consumers.

Given the consumer protection aspect of the FTC, it seems reasonable that the responsibility for collecting identity theft case data and providing statistics about the crime should fall under its umbrella, thus the FTC set up the Identity Theft Data Clearinghouse in November 1999. This clearinghouse allows victims of identity theft to report their crime to the FTC. The goal of this endeavor is to generate reliable records about the scope of identity theft in the United States. The data is used to understand the crime better and to detect developing trends. Internet users can access this information on the FTC Web site. In addition, consumers who visit this Web site can learn more about the "Deter, Detect, Defend" program that the Commission established to educate people about what to do if they are a victim of identity theft, and also what they can do to reduce their likelihood of becoming a victim.

Identity Theft 911
http://www. identitytheft911.com/home.htm

Identity Theft 911 started in 2003 with the goal of assisting in identity theft resolutions. Currently, the headquarters for Identity Theft 911 is located in Scottsdale, Arizona, and in 2008 the organization opened an office on the east coast, in Providence, Rhode Island. 911 offers educational information to help businesses and their clients gain a greater knowledge of identity theft and how to protect themselves from becoming victims. In addition, Identity Theft 911 offers assistance to victims.

The organization was founded to fill the need for an identity theft resolution specialist to partner with businesses. Adam K. Levin, one of the organization's co-founders, is the current Chairman of Identity Theft 911. His desire to start Identity Theft 911 stems from his interest in protecting and educating consumers. With over 30 years of experience to build upon Levin and other executives with experience in credit and financial services, law enforcement, and consumer advocacy worked together to found Identity Theft 911.

The Organization's leadership team is comprised of Levin, Matthew Cullina, and Sean Daly. Cullina is the Chief Executive Officer and has a background in the insurance industry. Daly is the President and Chief Financial Officer and is responsible for the financial aspects of the organization. His experience is in finance, business, and technology. Together, this group works to resolve the problems of identity theft and provide individual assistance while giving consumers the knowledge they need to protect themselves.

Identity Theft 911 also has a diverse group of members on its Advisory Council who come from various fields including finance, security, law enforcement, law, and technology. The members of the Advisory Committee offer additional insight and information on identity theft that assisting victims used to pursue the goal of the crime.

Identity Theft Partnerships in Prevention
http://www1.cj.msu.edu/~outreach/identity/

While the crime of identity theft was still in its infancy, Dr. Judith Collins created one of the first programs at a major university, the Michigan State University Identity Theft Partnerships in Prevention, now known as the Identity Theft Program. Dr. Collins sought out experts in the private security and law enforcement fields and brought them together for the purpose of establishing a program that offers training, conducts research, assists in investigations, and provides assistance to victims of the crime.

The initial research involved an identity theft case that took place at an international corporation. In this particular case, many of the corporate executives had their identities stolen by a person who was also employed by the company. This study became the basis on which future research was built. Tracy McGinley joined the staff in 2000 and Sandra Hoffman joined in 2001 as research assistants. Collins left the program in 2006 to take a job with the U.S. State Department in Washington, D.C. At that time, Sandra Hoffman was appointed interim director and was later appointed director. Tracy McGinley remains on the staff as an instructor. The program offers educational opportunities for victim assistance personnel and law enforcement officials at the local, state, and federal levels. The program's Web site provides step-by-step instructions in the form of worksheets for victims of identity theft to use in clearing their names.

Identity Theft Prevention and Mitigation Program—New York State Consumer Protection Board
http://www.nysconsumer.gov/

The New York Consumer Protection Board was established in 1970 and acts as a consumer advocate to protect the citizens of

New York. Its protection comes in a variety of methods. The Board investigates complaints, researches problems that arise, examines questionable business practices, offers educational information, works to bring about change through legislation, and speaks on behalf of consumers. The New York Consumer Protection Board addresses the issue of identity theft and works toward offering greater assistance residents of the state.

In 2008, Governor David A. Paterson signed legislation that required the creation of the Identity Theft Prevention and Mitigation Program, which is housed under the Consumer Protection Board, and the program went into effect in January 2009. The Identity Theft Prevention and Mitigation Program is designed specifically to help New Yorkers better understand identity theft and what to do if they become a victim.

The Web site for the Identity Theft Prevention and Mitigation Program is part of the New York Consumer Protection Board's Web site. As users access the homepage, they can read about the program and also click on various links to learn more about identity theft, including a video quiz show designed to test their knowledge about identity theft. In this quiz show format, users can watch contestants attempt to answer questions, and see the correct answers displayed. Other aspects of the Web site include ways to protect oneself from the crime and information on fraud schemes currently operating in the state. In addition, there are sample forms that can be used to document the steps that victims must take to restore their identities and a form to document their losses and expenses. This information can then serve as proof for restitution if the case is prosecuted.

Identity Theft Resource Center
http://www.idtheftcenter.org/index.html

Linda and Jay Foley started the Identity Theft Resource Center (ITRC) in 1999 under the Privacy Rights Clearinghouse. It was originally known as Victims of Crimes Extended Services (VOICES). In 2000, the name was officially changed to the Identity Theft Resource Center. Initially, Lindy Foley, a victim of identity theft, ran the ITRC alone. She started a support group for victims and spoke at national symposiums about the problem of identity theft. In 2001, as the center continued to grow, Jay Foley became its full-time director. ITRC also hired Sheila Gordon; she is currently the Director of Victim Services. By 2002, the ITRC was working with more than 150 victims and consumers each week. Their dedication and hard work earned them commendations for their fight against identity theft. In addition, the ITRC's reputation led law enforcement and other government agencies to make continual referrals to the organization. In 2003, the ITRC officially received 501(c)(3) nonprofit status. Also that same year, the ITRC conducted and published its first major study on identity theft. The study explored the impact that the crime has on its victims. Over the past six years, the ITRC has continued to conduct research on the impact of identity theft on victims. In addition, the organization continues to offer advice to lawmaker seeking new identity theft legislation both on the state and national levels. The ITRC and its successes have been featured in many national magazines. Realizing the need to continue to reach out to members of the community who may not have services available to them, the ITRC added a Spanish section to its Web site and also created the first teen video on identity theft, *Stolen Futures*.

The main goal of the ITRC is to offer quality victim assistance and to do so at no charge to the consumer. Although located in California, the ITRC serves victims located all over the country. Not only does the center seek to help victims, it also strives to educate people about identity theft and help them to develop quality policies and individual practices that can help to prevent the crime. Furthermore, the ITRC acts as a consultant to companies seeking specific advice about identity theft. The ITRC works to help both consumers and businesses that have been victimized. Those working for the ITRC realize that addressing the identity theft problem is not an easy task, and they recognize the need to continue to educate consumers and build support between consumers, private businesses, law enforcement agencies, and the government.

The ITRC Web site reveals its commitment to education. Numerous articles and surveys are available there. In addition, there is information aimed at diverse audiences.

Identity Theft Victims Advocate Network (IVAN)
http://s1.webstarts.com/ivan/

The Identity Theft Victims Advocate Network (IVAN) was started in 2006 in Colorado. The purpose of this organization is to assist victims of identity theft through a network of participants that include government and law enforcement agencies. There are currently over 60 IVAN members. Representatives from the

Division of Motor Vehicles, the Colorado Bureau of Investigation, Vital Records, the United States Postal Service, local law enforcement agencies, and attorneys are all part of the network. IVAN's Web site offers the names, jurisdictions/locations, and contact information for all the members, thus providing victims a centralized location where they can find assistances. The Web site also offers information about resources that are available at the state and federal level.

Institute of Consumer Financial Education (ICFE)
http://www.financial-education-icfe.org/default.asp

The Institute of Consumer Financial Education was founded by Loren Dunton and Paul Richard in 1982. It is a nonprofit organization based in San Diego, California that was created as a public education organization and designed to help people learn about ways to handle their money and their credit. The program is focused on teaching consumers how to control spending, increase savings, and use credit wisely. As with many programs, the institute's goal is to educate people about using money so that they are empowered to use it more wisely. The institute also offers assistance to businesses that wish to provide personal finance classes as an option for their employees.

In addition to teaching consumers how to handle their money better, the institute offers certification programs, including a Certified Credit Report Reviewer program, a Certified Home Equity Conversion Mortgage Specialist program (a.k.a., Reverse Mortgage Specialist), and a Certified Identity Theft Risk Management Specialist program. The institute developed the certification program used by Identity Theft Risk Management Specialists in response to the country's growing number of identity theft cases.

The program is designed to help law enforcement officials, financial planners, accountants, lawyers, debt counselors, and anyone else who may interact with consumers who have been victims of identity theft or who want to protect themselves from becoming victims. The program features five main areas of study. The first area focuses on understanding identity theft. The second area looks at credit reports, specialty reports, and public records and helps students to identify vulnerabilities. The third area focuses on risk management and resolution. The fourth area concerns consumer protection laws. The fifth area of the certification program is on the risks and concerns related to businesses.

International Association of Financial Crimes Investigators (IAFCI)
www.iafci.org

The International Association of Financial Crimes Investigators (IAFCI) is a nonprofit international organization located in El Dorado Hills, California with chapters throughout the world. Members of the IAFCI include law enforcement, personnel, prosecutors, private security specialists, and financial industry representatives. The IAFCI provides services and information about various fraud-related concerns, including financial fraud, fraud investigation, and fraud prevention methods. Its objective is to help foster a better understanding of the issues surrounding financial fraud and what can be done to stop it.

The IAFCI evolved from the International Association of Credit Card Investigators (IACCI), which was created in 1968 in response to the increasing number of credit card crimes. In 1996, the IACCI saw the need to include a larger variety of financial crimes in its mission and changed its name to the International Association of Financial Crimes Investigators. The IAFCI works to reduce and eliminate fraudulent financial transactions and to encourage its members to share intelligence information.

The organization offers its members many benefits, such as investigation assistance. IAFCI investigators work to track patterns of spending to determine a person's whereabouts and are able to use the information from financial transactions to determine the location of witnesses and suspects. The group also conducts annual training seminars throughout the world to help investigators learn more about current fraud schemes and how to investigate their cases more effectively. The IAFCI also works with manufacturers of transaction cards and checks to help them improve their current physical security and internal controls such as audits, storage, and delivery.

The IAFCI Web site offers information to both consumers and its members. The information aimed at the general public, for example, outlines eight basic fraud tactics: advance fee scams, employment scams, prizes that come with a price, money-making schemes, online auctions, bogus charities, identity theft, and products that are too good to be true. The Web site also has a section dedicated to identity theft that includes information about what to do if you are a victim and explains strategies for reducing the risk of victimization. Furthermore, the site offers a page of links to available public resources that are available. There is a members-only section of the Web site where members can share information about financial crimes, upcoming conferences, and other pertinent information.

Internet Crime Complaint Center (IC3)
http://www.ic3.gov

Originally known as the Internet Fraud Complain Center, the Internet Crime Complaint Center (IC3) is the product of a partnership between the Federal Bureau of Investigation (FBI) and the National White Collar Crime Center (NW3C). It is an online system that allows its users to file complaints about cyber crimes; these can range from identity theft complaints, to money laundering complaints, to intellectual property rights violations, or even computer hacking complaints. The purpose of developing the IC3 was to create a centralized location for gathering information on cyber crimes and to then use the data for research. Furthermore, the research can help to develop policies, regulations, and recommendations for law enforcement on both the domestic and international levels.

On the IC3 Web site, users can find scam alerts, fraud prevention tips, and statistics. Victims will find a straightforward reporting mechanism that informs law enforcement about potential violations.

Maryland Crime Victims' Resource Center (MCVRC): Identity Theft & Fraud Assistance
http://www.mdcrimevictims.org/

The Maryland Crime Victims' Resource Center (MCVRC) began as the Stephanie Roper Committee and Foundation, which was created as a means for addressing crime in Prince George's County, Maryland. The organization was named in memory of Stephanie Roper, a college student who was home visiting her family in 1982. While driving, her car broke down and two men stopped and kidnapped, raped, and tortured her for hours before killing her. In 2002, as the result of a merger, the committee's name changed to the Maryland Crime Victims' Resource Center. The MCVRC seeks to help victims in Maryland and focuses on providing advocacy, education, counseling, support groups, legal information, representation, and other assistance to victims of crimes. The MCVRC also offers free assistance to those who are victims of identity theft and fraud.

The Web site for the MCVRC offers a variety of information for victims of crime. In addition to explaining the creation of the MCVRC, the site also offers information about the center's board members, how to be a supporter, and copies of their newsletter. The site identifies specific information on crisis assistance, legal and financial help, victim notification, and resources that are available in the state of Maryland and throughout the country.

National Association of Consumer Advocates
http://www.naca.net/

The National Association of Consumer Advocates (NACA) is a nonprofit association whose members, mostly attorneys and consumer advocates, seek to represent the best interests of consumers. In order to accomplish this, NACA members are dedicated to sharing information and ideas with one another and representing consumers as they fight unfair business practices.

NACA offers a great deal of information on their Web site to help consumers understand their rights. The site offers specific information about consumers' rights when purchasing a new or used vehicle, including information on the lemon law. The site also informs consumers on their rights when dealing with debt collectors and when trying to correct issues on their credit report; it features a section on identity theft, military consumer rights, predatory lending practices, and student loans. Another section of the Web site assists consumers by listing attorneys and their areas of specialization or expertise.

National Check Fraud Center
http://www.ckfraud.org/

The National Check Fraud Center is a private organization located in Charleston, South Carolina. It focuses on offering assistance and information about counterfeit checks, fraud, and other white collar crimes. There are several components to the National Check Fraud Center, including the National Crime Alert Network. The network is designed to share information pertaining to check fraud and white collar crime among businesses, law enforcement officials, and financial institutions. The information shared with the network is in real time; this allows the network to help prevent fraud crimes from occurring by providing up-to-date information on scams and crimes that may impact businesses and financial institutions. The timely distribution of information is one of the network's key functions.

The Web site for the National Check Fraud Center offers a great deal of information about identity theft and other fraud-related crimes. Users may access many links to learn more about fraud crimes, liability, laws, and other factors relevant to white collar crime. The topics include information on bad check laws as they pertain to each state, a definition of check fraud, information about check washing, identity theft, counterfeit checks, and links to federal resources. In addition, the Web site provides a list of workshops and seminars that are available through the center.

National Fraud Information Center
http://www.fraud.org/

The National Consumers League established the National Fraud Information Center in 1992. Founded in 1899, the National Consumers League is the oldest nonprofit consumer advocacy group in the United States. The League was originally established to help promote fairness in the marketplace for both consumers and employees; this principle remains the League's focus today. It has fought to protect in-home workers from exploitation, to promote the Pure Food and Drug Act, to people for the passage of state minimum wage laws pertaining to women, to promote Social Security legislation, to support the concept of equal pay for equal work, and to support the enforcement powers of the Federal Trade Commission. In the 1980s, the League formed the Alliance Against Fraud in Telemarketing. This alliance later became the National Fraud Information Center, a joint effort by the National Consumers League, the Federal Trade Commission, the National Association of Attorneys General, and PhoneBusters of Canada.

The National Fraud Information Center is the only toll-free hotline designed to help consumers learn more about telemarketing schemes, offer consumers a place to call and speak to someone directly about potential telemarketing fraud, and to report possible telemarketing scams. The center is designed to fight the growing problem and irritations associated with telemarketing fraud and to help determine ways to improve the tools and resources available to those investigating it.

The Web site for the National Fraud Information Center offers valuable information on a variety of fraud schemes. It offers consumer advice and discusses current trends in telemarketing fraud, Internet fraud, scams against businesses, scams against the elderly, counterfeit drug information, and general fraud information.

National White Collar Crime Center (NW3C)
http://www.nw3c.org/index.cfm

The National White Collar Crime Center (NW3C) is a nonprofit organization focused on developing policies, practices, and training to address issues related to economic and technologically advanced crimes. The Institute for Intergovernmental Research (IIR) provides management performance, policy research, technical training, and activity analysis for the NW3C. For over 30 years, the NW3C has been the recipient of competitive grant funding.

The NW3C provides a variety of services. They offer training seminars to law enforcement agencies and other organizations in areas such as crime investigative techniques. There are many other training programs offered, too, such as those focusing on better understanding computer crimes. These classes vary, and may include courses on electronic evidence collection, data recovery, or even cellular telephone investigation. Other classes focus on financial crimes, intelligence analysis, and instructor developments. NW3C also offers an online Economic Crime Foundation Series program for its members and a three-day Identity Theft Investigations (IDTI) course that was developed for law enforcement officers and prosecutors.

Other services offered by the NW3C come in the more direct form of investigative support. The center does not have any independent investigative powers, but it is able to send analysts to assist in the investigative process. Ways in which analysts may assist law enforcement include the creation of financial transaction patterns, conducting network analysis, or even carrying out searches of public databases.

The NW3C's Web site contains information about the services offered to assist their members, a comprehensive list of the types of training available, data on the research that the center has done or is currently conducting, contact information for investigative services, and a list of partnerships that are available. The site also has answers to frequently asked questions about the center, press releases, and a listing of employment opportunities currently available.

OnGuard Online
http://www.onguardonline.gov

OnGuard Online is a Web site maintained by the Federal Trade Commission. Many other agencies and organizations provide valuable information for the site, too. OnGuard Online's partners include the U.S. Department of Justice, the Office of Justice Programs, the Department of Homeland Security, the Internal Revenue Service, the U.S. Postal Inspection Service, the Securities and Exchange Commission, the Naval Criminal Investigative Service, the U.S. Army Criminal Investigation Command, and many other organizations dedicated to protecting Internet users from fraud, scams, and other crimes. The Web site offers a plethora of information. Some of it is in the form of documents and reports. Other information is provided through online games and quizzes that test users' knowledge of identity theft, fraud scams, computer security, and other Internet related issues. There are also videos on the Web site that demonstrate how phishing occurs.

PhoneBusters—Canada
http://www.phonebusters.com/

PhoneBusters, the Canadian Anti-Fraud Call Centre that is managed by the Ontario Provincial Police, the Royal Mounted Police, and the Competition Bureau in Canada, was founded in 1993. The Ontario Provincial Police is the second largest police force in Canada. The Royal Mounted Police was founded in 1873 and is the national police service and an agency of the Ministry of Public Safety Canada. The Competition Bureau is an independent agency designed to protect competitive markets. Canadians believe that competition is a positive thing, not only for businesses but also for consumers, thus the Competition Bureau seeks to promote competitive markets and keep consumers informed so that they can make educated decisions. These three groups, whose interests focus on consumer information, protection, and law enforcement, manage the call center.

PhoneBusters plays an integral part in educating the public about fraudulent practices, especially telemarketing scams that are common and often hard to detect. Not only does PhoneBusters offer educational information about these scams, it also collects evidence, statistics, documents, tape recordings, and other important information that can be used by outside law enforcement agencies. PhoneBusters is considered the centralized Canadian agency for acquiring and maintaining information on telemarketing scams, fraud letters, and identity theft complaints. The data that PhoneBusters collects and analyzes helps to determine what the current trends are for these types of crimes and to discover what needs to be done to prevent these crimes from happening again. Originally, PhoneBusters was limited to the prosecution of offenders in Ontario and Quebec who were in violation of the Criminal Code of Canada, but today the call center also works with U.S.-based agencies through extradition treaties.

The PhoneBusters Web site is user-friendly and available in both English and French. Visitors to this site may access statistical information about the calls the center receives; this data is arranged so that viewers can compare current information with past statistics. Once a user selects the language he desires, he is directed to the home page, which offers a list of the latest scams reported to the center. These scams range from bomb threat e-mails to puppy scams. Puppy scams take place when someone places an advertisement to sell a puppy or other pet, even though in many cases he or she does not even have the animal. The seller often states that the owner has recently relocated to another country and needs to sell the pet because he or she can not take it with them. The advertisement requires that the buyer wire the fees in advance and to cover shipping and customs charges. Once the fees are paid, the pet is supposed to be shipped; however, the victim never receives the pet or hears from the seller again. The site also has a specific section devoted to identity theft. Once viewers select this option, they are directed to a page that talks about the types of identity theft scams that are most commonly reported, how to determine if one is a victim, and the steps to take to remedy the situation. The PhoneBusters slogan is "Fraud: Recognize It, Report It, Stop It."

President's Identity Theft Task Force
http://www.idtheft.gov/

In response to the growing concern about identity theft in the United States, President George W. Bush created a task force on identity theft through Executive Order 13402 in May 2006. Knowing that victims of identity theft face financial and emotional challenges as they try to reclaim their names, and recognizing that identity theft not only impacts individuals but also has a direct impact on the economy, Bush felt it was necessary to have government agencies work together to try and combat this problem. The President's Identity Theft Task Force was comprised of the Attorney General (Chairman of the President's Identity Theft Task Force), the Chairman of the Federal Trade Commission (co-Chair of the Task Force), the Secretary of the Treasury, the Secretary of Commerce, the Secretary of Health and Human Services, the Secretary of Veterans Affairs, the Secretary of Homeland Security, the Director of the Office of Management and Budget, the Commissioner of Social Security Administration, the Chairman of the Board of Governors of the Federal Reserve System, the Chairperson of the Board of Directors of the Federal Deposit Insurance Corporation, the Comptroller of the Currency, the Director of the Office of Thrift Supervision, the Chairman of the National Credit Union Administration Board, the Postmaster General, the Chairman of the Securities and Exchange Commission, and the Director of the Office of Personnel Management.

The mission of the task force's members was to develop a comprehensive plan for making the federal government more effective in its efforts to promote identity theft awareness, to prevent identity theft, to detect cases of identity theft, and to prosecute criminals who commit identity theft. The task force focused on several key aspects of the crime, one of which was to examine the role that law enforcement plays when dealing with identity theft. The task force identified the methods that were currently being used to combat the crime. Another area of focus was to assess the current educational efforts by the private and the public sectors to inform people about identity theft and how to protect their personal information. The third focus of the task force was to examine the safeguards that the government has used to prevent identity theft and to determine how these safeguards can be improved. In April 2007 the task force released a report to the public that detailed their findings and made recommendations for preventing the crime of identity theft. A subsequent report was released in October 2008 that outlined the actions that had been taken in response to the recommendations made in 2007.

Privacy Rights Clearinghouse
http://www.privacyrights.org/

Located in San Diego, California, the Privacy Rights Clearinghouse was founded in 1992 by Beth Givens, and she currently serves as its director. In 2005, Paul Stephen joined the organization. He uses his expertise in public policy, regulatory issues, and legislation to fulfill his responsibilities as the part-time Director of Policy and Advocacy. The Clearinghouse is a nonprofit organization dedicated to addressing the issues associated with identity theft. It seeks to educate and provide information to those who request it as well as serves as an advocate on behalf of consumers. Through education, the Clearinghouse focuses on demonstrating how technology can impact a person's privacy and what needs to be done to protect one's privacy in a society where technological advancements are taking place every day. Furthermore, the Clearinghouse works to provide information to all consumers about how their information is being used and what they can do to stop it from being available to so many different sources. The Clearinghouse also records complaints from consumers about issues that are privacy-related and offers assistance when possible. The organization maintains a consumer hotline where callers can report privacy-related abuses and request information on protecting themselves. The hotline's phone number is 619-298-3396.

Among other services, the Privacy Rights Clearinghouse has fact sheets available on their Web site in English and Spanish. These fact sheets pertain to various privacy issues and are written in an easy to understand format. The Clearinghouse works not only with consumers, but also with legislators to help develop policies to protect consumers' private information. Although the organization is not focused solely on identity theft, it deals with issues related to the crime. The Clearinghouse tries to detect potential problems within the acquisition of, maintenance, and access to identifying information even before an actual crime of identity theft takes place. The organization also breaks down privacy concern issues into smaller topics that allow for a more detailed understanding. These issues include financial privacy, Internet privacy, medical records privacy, telephone and telecommunications problems, public and government records privacy, and direct marketing concerns.

The Clearinghouse's Web site also offers a "Consumers Speak Out" page, which allows consumers to offer their input and share experiences in situations pertaining to privacy.

Stop Atlanta Fraud Empower (SAFE)
http://www.atlantava.org/default.asp

Stop Atlanta Fraud Empower (SAFE) is part of Atlanta Victim Assistance, Inc., a nonprofit organization that seeks to assist victims of crime and to strengthen them and their families. The Atlanta Victim Assistance program was founded in 1984 as the Victim Witness Assistance Program, and changed its name in 2005. The program specializes in helping victims of child abuse, domestic violence, identity theft, bank fraud, human trafficking, and the families of homicide victims. One of the public outreach programs that it offers is the Stop Atlanta Fraud Empower (SAFE) program, which is designed to provide education and support to help combat the identity theft and fraud problem in Atlanta, Georgia.

The SAFE program offers a three-part approach to address the problem of identity theft: education, advocacy, and training. Those working and volunteering within the SAFE program help victims file reports, address inaccuracies in their credit reports, and locate referral agencies to address other aspects of identity theft that are not covered by SAFE. The program also seeks to educate law enforcement officials about how to handle cases of identity theft and other fraud crimes more effectively. The group employs first responders to go to crime scenes or make home visits to offer support to victims. The assistance program also provides short-term counseling victims and their families. Details about the SAFE program can be found on the Atlanta Victim Assistance Web site.

United States Computer Emergency Readiness Team (CERT)
http://www.us-cert.gov/

In September 2003, the Department of Homeland Security and Carnegie Mellon University announced that they would partner to create the U.S. Computer Emergency Readiness Team (US-CERT), an agency that works toward preventing, protecting, and responding to cyber attacks on the Internet. Not limiting itself, US-CERT also partners with others in the private sector whose primary focus is on security.

Carnegie Mellon formed the first Computer Emergency Response Team/Coordination Center (CERT/CC) in 1988. The program was created in response to a worm that attacked computers and interrupted 10 percent of the systems connected to the Internet. The Carnegie CERT/CC is part of the Software

Engineering Institute, which is sponsored by the U.S. Department of Defense. The Carnegie Software Engineering Institute is federally funded and conducts research and develops products for the Department of Defense. The Carnegie Mellon CERT/CC issues alerts about potential cyber attacks and provides information about how to prevent them or how to recover from damages inflicted by such attacks.

US-CERT is located in Washington, D.C. and is part of the National Cyber Security Division in the Department of Homeland Security. There are over 250 organizations located around the world that are identified by the name "CERT"; however, US-CERT is only affiliated with the Carnegie Mellon program.

US-CERT is charged with helping to defend the United States from cyber attacks and to act as a source for the gathering and sharing of information between the private and public sectors. US-CERT's Web site is designed for audiences of varying levels. Within the site there are sections for both technical and novice users. The technical users section is aimed at those who are already familiar with computer security and are most likely the systems administrators. The novice section is written for the average home user or a business owner who is just beginning to learn about computer security. There is also a government section to help foster information sharing about cyber security among government agencies. Other options on the Web site include alerts, a place to report phishing attempts, vulnerabilities, and other incidents that might occur. In addition, the site features publications and information on ways to protect oneself from cyber attacks.

United States Department of the Treasury Financial Crimes Enforcement Network (FinCEN)
In 1990, the U.S. Department of the Treasury established the Financial Crimes Enforcement Network (FinCEN). Its main objective is to combat money laundering and other financial crimes in the United States and throughout the world. FinCEN is responsible for helping to protect the United States' financial infrastructure from possible corruption and crime, and it is the responsibility of the network's director to obtain and review banking records that may assist in the collection of intelligence information or which may be useful in investigations. In March 2004, FinCEN became a part of the Office of Terrorism and Financial Intelligence under the Department of the Treasury.

The FinCEN Web site is designed to provide information for a variety of financial institutions, including depository institutions, the insurance industry, casinos, money services businesses, securities and futures, and the precious metals/jewelry industry. Furthermore, the site offers information about financial fraud and identity theft crimes, including a section designed to inform users about the new fraud scams taking place and a section to help victims of identity theft.

Victims Initiative for Counseling, Advocacy, and Restoration of the Southwest (VICARS)
http://www.idvictim.org

The Victims Initiative for Counseling, Advocacy, and Restoration of the Southwest (VICARS) is a nonprofit law firm located in Texas. It is funded by a grant that was received as a result of needs identified in the reports of the President's Task Force on Identity Theft. VICARS was developed under the Texas Legal Services Center; its purpose is to help victims of identity theft and other forms of financial fraud. Their work is limited mostly to residents of Texas, New Mexico, Colorado, and Oklahoma. This victims' assistance program helps victims of identity theft in a variety of ways. They inform victims of their rights, help victims file identity theft complaints, dispute errors on credit reports, and document their cases.

VICARS maintains a Web site and a toll-free number to assist victims of identity theft. The Web site provides information to residents living in the four states. The "Victim's Toolkit" section, which is available in both English and Spanish, allows site visitors to learn what to do if they are a victim of identity theft. The toolkit features sample letters to send to credit reporting agencies, businesses, and collection companies. The toolkit also includes specific information on issues relating to medical and criminal identity theft. The Web site's links section connects visitors to other state and federal programs that offer information on identity theft. The news section keeps users updated on recent fraud schemes and trends, and the site also has a list of upcoming events during which VICARS will be distributing information and answering questions.

8

Resources

Print Resources

Books

Abagnale, Frank W. *The Art of the Steal: How to Protect Yourself and Your Business from Fraud, America's #1 Crime.* New York: Broadway Books, 2001.

This book describes the most common techniques used to defraud businesses and individuals. Through text and illustrations, the author gives advice on detecting vital document fraud, check fraud, counterfeit currency, Social Security number misuse, and other types of fraud plaguing modern society.

Abagnale, Frank W. *Stealing Your Life: The Ultimate Identity Theft Prevention Plan.* New York: Broadway Books, 2008.

Identity theft prevention is the subject of Frank Abagnale's latest book. Based on the author's experience as a con artist and his subsequent security consultant career, the author discusses the role of technology in the crime and offers specific options for deterring it. He describes how to detect the crime, how to determine where the compromise most likely occurred, and how to find out who the probable perpetrator is. The book also defines identity theft and talks about why it is a profitable crime.

Abagnale, Frank W. and Stan Redding. *Catch Me If You Can: The True Story of a Real Fake.* New York: Broadway Books, 2000.

This book is based on the author's personal knowledge of identity theft. It gives readers an intimate account of Abagnale's global exploits, which began when he was a teenager and continued nearly 25 years. While serving a prison term, the book chronicles how and why the famous con man came to the decision to change his life and try to make up for his past life of crime.

Arata, Michael J., Jr. *Preventing Identity Theft for Dummies.* **Indianapolis, IN: Wiley Publishing, 2004.**

This book is a comprehensive guide that provides strategies for deterring identity theft and also includes the resources victims need in order to reclaim their identities. Some of the subjects covered are reading credit reports, choosing safe account personal identification numbers, determining when it is appropriate to share personal information, safeguarding personal information, and avoiding the most common scams.

Biegelman, Martin T. *Identity Theft Handbook: Detection, Prevention, and Security.* **Hoboken, NJ: John Wiley & Sons, Inc., 2009.**

Identity theft as well as its connection to other crimes is discussed in this book. Among other issues, the author examines the global aspect of the crime, recent research, data breaches, and efforts of the criminal justice system to combat identity theft. Suggestions are also provided for preventing the crime.

Casey, Eoghan. *Digital Evidence and Computer Crime.* **San Diego, CA: Academic Press, 2001.**

This book, written to address the issues unique to investigating computer-related crimes, incorporates three disciplines: forensic, computer, and behavior sciences. It features case studies, step-by-step instructions, and hands-on exercises to help readers understand the role of digital evidence in all types of crimes. The companion CD contains exercises that compliment lessons in the book.

Collins, Judith M. *Preventing Identity Theft in Your Business: How to Protect Your Business, Customers, and Employees.* **Hoboken, NJ: John Wiley & Sons, Inc., 2005.**

A guide for businesses, this book provides step-by-step instructions for securing sensitive information in the workplace. It advocates the need for employees and managers to work together in fostering an honest workplace culture, developing security policies, and implementing security measures. Advice is also given on hiring practices. Hands-on exercises are provided to guide businesses through each step of achieving a workplace free of business and personal identity theft.

Collins, Judith M. *Investigating Identity Theft: A Guide for Businesses, Law Enforcement, and Victims.* **Hoboken, NJ: John Wiley & Sons, Inc., 2006.**

This book is a guide to developing a methodology for investigating identity theft cases. It was written for investigators, but can also be used by victims, law enforcement, and investigators employed in the public and private sectors. Real life case studies are used to illustrate the steps required to facilitate a successful resolution to identity theft cases. These case studies help investigators gain a better understanding of the crime, perpetrator, victim, technology, and the criminal justice system. A list of investigative resources is also included in the book.

Collins, Judith M., and Sandra K. Hoffman. *Identity Theft First Responder Manual for Criminal Justice Professionals.* **Flushing, NY: Looseleaf Law Publications, Inc., 2003.**

This training manual for police officers, attorneys, judges, prosecutors, and members of their respective staffs is divided into two parts. The first section serves as a guide for professionals as they assist identity theft victims and conduct investigations. The second section assists victims through the process of reclaiming their identities. The book contains a "Victim's Checklist" to guide victims through the process of collecting and documenting evidence pertaining to their cases. A stand-alone guide for victims is also available.

Cullen, Terri. *Complete Identity Theft Guidebook: How to Protect Yourself from the Most Pervasive Crime in America. The Wall Street Journal Series.* **New York: Three Rivers Press, 2007.**

Some of the major information breaches of recent years and the responses to them by the affected businesses are discussed in this book. It examines the most common types of identity theft, such as credit card fraud, and offers suggestions on how to avoid becoming a victim. In addition, a guide to reclaiming a stolen identity is provided; the guide includes letter and form templates suitable for use by victims.

Doerner, William G. and Steven P. Lab. *Victimology.* **4th ed. Cincinnati, OH: LexisNexis Publications, 2005.**

This book offers a general understanding of the key concepts associated with the study of victimology. It explores many specific crimes such as spousal, elder, and child abuse and how victims respond to these crimes. The book also provides insight into victim empowerment strategies and what the criminal justice system can do to address victims' needs.

Frank, Mari J. and Dale Fetherling. *From Victim to Victor: A Step by Step Guide for Ending the Nightmare of Identity Theft.* **2nd ed. Laguna Nigel, CA: Porpoise Press, 2005.**

Mari Frank, an attorney and identity theft victim, wrote this book as a response to the theft of her identity in 1996. The book is a complete guide to helping victims work through the process of clearing their names. The accompanying CD contains ready-to-use forms and letters.

Garner, Bryan A., ed. *Black's Law Dictionary.* **7th ed. St. Paul, MN: West Group, 1999.**

This comprehensive dictionary includes over 24,000 legal definitions that are clear and concise. It also contains government-related information such as the Constitution of the United States.

Hemphill, Ronald. *Rollin: True Confessions of a Former Identity Thief.* **Federal Way, WA: D'Lanor Publishing, 2005.**

This book chronicles the life of a former ringleader of a multi-million dollar identity theft organization. Without being a how-to manual, it demonstrates how a network is formed and how it operates. The author, now dedicated to eradicating identity theft, offers suggestions on securing sensitive information.

Karmen, Andrew. *Crime Victims: An Introduction to Victimology.* **5th ed. Belmont, CA: Thomson Publishing, 2003.**

Crime victims are the focus of this book. It defines victimology and discusses its history. The book explores many types of crimes, including assault, rape, and robbery, and looks at how victims typically respond to each of these crimes. It also provides insight into how the criminal justice system deals with victims and demonstrates how to transform the system to meet victims' needs.

Lininger, Rachael, and Russell D. Vines. *Phishing: Cutting the Identity Theft Line.* **Indianapolis, IN: Wiley Publishing, 2005.**

This book provides an in-depth examination of phishing, including how it evolved over time to incorporate malicious codes, and why it leads to identity theft. Technical information is given to help businesses and individuals reduce phishing occurrences. The book includes strategies for an effective response should an incident occur. Pictures and diagrams illustrate phishing Web sites, phishing e-mails, and the execution of various phishing scams.

May, Johnny R. *Johnny May's Guide to Preventing Identity Theft: How Criminals Steal Your Personal Information, How to Prevent it, and What to do if You Become a Victim.* **Bloomfield Hills, MI: Security Resources Unlimited, LLC, 2004.**

Written by a security professional, this book is a comprehensive guide on how to prevent personal and business identity theft. It includes a thorough definition of identity theft, describes the role of technology in the crime, and explains how the crime is committed. Step-by-step instructions are also provided to assist victims in reclaiming their identities.

McMillan, Edward J. *Policies and Procedures to Prevent Fraud and Embezzlement: Guidance, Internal Controls, and Investigation.* **Hoboken, NJ: John Wiley & Sons, Inc., 2006.**

This book is written for accountants, auditors, managers, and investigators, regardless of the size or type of business with which they are associated. It provides the tools needed to implement policies and procedures for protecting organizations against fraud and individuals against identity theft. It leads readers through a risk assessment process ranging from procedures for hiring personnel to forensic accounting. Included in the book are numerous forms, checklists, and sample documents.

Stickley, Jim. *The Truth about Identity Theft. The Truth about Series.* **Upper Saddle River, NJ: FT Press, 2008.**

Stickley, a security expert, has breached the security of all types of institutions across the United States as part of his job. Included in this book are detailed examples about the online and offline methods used to steal identities and the preventative measures that can be instituted by both individuals and businesses.

Sullivan, Bob. *Your Evil Twin: Behind the Identity Theft Epidemic.* **Hoboken, NJ: John Wiley & Sons, Inc., 2004.**

This book covers many facets of identity theft. Some of the most notorious heists of high-profile victims are covered, including hacking incidents carried out over the Internet. The author scrutinizes responses to the crime by the financial industry, law enforcement, and legislators. Advice for preventing identity theft is also provided.

Weisman, Steve. *50 Ways to Protect Your Identity and Your Credit: Everything You Need to Know about Identity Theft, Credit Cards, Credit Repair, and Credit Reports.* **Upper Saddle River, NJ: Prentice Hall, 2005.**

Real-life case examples are used in this book to illustrate how identities are stolen. The book offers advice on detecting identity theft scams and preventing victimization. Should the crime occur, it covers the steps victims need to take in order to clear their names. The book also discusses legislation such as The Gramm-Leach-Bliley Act and FACTA. Forms and letter templates are included in the book.

Journals and Magazines

Allison, Stuart F. H., Amie M. Schuck, and Kim Michelle Lersch. 2005. "Exploring the crime of identity theft: Prevalence, clearance rates, and victim/offender characteristics." *Journal of Criminal Justice* **33 (1): 19–29.**

This article was written in response to the need for more empirical research on the topic of identity theft. Data for the study was collected from a Florida police department. The authors discuss common characteristics of the perpetrators as well as their victims. The article addresses the fact that, while the volume of identity theft cases continues to grow, the number of perpetrators convicted of the crime continues to decline.

Berghel, Hal. 2000. "Identity Theft, Social Security Numbers, and the Web." *Communication of the ACM* **43 (2): 17–21.**

The author of this article addresses privacy concerns related to the overuse of Social Security numbers (SSNs), computer technology, and the Internet. Since SSNs are commonly used as personal identifiers by public and private entities, the author points out how this practice makes individuals vulnerable to identity theft. The article contends that the use of SSNs for anything other than credit purposes exposes individuals to unnecessary risk and warns that SSNs should not be used as a record-keeping tool. As technology advances and reliance on the Internet increases, the author discusses concerns about future online privacy and security.

Boyter, Jennifer Horne. 2009. "Crimes in Another Name: States Trying to Address Criminal Identity Theft." *State News (Council of State Governments)* **52 (1): 32–33.**

This article explores the issues surrounding criminal identity theft. As defined in the article, criminal identity theft occurs when an offender is questioned about or arrested for committing a felony or misdemeanor and provides law enforcement officials with someone else's identifying information. The author discusses the many problems encountered by victims as they work through the process of removing criminal charges from their records. Additionally, the article describes the programs implemented by different state governments to assist victims in clearing their names and to protect them from future victimization.

Britt, Phillip. 2009a. "Identity Thieves Hit a New Low." *Information Today* **26 (2): 1–44.**

This article predicts that incidences of identity theft will drastically increase in the near future due, in part, to the economic recession. Although the article discusses the prevalence of the crime, it focuses mainly how and why thieves steal the identities of recently deceased persons and the strategies to prevent it.

Britt, Phillip. 2009b. "Tax-Time Phishing Scams Out to Lure the Unsuspecting." *Information Today* **26 (4): 17.**

According to this magazine article, the threats to personal information and the potential for identity theft increases during tax season. Focusing on the 2009 tax season, the author noted an increase in the number of phishing scams alleged to be from the U.S. Internal Revenue Service and other agencies. In the article, the U.S. Computer Emergency Readiness Team warned of a new e-mail scam that invites recipients to apply for stimulus package funds.

Choice. 2008. "10 threats to your good name." (October): 12–16.

This article provides information on identity theft that is specific to the country of Australia. The author states that 499,500 citizens became victims in 2007. The article names the top 10 threats that put Australians at risk of becoming victims of identity theft.

Computer Fraud & Security. 2008. "TJX hackers caught." 8:1–2.

This article chronicles the TJX security breach and the arrests that have been made in the case. It states that 11 individuals, including three U.S. citizens, were charged with hacking into the TJX database and stealing customers' information, including credit and debit card numbers. The article alleges that the group was also responsible for several other security breaches.

Consumer Reports. 2009. "Debit-card dilemma." 74 (3): 8.

This article examines the risks associated with the use of debit cards. It explains that when a debit card is used to make a purchase, the cash comes out of the cardholder's checking or savings account. However, a compromised debit card can lead to many problems for the cardholder. The article discusses how thieves steal debit card information and provides options to help consumers keep their debit cards safe.

Goldsborough, Reid. 2008. "Phishing Away Your Identity." *Tech Directions* **67 (8): 12.**

The connection between phishing and identity theft is addressed in this article. The author gives a brief history of how phishing began and how it has evolved over the years.

Goodman, Eduard F. 2008. "Your Duty if You Discover a Data Breach." *GPSolo* **25 (8): 16–19.**

This article offers readers a different approach to identity theft because it is written by an attorney to inform others in the profession of their responsibilities should a data breach occur at their law firms. The author discusses the ethical and legal obligations for disclosing a breach without jeopardizing their law careers. Furthermore, the author predicts that breach coverage insurance will be available by 2013 and become as commonplace as malpractice insurance.

Greenberg, Andy. 2008. "Stop, Thief." *Forbes* 181 (11): 60.

This article is a review of cutting-edge technology and how it can be used to prevent identity theft. The author provides examples of many security options ranging from the receipt of a text message from the bank when an online transaction is attempted to biometric authentication.

Groc, Isabelle. 2008. "Payback for ID Theft." *PC Magazine* 27(3): 20.

This article was written prior to the passage of the Identity Theft Enforcement and Restitution Act which became federal law in 2008. One provision of the Act discussed in the article is that victims will have the opportunity to seek restitution if their imposter is convicted. While the bill may appear to be a solid attempt to help address the plight of victims, the article points out that only a small number of victims will benefit since very few identity theft cases are investigated.

Higgins, Michael. 1998. "Identity Thieves." *ABA Journal* 84 (10): 42–48.

This article outlines the responses to the identity theft problem in the United States during the 1990s, as it was during the 1990s that the phrase *identity theft* was coined. According to the article, the federal government reacted by holding training seminars, summits, and legislative hearings in efforts to solve the problems associated with this crime.

***Information Management Journal.* 2006. "Does FACTA Go Far Enough?" 40 (6): 11.**

The Fair and Accurate Credit Transaction Act (FACTA) that became federal law in 2003 is the subject of this article. A provision of FACTA that became effective in 2005, the Disposal Rule, mandates the proper destruction and disposal of records containing credit information. However, this article argues that the law is not board enough to cover all of the personal information routinely collected and destroyed by businesses. It concludes that while FACTA is a good piece of legislation, it does not do enough on its own to protect consumers from identity theft.

Jackson, Margaret and Julian Ligertwood. 2006. "Identity Management: Is an Identity Card the Solution for Australia?" *Prometheus* **24 (4): 379–387.**

This article examines the benefits and consequences of establishing a national identity card program in Australia that is based on the model utilized in the United Kingdom. The authors begin by offering a historical perspective on the use of national identity cards in Australia. Although national identifiers have been temporarily implemented in the past, the article discusses the potential benefits of establishing an identity card program such as improving the efficiency of the government and detecting fraud. The article also talks about the legal and social implications that could arise. However, the authors offer other options that would protect the privacy of citizens and secure personal data.

Koops, Bert-Jaap, et al. 2009. "A Typology of Identity-Related Crime." *Information, Communication & Society* **12 (1): 1–24.**

This article begins by acknowledging that a standardized, widely accepted, inclusive definition of identity-related crimes is nonexistent. The authors developed the typology to address this problem. The article states that the information can be used as a building block for subsequent research, to enhance policy making decisions, and to aid in the development of preventive measures.

Lacey, David and Suresh Cuganesan. 2004. "The Role of Organizations in Identity Theft Response: The Organization-Individual Victim Dynamic." *Journal of Consumer Affairs* **38 (2): 244–261.**

This study examines the relationship between identity theft and the role of organizations in detecting identity theft, serving as the location where identities are used or abused, and serving as a location where identity theft can be addressed to ensure a level of responsibility in protecting sensitive information, and responding to victims of the crime. After analyzing the data, the authors found that many factors influence an organization's ability to anticipate identity theft incidences and respond to victims of the crime. One example cited in the study was employee training. The study found that most organizations provide training either at the time the employees are hired or do not provide training at all. Even though this research involved organizations located in Australia, the authors suggest that the results are internationally applicable.

Lankford, Kimberly. 2008. "Your ID-Theft Prevention Kit." *Kiplinger's Personal Finance* **62 (4): 72–74.**

The author of this article discusses everyday activities that make individuals vulnerable to identity theft and how to avoid becoming victims. It also covers the types of personal information that are most desired by identity thieves. Additionally, the article explains how credit reports are useful tools for detecting victimization.

Lee, Victor. 2008. "Biometrics and Identity Fraud." *Biometric Technology Today* **16 (2): 7–11.**

This article acknowledges that identity theft is a growing concern and addresses the connection between biometrics and identity fraud. The author discusses the monetary losses sustained in the United Kingdom and the United States as a direct result of the crime and argues that biometric technologies have the potential to reduce those losses. The article addresses how biometrics technologies can improve the identification and authentication systems that are currently in use. It addresses the vulnerabilities of biometric systems and how to secure the technology. The author also discusses the publics' reaction to using biometrics as a means of preventing identity theft.

Linnhoff, Stefan and Jeff Langenderfer. 2004. "Identity Theft Legislation: The Fair and Accurate Credit Transactions Act of 2003 and the Road Not Taken." *Journal of Consumer Affairs* **38 (2): 204–216.**

The authors of this article address the Fair and Accurate Credit Transactions Act of 2003 (FACTA) as it relates to identity theft. The article examines the provisions of the Act that help combat the crime such as giving consumers free access to their credit reports every 12 months, prohibiting organizations that process credit card payments from printing the complete number on receipts, and requiring credit card companies to confirm address change requests before updating the cardholders' accounts. Next, the article discusses proposed legislation and its effectiveness in preventing identity theft. The authors conclude that, while FACTA improves the manner in which sensitive information is protected, there are issues that must addressed such as the overuse of Social Security numbers as personal identifiers.

LoPucki, Lynn M. 2001. "Human Identification Theory and the Identity Theft Problem." *Texas Law Review* **80 (1): 89–136.**

This article reviews the Human Identification Theory and applies it to the identity theft issues that plague modern society. LoPucki addresses the role of identification as it relates to consumers and their ability to obtain credit. Since past approaches have been ineffective, the author suggests an identification system that would be effective in combating identity theft. The system would give consumers the option of managing the flow of their own personal information. At the same time, it would provide the credit industry with an identity verification method that protects consumer privacy.

Lynch, Jennifer. 2005. "Identity Theft in Cyberspace: Crime Control Methods and Their Effectiveness in Combating Phishing Attacks." *Berkeley Technology Law Journal* **20(1): 259–300.**

This article discusses identity theft and phishing, a common method used to steal identities. The author examines the increasing number of phishing attacks and the costs associated with identity theft. Also, the article explores statistics that are associated specifically with the phishing aspect of identity theft and addresses crime control strategies that have been utilized on the primary, secondary, and tertiary levels. Primary control strategies address society as a whole and focus on the root causes of the problem. Secondary control strategies identifies those who are most at risk of becoming victims and offers them information about how to protect themselves. On the tertiary level, a crime is addressed after it happens and the response is aimed at deterring future occurrences. The author explains how each of the crime control strategies is being used to fight identity theft. In conclusion, the article states that it is essential to utilize all levels of crime control in combating phishing attacks as well as identity theft.

"Medical Identity Theft." 2008. *Biomedical Safety & Standards* 38(18): 137–139.

This article was written to specifically address cases of medical identity theft within the United States. It discusses the Federal Trade Commission's data analysis of medical identity theft for the year 2005. Medical identity theft is defined and recommendations for combating the crime are provided in the article.

Milne, George R. 2003. "How Well do Consumers Protect Themselves from Identity Theft?" *Journal of Consumer Affairs* 37(2): 388–402.

This exploratory research was conducted to determine the degree to which consumers implement measures to protect themselves from becoming victims of identity theft. The author discusses the results of a self-report survey. Two sample groups participated in the project. One group consisted of college students who, on average, were 21 years of age. The other group was nonstudents whose average age was 36. The research found that both groups did not practice the same types of preventative measures. For example, students were more likely to give their Social Security numbers as identification when cashing checks than nonstudents. The findings also show that some preventative measures were barely utilized by either group such as reviewing their credit reports. The author concludes that there are specific areas in which further consumer education is necessary.

Pastrikos, Catherine. 2004. "Identity Theft Statutes: Which Will Protect Americans the Most?" *Albany Law Review* 67(4): 1137–1157.

This article examines some of the state and federal identity theft legislation enacted in the United States. The author discusses the Identity Theft and Assumption and Deterrence Act of 1998, a federal law, and the state statutes adopted in Arizona, California, and New York. The strengths and weaknesses of each law are explored. Based upon the strengths, the author proposes a new statute that would effectively address the identity theft problem.

Saunders, Kurt M. and Bruce Zucker. 1999. "Counteracting Identity Fraud in the Information Age: The Identity Theft and

Assumption Deterrence Act." *International Review of Law, Computers & Technology* 13 (2): 183–192.

This article explores the issues surrounding identity theft and the potential effects of federal legislation. First, the authors define identity theft and examine the problems associated with the crime. The next section explores the importance of identity in modern society from both a sociological and practical perspective. The authors discuss the need for identity verification as well as the need to protect personal information. Lastly, the authors assess the Identity Theft and Assumption Deterrence Act of 1998 and its potential role in protecting the privacy of U.S. citizens.

Seltzer, Larry. 2008. "Measuring Identity Theft at Top Banks." *PC Magazine* 27 (7): 104.

The author of this article reports the findings of a study conducted at the University of California's Berkeley Center for Law and Technology. The purpose of the research was to ascertain the major institutions that are most often targeted by identity thieves. Researcher, Chris Hoofnagle, contends that financial institutions should disclose identity theft statistics so consumers can make informed decisions when choosing a bank with which to do business. Statistics should include how many times identity theft was attempted as well as the number of times it occurred, the method used, and the type of account targeted. The author of the study proposes that this information ought to be voluntarily disclosed by the banking institutions.

Sharp, Tracy, et al. 2004. "Exploring the Psychological and Somatic Impact of Identity Theft." *Journal of Forensic Sciences (ASTM International)* 49 (1): 131–136.

This article examines identity theft from the victims' perspective. It discusses the psychological and somatic impact of the crime and pinpoints some of the most effective coping mechanisms. The article is based upon the results of an exploratory study in which victims completed a questionnaire. Based upon the responses, the authors determined that victims of identity theft experienced higher levels of psychological and physical difficulties than non-victims. The study also found that victims whose identity theft problems were unsettled continued to suffer as compared to victims whose cases had been resolved. As noted in the article, victims reported that one of the most effective coping techniques was active participation in working through the problems associated with the crime.

Smith, Lamar. 2008. "The New Challenges of Cybercrime." *Federal Sentencing Reporter* 20(5): 356.

Lamar Smith, member of the Committee on the Judiciary, House of Representatives, wrote this article to address the challenges facing the United States pertaining to cybercrimes. From a historical perspective, the author notes that criminal law has always been a reactive response to crime. In addition to responding to cybercrimes, the author demonstrates that it is also essential for the U.S. government to become proactive in the battle against it. By looking forward to new technologies and how they can be exploited, proactive measures can be instituted to deal with the issues inherent in a virtual world.

Sullins, Lauren L. 2006. "'Phishing' for a Solution: Domestic and International Approaches to Decreasing Online Identity Theft." *Emory International Law Review* 20 (1): 397–433.

This article addresses online identity theft and phishing, a technique used to trick individuals into revealing their personal information. It discusses the impact that phishing and identity theft has on consumers as well as corporations. The author contends that identity theft jeopardizes the future of Internet-based transactions because consumers will lose trust in the authenticity of Web sites.

Sullivan, Clare. 2009. "Is Identity Theft Really Theft?" *International Review of Law, Computers & Technology* 23 (1/2): 77–87.

The author of this article discusses identity theft in the United Kingdom. It builds upon a previous article in which the concept of identity and the definition of identity theft were discussed in the context of the UK Identity Cards Act of 2006. The author explores the idea that an identity is not comparable to an individual's material possessions that can be stolen. Rather, an identity may be considered an emerging legal concept that is not subject to theft.

Sullivan, Richard J. 2008. "Can Smart Cards Reduce Payments Fraud and Identity Theft?" *Economic Review* 93 (3): 34–62.

The author of this article offers insight into the use of smart cards as a means for reducing payments fraud and identity theft. The article outlines the costs related to fraud cases, including identity theft, since payments fraud frequently involves a stolen identity. The author suggests that the use of smart cards would result in a savings for the financial industry, merchants, consumers, and law enforcement agencies. In addition, the author states that smart cards would provide a more secure and efficient payment system. The author also compares the strengths and weaknesses of the security features available through smart card technology.

Swartz, Nikki. 2008. "FTC Settles with TJX, Data Brokers." *Information Management Journal* 42 (4): 14.

The author of this article writes about three companies that reached settlements with the Federal Trade Commission (FTC) for failing to protect personal information. According to the article, a hacker gained access to TJX's computer network and stole debit and credit card information belonging to the retailer's customers. The other cases involved data brokers Reed Elsevier and Seisint who allowed criminals to access their databases containing the sensitive information of U.S. consumers.

Swartz, Nikki. 2009. "Will Red Flags Detour ID Theft?" *Information Management Journal* 43 (1): 38–41.

This article explains the "red flags" rule and its potential role in reducing the losses that victims and businesses incur. The Identity Theft Red Flags program revised the Fair and Accurate Credit Transactions Act of 2003 (FACTA) to require specific entities, such as banks, to develop and implement an identity theft prevention program. The author also presents the arguments of proponents and advocates regarding the effectiveness of the rule in combating the identity theft problem.

Tynan, Dan, Tim Moynihan, and Tom Spring. 2008. "Identity Protectors: Who Can You Trust?" *PC World* 26 (6): 105–112.

This article is a review of some of the identity theft protection services that were available to consumers as of 2008. The services offered by six different companies were tested to determine if the services were effective in protecting against identity theft and if the protection was worth the price of the services. The article reported that four of the companies offered services designed to protect against financial identity theft and did not address other types of the crime. The authors concluded the article with a list of steps consumers can take to reduce the risk of becoming victims of identity theft.

Vijayan, Kaikumar. 2008. "Feds Nab More Members of Alleged Identity Theft Gang." *Computerworld* **42 (48): 8.**

In this article, the author discusses the arrests of several individuals and their alleged involvement in a multimillion, global, cybercrime network. The article examines the techniques used by the suspects to facilitate the theft of over $2.5 million from banks and credit unions. It also discusses the underground market and the amount and type of personal information that is sold in this venue.

White, Anthony E. 2005. "The Recognition of a Negligence Cause of Action for Victims of Identity Theft: Someone Stole my Identity, Now Who is Going to Pay for It?" *Marquette Law Review* **88 (4): 847–866.**

This article is an in-depth discussion of identity theft. The author explores the background of the crime, defines identity theft, and explains how and why the crime happens. In addition, the article examines responses to the crime in the form of civil litigation and legislative actions. Some of the laws discussed are the Gramm-Leach-Bliley Act, the Fair Credit Reporting Act, and the Database Breach Notification Security SB 1386 Act.

White, Michael D. and Christopher Fischer. "Assessing Our Knowledge of Identity Theft." 2008. *Criminal Justice Policy Review* **19 (1): 3–24.**

The authors of this article explore the many unanswered questions pertaining to identity theft. They point out that the crime continues to escalate; yet knowledge of the topic is relatively limited. According to the article, there is much to learn about identity theft such as how often it occurs, the amount of losses incurred by victims, the nature of the crime, and a definitive profile of the victims and the perpetrators. The authors identify many obstacles that must be overcome if a greater understanding of the crime is to be realized. The article states, for example, that the inconsistencies between the state and federal definitions of identity theft need to be addressed.

Winterdyk, John and Nikki Thompson. 2008. "Student and Non-Student Perceptions and Awareness of Identity Theft." *Canadian Journal of Criminology & Criminal Justice* **50 (2): 153–186.**

This article opens by offering some statistical information about identity theft in Canada. Although Canadian scholars are beginning to do more research on the topic, the authors note that most of the available research is generated in the United States. The article then provides a comparison of the research conducted in both countries. U.S. researchers tend to focus on law enforcement approaches for detection and prevention of the crime. On the other hand, Canadian researchers mainly concentrate on how individuals can protect themselves from becoming victims of identity theft. The authors conducted a self-report study to assess how well college students and nonstudents understood the crime and the methods that they can use to protect themselves. Based upon the results, the authors offer information that can be useful in policy decisions and suggest techniques to help educate the public about identity theft.

Pamphlets/Booklets

Federal Trade Commission. *Take Charge: Fighting Back Against Identity Theft.* **Washington, DC: Author, 2006. http://www.ftc.gov/bcp/edu/microsites/idtheft/become-a-partner.html. Accessed March 31, 2009.**

This booklet guides victims of identity theft through the process of reclaiming their identities. It includes charts, letter templates, and the Identity Theft Affidavit. The booklet is available in English and Spanish, and can be downloaded in PDF form from the FTC's Web site. Copies may also be ordered directly from the FTC.

Federal Trade Commission. *Talking About Identity Theft: A How-to Guide.* **Washington, DC: Author, n.d. http://www.ftc.gov/bcp/edu/microsites/idtheft/become-a-partner.html. Accessed March 31, 2009.**

The purpose of this booklet is to provide the tools necessary for implementing an awareness program in a community or workplace. It includes a definition of identity theft, information about assisting victims, deciding on a location to hold a seminar, and issuing a statement to the media regarding the event. The booklet is available in English or Spanish, and can be downloaded from the Web site in PDF form or may be ordered from the FTC. A companion PowerPoint presentation is also available on the Web site.

Federal Trade Commission. *AvoID Theft: Deter, Detect, Defend. Fighting Back against Identity Theft.* **Washington, DC: Author, n.d. http://www.ftc.gov/bcp/edu/microsites/idtheft/become-a-partner.html. Accessed March 31, 2009.**

This pamphlet, written for consumers, outlines how to protect personal information and how to take action, should an identity theft occur. The pamphlet is available in English or Spanish, and can be downloaded from the FTC's Web site in PDF form or ordered from the FTC.

Federal Trade Commission. *AvoID Theft: Deter, Detect, Defend. Military Personnel & Families. Fighting Back against Identity Theft.* **Washington, DC: Author, n.d. http://www.ftc.gov/bcp/edu/microsites/idtheft/become-a-partner.html. Accessed March 31, 2009.**

This pamphlet addresses issues related to identity theft that are unique to military personnel and their families. It outlines how to protect personal information and how to take action should an identity theft occur. The pamphlet can be downloaded from the FTC's Web site in PDF form, or may be ordered from the FTC.

Nonprint Resources

AARP. 2004. *One identity theft victim's 'living hell.'* **Available at: http://www.aarp.org/bulletin/yourlife/Articles/a2004-01-28-livinghell.html. Accessed January 23, 2007.**

The article chronicles one woman's experience as a victim of identity theft. It discusses the problems she encountered as a result of another person using her identifying information following an automobile accident. The victim in this case received medical bills in her name and she was sued by another person who was injured.

Anti-Phishing Working Group. 2008. *Phishing activity trends: Report for the month of November, 2007.* Available at: http://www. antiphishing.org/reports/apwg_report_nov_2007.pdf. Accessed April 2, 2009.

The Anti-Phishing Working Group (APWG) is an organization dedicated to eradicating fraud, such as identity theft, perpetrated by online tactics such as phishing, pharming, and spoofing. It was founded in 2003 and is the largest repository of its kind. Members include law enforcement agencies, financial institutions, retailers, Internet service providers, and solution suppliers. APWG tracks phishing incidents, phishing Web sites, spoofed e-mails, and malicious crimeware. The findings are published once a month in the *Phishing Activity Trends Report.* The November 2007 report notes that phishing incidents decreased, yet at the same time there was an increase in phishing e-mails targeting business recipients (e.g., executives and employees). The goal of these e-mails was to commit business identity theft.

California Department of Motor Vehicles. 2007. *DMV Investigators Arrest Fresno Dealer on Charges of Identity Theft* Available at: http://www.dmv.ca.gov/pubs/newsrel/newsrel07/2007-7_10. htm. Accessed April 2, 2009.

This news release by the California DMV is an example of business owners accused of stealing the identities of their customers. The California DMV is the governmental agency responsible for issuing drivers' licenses, state identification cards, and vehicle registrations. All documents submitted (applications, proof of legal presence, medical reports, driver tests, alcohol program completion certificates, etc.) are reviewed for possible fraud. If fraud is detected, the DMV participates in the investigation and prosecution of the wrongdoers. Since identity theft often involves a driver's license or state identification card, the DMV's Web site offers information to victims and businesses about preventing the crime. News releases are also available on the Web site dating from 2004 to the present.

Collins, Judith M. and Sandra K. Hoffman. 2004. *Identity theft: Predator profiles.* Unpublished Paper, School of Criminal Justice, Michigan State University.

This exploratory research was conducted by researchers of the Michigan State University's Identity Theft Program. At the time of the research, it was the only comprehensive, on-campus program consisting of training, victim advocacy, research, and investigative service or support. This research is one of the first studies to offer a profile of perpetrators of identity theft. The study provides a foundation upon which to base future research. The data was collected between 1999 through 2002 and was gleaned from 486 sources across the nation through systematic online searches that utilized search engines and databases.

Deloitte Services LP. 2004. *The Titans Take Hold. How Offshoring has Changed the Competitive Dynamic for Global Financial Services Institutions.* **Available at: http://www.deloitte.com/dtt/cda/ doc/content/Offshoring%20Final%281%29.pdf. Accessed January 16, 2006.**

This article discusses the practice of offshoring and clarifies some of the confusion surrounding it by first defining and identifying the distinction between offshoring and outsourcing. Then, the article talks about the benefits of offshoring as it pertains to the financial industry and addresses the risks associated with it. The article also explores some of the issues that should be taken into account when planning to offshore such as regulatory compliance, cost effectiveness, emergency preparedness, and protecting intellectual property.

Federal Bureau of Investigation. 2006. *Financial Crimes Report to the Public, Fiscal Year 2006.* **Available at: http://www.fbi.gov/ publications/financial/fcs_report2006/financial_crime_2006. htm. Accessed June 2, 2007.**

The U.S. Federal Bureau of Investigation (FBI) is responsible for the investigation of fraud, theft, and embezzlement that occurs within the financial community. This report represents the Bureau's investigations and findings for the fiscal year 2006 and covers elements from various units within the FBI, offering an indicator of the latest crime trends. The crimes summarized in this report include: corporate fraud, securities and commodities fraud, health care fraud, mortgage fraud, identity theft, insurance fraud, mass marketing fraud, asset forfeiture, and money laundering.

Federal Trade Commission. n.d. *Consumer Sentinel/Military.* **Available at: http://www.ftc.gov/sentinel/military/index.shtml. Accessed April 6, 2009.**

The Consumer Sentinel/Military database was founded in 2002 and is run by the Federal Trade Commission. The online portal collects consumer complaints from military personnel and their families; this data is then used as a means to analyze identity theft trends among military personnel and to offer advice on ways to protect themselves, especially during times of deployment.

Federal Trade Commission. 2001. *Identity Theft Victim Complaint Data: Figures and Trends on Identity Theft, January 2000 through December 2000.* **Available at: http://ftc.gov/bcp/edu/mi crosites/idtheft/downloads/clearinghouse_2000.pdf. Accessed April 2, 2009.**

This national statistical data, presented in the form of colorful charts and graphs, depicts complaints filed by identity theft victims. Covering the year 2000, it is the first report available for a complete year. The statistical information was compiled from databases maintained by the Federal Trade Commission (FTC). The report may be downloaded in PDF form from the FTC's Web site.

Federal Trade Commission. 2007. *Consumer Fraud and Identity Theft Complaint Data, January—December 2006.* **Available at: http://www.ftc.gov/sentinel/reports/sentinel-annual-reports/ sentinel-cy2006.pdf. Accessed April 3, 2009.**

This national statistical data, presented in the form of colorful charts and graphs, depicts complaints filed by identity theft and consumer fraud victims with the Federal Trade Commission (FTC). The annual report compares 2006 data with that from 2004 and 2005 and provides detailed statistics for each state. The report may be downloaded in PDF form from the Consumer Sentinel Web site.

Federal Trade Commission. 2008. *Consumer Fraud and Identity Theft Complaint Data: January—December 2007.* **Available at: http://www.ftc.gov/sentinel/reports/sentinel-annual-reports/ sentinel-cy2007.pdf. Accessed April 3, 2009.**

This file offers a national look at the issue of identity theft. It allows readers to examine the problem of identity theft through the use of colorful charts, tables, and graphs. The information in this report was collected by the Federal Trade Commission and the report depicts complaints filed by identity theft and consumer fraud victims. The annual report compares 2007 data with that from previous years. It also provides detailed statistics for each state. The report may be downloaded in PDF form from the Consumer Sentinel Web site.

Gayer, Jennette. 2003. *Policing Privacy: Law Enforcement's Response toIdentity Theft.* CALPIRG Educational Fund. Available at: http://www.calpirg.org/home/reports/report-archives/ campaign-finance-reform/campaign-finance-reform/ policing-privacy-law-enforcements-response-to-identity-theft#dzyQhMxIWX4i6d33b6aLPg. Accessed April 3, 2009.

This is a summary of the information gleaned from interviews with law enforcement personnel in cities that have elevated incidences of identity theft. The research was conducted by the CALPIRG Education Fund, a nonprofit organization based in California. As consumer advocates, the organization does research and publishes their findings on issues ranging from health care-related issues to privacy issues.

Gordon, Gary R., et al. 2007. *Identity Fraud Trends and Patterns: Building a Data-Based Foundation for Proactive Enforcement.* Available at: http://www.utica.edu/academic/institutes/ecii/publi cations/media/cimip_id_theft_study_oct_22_noon.pdf. Accessed February 27, 2008.

This research was done by the Center for Identity Management and Information Protection (CIMIP) at Utica College, a center that was founded in 2006. CIMIP is a joint research initiative made up of public and private entities. One of their goals is to provide proactive solutions to the growing problem of identity theft. The nature of this research was designed to assist law enforcement in the development of strategies to control and prevent the crime. While many research projects focus specifically on the victims, this project concentrates mainly on the offenders. The study addresses one of the concerns expressed in the President's Identity Theft Task Force report, the lack of information pertaining to the perpetrators of identity theft. The data used in this study came from the identity theft case files of the U.S. Secret Service from 2000 to 2006. Based upon the data analysis and the understanding gained through the research, the authors offer several suggestions that would allow the criminal justice system to take a proactive stance in controlling or preventing identity theft.

Greenfeld, Lawrence A. and Tracy L. Snell. 1999. *Women Offenders.* **Revised October 3, 2000. U.S. Department of Justice, Bureau of Justice Statistics. NCJ 173688. Available at: http://www.ojp. gov/bjs/pub/pdf/wo.pdf. Accessed February 29, 2008.**

This report analyzes the trends surrounding women offenders and explores the aggregate statistics regarding them. The authors discuss the number and types of violent crimes committed by females as compared to males. Several factors are considered such as the offender's race, offender's relationship to the victim, location of the crime, age of the victim and offender, and the role of alcohol, drugs, or weapons in commission of the crime. The report provides specific data pertaining to the number of women who commit murder, including those who murder their children and stepchildren. The authors discuss the demographic information associated with arrest data, conviction rates, and incarceration of females in the prison system. The report addresses the frequency with which woman commit violent, property, and drug felonies. It also examines the common characteristics of incarcerated women such as race, age, and marital status, level of education, age of their children, economic situation, health problems, and criminal history. Lastly, the recidivism rate among women is discussed. The data for this report was gleaned from many sources including the National Crime Victimization Survey, the Uniform Crime Reporting program, and the National Corrections Reporting Program.

Helmkamp, James, Richard Ball, and Kitty Townsend, eds. 1996. *Definitional Dilemma: Can and Should There be a Universal Definition of White Collar Crime?* **Proceedings of the academic workshop of the National White Collar Crime Center and West Virginia University, West Virginia. Available at: http://www.nw3c. org/research/site_files.cfm?mode=p. Accessed April 3, 2009.**

The workshop was sponsored by the National White Collar Crime Center (NW3C) and West Virginia University. It was held to provide an opportunity for experts on white collar crime to come together and discuss two main issues, the lack of research on the subject and the lack of a universally accepted definition of white collar crime. Bill McDonald, NW3C chairman of the Board of Directors, suggested that the term *white collar crime* contributes to the perception that economic crimes are not serious crimes. He discussed changing the name altogether to reflect the harm perpetrated upon victims such as individuals, businesses, and the financial market. His comments were followed by three days of academic presentations given by experts from 15 colleges and universities across the United States. At the end of the workshop, participants agreed on a definition of white collar crime.

Identity Theft 911 Knowledge Center. 2005. *Identity Theft:* **The Meth Connection. Available at: http://www.identitytheft911.org/ articles/article.ext?sp=81. Accessed June 25, 2007.**

This brief online article outlines legislation proposed by U.S. Senator Maria Cantwell of Washington to authorize a study to determine if there is a relationship between identity theft and the use of methamphetamines. At the time of the proposed legislation, no research had been conducted in this area. The proposed study would focus on the sentences commensurate with crimes committed in which both methamphetamine and identity theft are involved, the need for creating a database to facilitate information sharing among law enforcement agencies, and types of identity theft crimes that are most often associated with the use of methamphetamines.

Identity Theft 911, LLC. 2008. *Identity Theft in Arizona.* **Available at: http://identitytheft911.org/attachment.do?sp=0408. Accessed April 3, 2009.**

This white paper is unique because it addresses identity theft issues pertaining to the state of Arizona. According to the report, this state led the nation in the highest number of victim complaints filed for five consecutive years. The paper examines the root causes behind the explosion of the identity theft in Arizona, with the goal of gaining a better understanding of the crime and offering potential remedies to the problem. Statistics provided by the Federal Trade Commission's annual reports are analyzed. In the report, the connection between identity theft, specifically employment fraud and illegal immigration, is examined. It discusses the marked increase in the numbers of children who became victims of the crime between 2003 and 2006. The report also examines the connection between identity theft and methamphetamine use. The white paper talks about some of the initiatives that have been undertaken in Arizona to combat the crime such as the establishment of Investigation Jurisdiction Protocol to aid police agencies in the Phoenix area in taking victim complaints.

Internal Revenue Service. 2005. "Examination Techniques for Specific Industries (Direct Sellers)," In *Retail Industry Audit Technique Guide (ATG)*. http://www.irs.gov/businesses/small/ article/0,,id=141491,00.html#top. Accessed December 27, 2005.

This audit guide is published by the Internal Revenue Service (IRS) and is available online in PDF and HTML formats. For ease of use, the guide is divided into chapters. The third chapter discusses electronic business (e-business) and how it is constantly growing, changing, and evolving. It explores the types of business transactions that are routinely conducted online in addition to shopping. The chapter then provides techniques to aid IRS auditors in determining if a company is engaged in e-business.

Jabaily, Bob, ed. 2004. "Credit history: The Evolution of Consumer Credit in America." *The Ledger* Spring/Summer. Available at: http://www.bos.frb.org/education/ledger/ledger04/sprsum/ credhistory.htm. Accessed April 2, 2009.

This article outlines the history of credit from 1810 forward. It explores how technology made it possible for Americans to enjoy leisure time, which triggered the invention of various forms of credit, including credit cards. *The Ledger* is published two times annually by the Federal Reserve Bank of Boston to promote education on economic topics. It is available online in HTML and PDF formats from 1997 to the present . Consumers may also subscribe to free print issues for home delivery.

Lyzhina, Svetlana, and Zaghid Yusoupov, trans. "The Unsolved Riddle of Princess Anastasia." *Pravda* (Russia) (July 13) http://eng lish.pravda.ru/main/18/90/363/13367_Nicholas.html. Accessed April 3, 2009.

This article documents some of the many imposters of Anastasia Nikolayevna Romanova, the daughter of Tsar Nicholas of Russia. After the execution of Nicholas' family, many women claimed to be the princess and told stories about how they escaped death. The author examines the stories of three of the most convincing imposters.

McMillan, Robert. 2006. "Paris Hilton Accused of Voice-Mail Hacking." *PC World*. http://www.pcworld.com/article/id,126923/ article.html. Accessed June 22, 2007.

This article uses a Hollywood experience to demonstrate how easy it is to break into mobile phone voicemail accounts. The article also talks about Tim Murphy, a U.S. Representative, who was a victim of spoofing. The author explains how technology has spawned new business opportunities, selling caller ID spoofing services. In the article, one vendor, SpoofCard.com, advocates that there are legitimate uses for the technology despite the fact it has been used to hack into voicemail accounts and for carrying out telemarketing scams. Finally, the author offers a solution to the problem. A security expert suggests that hackings could be eliminated if all cell phone companies required their customers to place passwords on their voicemail accounts.

Morris, Robert G., II. 2004. *The Development of an Identity Theft Offender Typology: A Theoretical Approach*. Available at: http:// www.shsu.edu/~edu_elc/journal/research%20online/re2004/ Robert.pdf. Accessed March 9, 2008.

This research project was conducted at Sam Houston State University, College of Criminal Justice and published in *The Graduate Research Journal*. The journal, which is only published online twice a year, offers a place for students to share their research with the academic community and those working in related fields. The purpose of this particular exploratory research is to provide a foundation for future research regarding identity theft perpetrators in order that solutions for combating the crime might be forthcoming. The author points out that little empirical research exists on this topic so data and information gathered from a police department are the major sources utilized in the study. The author begins with a general discussion of the nature of the identity theft problem and the government's reactions to the crime. The author then examines who commits identity theft and why they commit it.

Newman, Graeme R. and Megan M. McNally. 2005. *Identity Theft Literature Review*. Document No. 210459. Available at: http://www. ncjrs.gov/pdffiles1/nij/grants/210459.pdf. Accessed March 1, 2008.

The authors of this literature review received a grant from the U.S. Department of Justice to conduct an assessment of existing research and available resources related to identity theft. The goal of the review is to determine the identity theft topics that warrant research in the future. Many possibilities are identified and they encompass nearly every aspect of the crime. For example, more research is needed to ascertain the extent that organized crime is involved in identity theft. Such research may discover a means to prevent identity theft from becoming a tool for crime syndicates. This report is available online, or paper copies can be ordered from the National Criminal Justice Reference Service (NCJRS) Web site.

Glossary

$299 ring   A type of scam in which Medicare recipients are targeted and offered additional coverage. Scammers take payments over the phone by requesting the victim's credit card or checking account information.

aggravated identity theft   The unlawful transfer, possession, or use of another person's identifying information related to the commission of specific felonies. For example, a terrorism conviction involving stolen personal information or false identification documents results in two sentences (i.e., one for the terrorism conviction and an additional five-year sentence for aggravated identity theft).

better business bureau (BBB)   According to its mission statement, the BBB is a private, non-profit organization founded in 1912 to promote trust between consumers and businesses in the marketplace.

business identity theft   The use of identifying information pertaining to a company or corporation without its knowledge and with the intent to aid or abet in any unlawful activity such as obtaining services, merchandise, money, and/or credit, committing felonies and/or misdemeanors, or filing for bankruptcy.

check cleaning (washing)   A process by which household chemicals are utilized to remove the handwritten information from a check, leaving only the preprinted information placed on the check at the time of ordering.

child identity theft   The fraudulent use of the identifying information of a minor with the intent to aid or abet in any unlawful activity such as obtaining services, merchandise, money, and/or credit, committing felonies and/or misdemeanors, or filing for bankruptcy.

common identifiers   Personal information that might be targeted for identity theft, including a person's name, address, and telephone number.

consumer sentinel   A database maintained by the Federal Trade Commission that contains the complaints of victims of identity theft, scams, and other types of fraud. The database is accessible to approved users, including law enforcement personnel, consumer protection agencies in the United States and abroad, state and federal Attorneys General offices, and Department of Defense personnel.

credit card fraud   When an unauthorized person opens credit cards in someone else's name, uses someone else's credit card, or instigates changes to someone's credit card information without the knowledge or permission of the credit card holder.

do not call registry   A program created by the federal government in 2003 to allow consumers to remove their home and cell phone numbers from telemarketing call lists.

Dumpster diving   The act of searching through the trash of residences or businesses in order to locate personal information that can be used to commit identity theft.

federal trade commission (FTC)   Created in 1914 by the Federal Trade Commission Act, the FTC is an independent agency of the federal government designed to promote consumer protection and to help eliminate and prevent anti-competitive business practices.

financial identifiers   Personal identifying information that is associated with an individual's finances. This may include account numbers that are issued by banks, credit unions, and credit card companies.

fraud alert   An official notification a person places on their credit bureau reports. This alert tells creditors to contact the claimant prior to opening any new accounts or making any changes to his or her existing accounts.

government issued identifiers   Personal information that is assigned to an individual by the government for record-keeping purposes. Social Security numbers are an example of government issued identifiers.

Gypsy scammers   A group of people who travel from one area to another to commit fraud and other crimes. The group does not establish residency, thus making it harder to track them. Often times, the scams are committed under the guise that the scammers are going to perform some type of service. They collect the money up-front and then never return to complete the job.

hacker   Someone who gains unauthorized access to computer databases, computer networks, or other technological device.

hacking   The process of gaining unauthorized access to a computer database, computer network, or other technological device.

health insurance portability and accountability act (HIPAA)   This act was passed by Congress in 1996 and designed to address issues of security and efficiency within the nation's health care system.

identity theft   According to federal law, identity theft is the transfer or use of another person's *identifying information* without their knowledge and with intent to aid or abet in any unlawful activity such as obtaining services, merchandise, money, and/or credit, committing felonies and/or misdemeanors, or filing for bankruptcy.

identity theft assumption and deterrence act of 1998   This Act, passed by Congress in October 1998 to amend 18 U.S.C. § 1028, makes it a federal offense for a person to transfer or use the personal identifying information of another with the intent to commit a crime or to aid in the commission of other crimes. It also enhanced the penalties when identity theft is committed in order to facilitate drug trafficking and violent crimes. The Act also mandated that the Federal Trade Commission establish a centralized complaint and education service for victims of identity theft.

identity theft clearinghouse   A database established by the Federal Trade Commission as mandated by the Identity Theft and Assumption Deterrence Act of 1998. Launched in November 1999, the database collects identity theft complaints directly from victims.

identity theft networks   A group of individuals who work together to commit identity theft. The networks resemble organized crime in that the information and the benefits are commonly shared. Some networks are made up of smaller groups that offer certain specializations necessary to perpetuate the identity thefts.

identity theft penalty enhancement act   This Act, passed by Congress in 2004 to amend 18.U.S.C. § 1028, created the offense of aggravated identity theft and implemented mandatory sentences. The Act also mandates that those convicted of aggravated identity theft must serve out their sentences instead of being placed on probation.

living trust   A trust created during the lifetime of the grantor.

medical identity theft   This occurs when someone receives medical services, equipment, or doctor visits using the identity of another person without that person's knowledge.

military sentinel   A database established in September 2002 by the Federal Trade Commission. The database collects identity theft and fraud-related complaints from members of the armed forces, military civilian employees, and their families.

mystery shopping providers association   Established in 1998, this is the largest professional trade association dedicated to improving service quality using anonymous resources (http://www.mysteryshop.org/).

Nigerian 419 scam   A type of money transfer fraud or advance fee fraud named after the Nigerian criminal code it violates. Victims are promised large sums of money upon paying an advance fee or tax and providing bank account information. All scams of this nature are called Nigerian 419 Scams, even though they may not originate in Nigeria.

offshoring The practice of employing third-party vendors located outside the United States to perform jobs requiring access to the personal identifying information of U.S. citizens, such as medical records and income tax returns.

OPT-OUT A program that gives consumers the option of removing their names from marketing lists to reduce the amount of pre-approved credit card offers and promotional materials they receive by mail.

passport program (Ohio) A pilot program developed in the state of Ohio in which law enforcement officials forward information to the Attorney General's office in cases of identity theft. Victims then receive a passport identification card providing them with documentation of their victimization.

personal identifying information Personal identifiers distinguish one person from all other people. There are four basic types of identifiers: common identifiers, government issued identifiers, financial identifiers, and other identifiers. "Other identifiers" is a category that encompasses the identifiers that do not fall into the first three categories. Other identifiers include medical record information, employee identification numbers, student identification numbers, and biometric data.

phantom seller scam An online auction scam in which a seller has friends and family members create bogus feedback to give the impression that the seller is reliable.

phishing Sending deceptive e-mails for the purpose of tricking recipients into providing their personal information.

phone or utilities fraud The use of a person's identifying information to obtain phone or other utility services without their knowledge.

pre-texting Making deceptive telephone calls for the purpose of tricking individuals into providing their personal identifying information.

search engine An online database of Web pages and programs through which users can search for information on a specific topic.

security breach The unauthorized access to personal identifying information of those who have had contact with the institution targeted. This access may be the result of lost, stolen, unsecured, or even mishandled personal identifying information. This type of attack has the potential for hundreds or thousands of victims, depending on the target.

skimmer A small electronic device used to read and/or record the information on the magnetic strips of debit and credit cards.

skimming   A method used to capture debit and credit card information with a small electronic device called a skimmer.

spam   Sending numerous copies of the same e-mail to various Internet users in an attempt to reach recipients who would not normally receive the message. It is often used for commercial advertising, get-rich-quick schemes, or quasi-legal services.

third-party billing   The process of an operator-assisted telephone call in which the cost of the call is charged to a third party, separate from the caller, or the person receiving the phone call.

verified internet pharmacy practice sites (VIPPS)   An online database initiated by the National Association of Boards of Pharmacy to help consumers identify legitimate pharmacies licensed to conduct business on the Internet.

vishing   A combination of pre-texting, phishing, and/or the use of advanced voice technology for the purpose of tricking individuals into providing their personal information. This practice is also known as "voice phishing."

war dialers   An automated dialing program that allows scammers to call numerous numbers simultaneously.

Index

Abagnale, Frank, Jr., 140
Afghanistan, 117
age of perpetrators, 23–24
age of victims, 32–34
Al-Qaeda, 27–28, 92, 93, 117
Allie, Mohamed, 112
Anderson, Anna, 9
Anti-Phishing Working Group, 199–200
arrests for crimes, 43
Ashcroft, John, 140–141
Asia, 113–115
attempted identity theft, 29
attributed identity, 101
Automatic Teller Machines (ATMs), 79
"AvID Theft: Deter, Detect, Defend" (FTC), 66
Aylmer, John, 6–7

background and history, 1–39
bank fraud, 29, 30
Bank of America, 11, 73–74
bank robbery, first documented multinational Internet bank robbery, 12–13
banking/credit/financial data breaches, 59, 60, 61
Beers, Rand, 116
Belgium, 102
benefits fraud, 29, 30
Better Business Bureau (BBB), 76

bills and account statements, 80
Bin Laden, Osama, 91, 93
biographical identity, 101
biographical sketches, 139–161
biometric identity, 101
birth certificates, 2, 98
    and terrorists plots, 116
Bliley, Thomas Jerome, Jr., 141–142
border security, Canada and US., 94
Bowen, Debra, 142
Boyer, Amy, 15–16
breeder documents, 2
British Crime Survey, 104
business data breaches, 59, 61
business identity theft, 3–5
business interactions, 75–76
businesses
    data breaches, 59, 61
    early detection procedures, 42, 43–44

Cade's Rebellion of 1450, 6–7
Calderon, Charles, 143
Canada, 89–100
Canadian Security Intelligence Service (CSIS), 91
Canadian Social Insurance Number (SIN), 98–99
Cantwell, Maria, 143–144
Carter, Steve, 144–145

categories of perpetrators,
18–19
Chicago debacle, 11–12
ChoicePoint incident, 52–53
Chugaev, Aleksey, 111
Citibank, 12–13
Cogdill, David, 145–146
collection agencies, 42
computer security systems, 79
computers and other electronic
devices, discarding, 79–80
Consumer Sentinel, Federal
Trade Commission (FTC),
65, 67, 95
Coppolino, Justine, 4
corporate identity crime,
defined, 103
corporate identity fraud,
defined, 103
corporate identity theft, 103
costs, of identity theft, 62.
See also financial losses
country of origin of perpetrators, 26
credit and debit cards, 77
credit bureaus, 66
credit card fraud, 29, 30, 31
charges on statements, 42
Chicago debacle, 11–12
early case of, 13–15
existing credit cards only,
44–45
credit monitoring for identity
theft, 1
credit reporting bureaus, 50
credit reports, 1, 43, 50, 80
Fair Credit Reporting Act
(FCRA), 80
creditors, 42, 50
criminal history of perpetrators, 25–26
criminal justice system
responses from, 72–73
victims' experiences, 50
CSIS. *See* Canadian Security
Intelligence Service

Cuccinelli, Ken, 146
Czar Nicholas II and his family,
8–9

Dahoumane, Abdelmajid, 93
data and documents, 163–197
Executive Summary Consumer
Fraud and Identify Theft
Complaint Data (January–
December 2008), 163–164
Identity Theft and Assumption
Deterrence Act (amended
1998), 173–180
President's Identity Theft
Force (April 2007), 165–173
Title V of the Gramm-Leach-
Bliley Act (1999), 180–197
data breaches, 59–61
banking/credit/financial, 59,
60, 61
businesses, 59, 61
educational institutions, 50, 60,
61
government/military, 59, 60,
61
medical/healthcare, 59, 61
Demara, Ferdinand Waldo, Jr.,
9–10
"The Development of an Identity
Theft Offender Typology:
A Theoretical Approach"
(Morris), 17–18
Diners Club, 11
Dinerstein, Marti, 108, 109
Directory of Organizations,
Associations, and Agencies,
199–221
discarding computers and other
electronic devices, 79–80
document shredding, 82
Docusearch, 15–16
Doha, Abu, 92
driver's licenses, 2, 98, 104
and illegal immigrants, 107
and terrorist plots, 116
drug trafficking, 89, 111

e-commerce, 13–15
E. H. Ferree Company, 10–11
early credit card fraud, 13–15
early detection procedures,
      by businesses, 42
early detection products for
      identity theft, 1
educated citizens, 81
educational institution data
      breaches, 50, 60, 61
EFTs (electronic funds transfers),
      30
EIN (employer identification
      number), 4
Electronic Crimes Task Forces
      and Working Groups,
      200
electronic funds transfers (EFTs),
      30
emotional and medical concerns,
      47–48
employer identification number
      (EIN), 4
employment of perpetrators
      in private businesses
      and financial industry,
      51–52
employment-related fraud, 29, 30,
      31
Equifax, 66
ethnicity of perpetrators,
      24–25
evading law enforcement, 30
Executive Summary Consumer
      Fraud and Identify
      Theft Complaint Data
      (January-December 2008),
      163–164
Experian, 66
"Exploring the Crime of Identity
      Theft: Prevalence,
      Clearance Rates: and
      Victim/Offender Charac-
      teristics"
   affiliation with other
      criminals, 28

age of perpetrators, 24
ethnicity and race of
      perpetrators, 24–25
gender of perpetrators, 20

Fair Credit Reporting Act
      (FCRA), 80
familial identity theft, 46–47
fax machines, 82
federal offense, identity theft
      as, 1
Federal Trade Commission
      (FTC), 201–202
   age of victims, 33–34
   "AvID Theft: Deter, Detect,
      Defend," 66
   Consumer Sentinel, 65, 67,
      95
   data from victims, 53
   identity theft complaints, 22
   Identity Theft Data Clearing
      House, 65–68
   "Identity Theft Survey Report,"
      44
Feinstein, Dianne, 146–147
Fighting Back Against Identity
      Theft (FTC web site), 81
financial accounts, 2
financial losses, 41–42, 48, 49.
      See also costs
financial security, 47
first documented multinational
      Internet bank robbery,
      12–13
first Internet murder, 15–16
Foley, Linda, 147–148
Frank, Mari, 148–149
Franklin National Bank, 11
fraud, identity theft as, 21
FTC. *See* Federal Trade
      Commission

gender of perpetrators, 19–23
geographical location of victims,
      31–32
Giverns, Beth, 149

government documents or
   benefits fraud, 29, 30
government-issued identification
   records, 2
government/military data
   breaches, 59, 60, 61
government responses to identify
   theft, 64–72
   "AvID Theft: Deter, Detect,
      Defend" (FTC), 66
   Consumer Sentinel Network,
      65, 67
   Identity Theft and Assumption
      Deterrence Act of 1998,
      64–65
   Identity Theft Data Clearing
      House, 65–68
   Identity Theft Enforcement and
      Restitution Act of 2008,
      68–69
   Identity Theft Penalty Enhance-
      ment Act of 2004, 68
   Identity Theft Prevention and
      Mitigation Program, 71–72
   identity theft task forces, 70–71
   National Data Privacy Day, 71
   passport programs, 70
   state-level legislative responses,
      69–72
   See also solving identity theft
Gramm, William Philip, 149–150
Great Depression, 10
The Great Imposter, 9–10

"Hacking, Why Not?," 117
Hannachi, Abderraouf, 91
Health Information Portability
   and Accountability Act of
   1996 (HIPAA), 81
Helen Remsburg v. Docusearch,
   16
Henry VI (Shakespeare), 7
HIPPA. See Health Information
   Portability and Account-
   ability Act of 1996
hiring practices, 83

history of identity theft, 5–16
   Cade's Rebellion of 1450, 6–7
   Chicago debacle, 11–12
   Czar Nicholas II and his family,
      8–9
   early credit card fraud, 13–15
   first documented multinational
      Internet bank robbery,
      12–13
   first Internet murder, 15–16
   the Great Imposter, 9–10
   Jacob and Esau, 6
   most misused Social Security
      number (SSN) in history,
      10–11
   Sarah Wilson in Colonial
      America, 7–8
Home Office Identity Fraud
   Steering Committee
   (United Kingdom), 103
human trafficking, 89, 111

identity cards, 102
   Mexico, 107
   South Africa, 113
   United Kingdom, 106
identity documents, 116
identity fraud
   defined, 103, 115
   and terrorist plots, 116
Identity Fraud—The UK Manual,
   104
"Identity Fraud and Transnational
   Crime," 94–95
"Identity Fraud Trends and
   Patterns: Building a Data-
   Based Foundation for
   Proactive Enforcement,"
   51–52
   affiliation with other crimes,
      27
   affiliation with other criminals,
      28
   age of perpetrators, 23–24
   country of origin of perpe-
      trators, 26

criminal history of perpetrators, 26
ethnicity and race of perpetrators, 25
gender of perpetrators, 20
Identity Theft 911, 202–203
identity theft
  and Al-Qaeda, 27–28
  business, 3–5
  defined, 1–5, 103, 115
  as federal offense, 1
  as fraud, 21
  hidden costs of, 62
  and illegal immigration, 32
  and the Internet, 13–15
  personal, 2–3
  by state, 31–32
  statistics for 2008, 29
  and terrorist plots, 116
  as white collar crime, 21
  See also solving identity theft; types of identity theft
"Identity Theft: Predator Profiles," 52, 53
  affiliation with other crimes, 27
  affiliation with other criminals, 27
  age of perpetrators, 23
  criminal history of perpetrators, 26
  gender of perpetrators, 20, 21
Identity Theft and Assumption Deterrence Act of 1998, 64–65
Identity Theft and Assumption Deterrence Act (amended 1998), 173–180
Identity Theft Enforcement and Restitution Act of 2008, 68–69
identity theft marriages, 113
Identity Theft Partnerships in Prevention, 203
Identity Theft Penalty Enhancement Act of 2004, 68

Identity Theft Prevention and Mitigation Program, New York Consumer Protection Board, 71–72, 203–204
Identity Theft Resource Center, 42, 45, 204–205
"Identity Theft Survey Report," Federal Trade Commission (FTC), 44
identity theft task forces, 70–71
Identity Theft Victims Advocate Network, 205–206
identity thief categories, 18–19
  circumstantial, 18
  professional, 18–19
  semi-pro, 18
  survivalist, 19
  See also types of identity theft
Ikhlef, Mourad, 92
illegal immigrants, 107
  and identity theft, 32
immigration policies
  Canada and US, 94
  Mexico and US, 108
impersonation, 5
Indonesia, 117
information collected by organizations, 81–82
Institute of Consumer Financial Education, 206
Instituto Federal Electoral, Mexico, 107, 109
insurance for identity theft, 1
Internal Revenue Service (IRS), 4
International Association of Chiefs of Police and Bank of America, 73–74
International Association of Financial Crimes Investigators, 207–208
international organized crime, 94–95

Internet
 first documented multinational
  Internet bank robbery,
  12–13
 first Internet murder, 15–16
 and identity theft, 13–15
 purchases on, 76
 service providers, 14
Internet Crime Complaint Center,
 208
IRS (Internal Revenue Service), 4

Jacob and Esau, 6
Japan, 114
job procedures in businesses, 82

Kaine, Timothy M., 150–151
Karelov, Roman, 111
Kourani, Fadi, 109
Kyl, Jon, 151

Leach, James Albert Smith,
 151–152
Leahy, Patrick, 152–153
Levin, Vladimir, 12–13
loan fraud, 29, 30
lost productivity in the workplace,
 42
Lyakhov, Artur, 110

Madigan, Lisa, 153
mail protection, 77–78
marriages of convenience, 112
Maryland Crime Victims'
  Resource Center: Identity
  Theft & Fraud Assistance,
  208–209
Mashokwe, Leslie, 113
matriculas consulares, 107–109
May, Johnny, 153–154
medical concerns, 47–48
medical fraud, 54–56
medical/healthcare data
  breaches, 59, 61
methods of detection and time
  lapse, 42–44

Mexico, 107–109
Millennium Bomber, Ressam,
  Ahmed, 90–94
Miller, Noel, 5
Miskini, Abdelghani, 94
modus operandi (MO) of perpetrators, 16–17
Morris, Robert II, "The Development of an Identity Theft
  Offender Typology: A
  Theoretical Approach,"
  17–18
most misused Social Security
  number (SSN) in history,
  10–11
mother's maiden name, 2, 82
motives of perpetrators, 16, 17
murder, first Internet murder,
  15–16

National Association of Boards
  of Pharmacy (NAPB), 76
National Association of Consumer
  Advocates, 209
National Check Fraud Center,
  209–210
National Data Privacy Day, 71
National Fraud Information
  Center, 210–211
National Identity Register (NIR)
  database, UK, 106–197
National White Collar Crime
  Center, 211–212
 "White Collar Crime Statistics,"
  21–22
new accounts and other frauds,
  44–45
Nizamov, Radik, 111
non-credit card accounts,
  44–45

O'Carroll, Patrick, 116
offshoring identities, 57–59
Oller, Thomas, 154
O'Neil, Kevin, 107
OnGuard Online, 212

opportunity takers or makers, 17–19
organized criminal syndicates, 58–59
See also international organized crime; Russian Organized Crime
Ostergren, Betty, 155

passport programs, 70
passports, 2
Canada, 89, 98
United Kingdom, 104, 106
password protection, 78
Paterson, David A., 155–156
perpetrators, 16–29
affiliation with other crimes, 27
affiliation with other criminals, 27–29
age, 23–24
categories of, 18–19
ChoicePoint incident, 52–53
country of origin, 26
criminal history, 25–26
employment in private businesses and financial industry, 51–52
ethnicity, 24–25
gender, 19–23
"Identity Theft: Predator Profiles," 52
modus operandi (MO), 16–17
motives, 16, 17
opportunity takers or makers, 17–19
phishing e-mail, 51
sources and methods for accessing identities, 51–53
personal identifying information, 2
of customers, employees, and vendors of businesses
personal identity theft, 2–3
Petro, James, 156–157
phishing activity, 51, 74–75, 114

PhoneBusters (Canada), 95–96, 212–213
Police and Justice Act of 2006 (UK), 105
Poochigian, Charles, 157
President's Identity Theft Task Force (April 2007), 165–173
President's Identity Theft Task Force (May 2006), 213–214
prevention measures, solving identity theft, 62
Privacy Act of 1983 (Canada), 99–100
Privacy Rights Clearinghouse, 215
private and public partnerships, solving identity theft, 73–74
problems, controversies, and solutions, 41–87
proprietary information storage, 82
protecting personal information, 74–81
Automatic Teller Machines (ATMs), 79
awareness, 74
Better Business Bureau (BBB), 76
bills and account statements, 80
business interactions, 75–76
computer security systems, 79
credit and debit cards, 77
credit reports, 80
discarding computers and other electronic devices, 79–80
educated citizens, 81
Internet purchases, 76
mail protection, 77–78
National Association of Boards of Pharmacy (NAPB), 76
password protection, 78
phishing, 74–75
shoulder-surfing, 79
shredding documents, 78
skimming, 77

protecting personal information
(*continued*)
Social Security number (SSN), 74
unsolicited mail, 77–78
Verified Internet Pharmacy
Practice Sites (VIPPS), 76
vishing, 75
See also solving identity theft
protecting workplace information,
81–83
fax machines, 82
Health Information Portability
and Accountability Act of
1996 (HIPAA), 81
hiring practices, 83
information collected by
organizations, 81–82
mother's maiden names, 82
proprietary information storage,
82
security policies and job procedures, 82
shredding documents, 82
Social Security number (SSN),
81, 82
See also solving identity theft

refugee policies, Canada, 89
Reid, Michael, 97–98
responsibility theories, solving
identity theft, 63–64
Ressam, Ahmed, Millennium
Bomber, 90–94
restoration period and types of
identity theft, 44–45
Romanova, Anastasia Niko-
layevna, 8–9
Roosevelt, Franklin D., 10
Russia, 109–111
Russian Organized Crime, and
fraud, 109, 110, 111

Salgado, Carlos Felipe, Jr., 14
security policies, 82
September 11, 2001, 115
Shakespeare, William, *Henry VI*, 7

shoulder-surfing, 79
shredding documents, 82
Simitian, Joe, 157–158
SIN. *See* Canadian Social
Insurance Number
Single Points of Contact (SPOC)
network, 104–105
skimming, 77
Sloan, Shovana, 17
Social Security Act (1935), 10
Social Security Administration, 11
Social Security number (SSN),
116–117
abuse of, 2, 31
defined, 3
and illegal immigrants, 107, 109
most misused in history, 10–11
protecting personal information,
74
protecting workplace information, 81, 82
solving identity theft, 62–83
criminal justice system
response, 72–73
Fighting Back Against Identity
Theft (FTC web site), 81
prevention measures, 62
private and public partnerships,
73–74
responsibility theories, 63–64
victim blaming, 63, 64
victim-defending, 63–64
See also government responses
to identify theft; protecting
personal information;
protecting workplace
information
*Sourcebook of Criminal Justice
Statistics*
age of perpetrators, 23
ethnicity and race of perpetrators, 24, 25
gender of perpetrators, 19, 21
sources and methods for accessing
identities, 51–53
South Africa, 112–113

South Korea, 114
Spain, 102
Specter, Arlen, 159
SSN. *See* Social Security number
standardized definitions of identity theft, 100–101, 103–104, 118
state-level legislative responses, 31–32, 69–72
statistics for identity theft in 2008, 29
Steffer, Fred, 112
Stop Atlanta Fraud Empower, 216
Strategic Council for the Competition Bureau of Canada, studies by, 95–96
Suzanne Sloane v. Equifax Information Services, 17

tax returns, 4
    fraudulent, 30, 31
telephone or cell phone bills, 42
telephone or utilities fraud, 29, 30
terrorism, 89, 90
terrorist plots, and identity theft, 116
Thomas, Nicholas, 114, 115
threat to international and homeland security, 115–118
    transnational crimes, 89
    See also worldwide perspective
time lapse and methods of detection, 42–44
Title V of the Gramm-Leach-Bliley Act (1999), 180–197
Torlakson, Tom, 159–160
transnational crimes, 89
TransUnion, 66
trends and special issues, 53–62
    medical fraud, 54–56
    offshoring identities, 57–59
    organized criminal syndicates, 58–59
    real estate fraud, 56–57
    tax fraud, 54
    See also data breaches

types of identity theft, 29–31
    attempted identity theft, 29
    bank fraud, 29, 30
    credit card fraud, 11–12, 13–15, 29, 30, 31
    employment-related fraud, 29, 30, 31
    existing credit cards only, 44–45
    existing non-credit card accounts, 44–45
    government documents or benefits fraud, 29, 30
    loan fraud, 29, 30
    new accounts and other frauds, 44–45
    other identity theft, 29, 30–31
    phone or utilities fraud, 29, 30
    and the restoration period, 44–45
    See also identity thief categories

underground marketplace, 116
Uniform Crime Reporting system (US), 104
United Kingdom, 100–107
United States Computer Emergency Readiness Team, 216–217
United States Department of the Treasury Financial Crimes Enforcement Network, 217–218
United States of America v. ChoicePoint, 52–53
unsolicited mail, 77–78
utilities fraud, 29, 30
utility services interruptions, 42

Verified Internet Pharmacy Practice Sites (VIPPS), 76
victim blaming, solving identity theft, 63, 64
victim-defending, solving identity theft, 63–64

victims, 29–34
  age, 32–34
  geographical location, 31–32
  see also types of identity theft
victims' experiences, 41–51
  criminal justice system, 50
  effects on relationships,
    46–47
  emotional and medical
    concerns, 47–48
  familial identity theft, 46–47
  financial losses, 41–42, 48, 49
  financial security, 47
  lost productivity in the work-
    place, 42
  methods of detection and time
    lapse, 42–44
  types of identity theft and the
    restoration period,
    44–45
Victims Initiative for Counseling,
    Advocacy, and Restoration
    of the Southwest, 218
vishing, 75

Wahid, Abdul, 5
weapon trafficking, 111
Whitcher, Hilda Schrader, 11
white collar crime, 21–22
"White Collar Crime Statistics,"
    National White Collar
    Crime Center (NW3C),
    21–22
Wilson, Sarah, 7–8
"Women Offenders," 21
worldwide perspective, 89–121
  Asia, 113–115
  Canada, 89–100
  Mexico, 107–109
  Russia, 109–111
  South Africa, 112–113
  United Kingdom, 100–107
  See also threat to international
    and homeland security
Wyland, Mark, 160–161

Youens, Liam, 15–16

Zubaydah, Abu, 91

About the Authors

SANDRA K. HOFFMAN is the Director of the Identity Theft Program at Michigan State University, School of Criminal Justice, East Lansing, Michigan. She holds a Bachelor of Arts degree in Human Services. Sandra is the coauthor of the book *Identity Theft First Responder Manual for Criminal Justice Professionals* and its companion manual, *Identity Theft Victims' Assistance Guide*. Sandra is also an Identity Theft Specialist for the Adrian Charter Township Police Department.

TRACY G. MCGINLEY holds a Masters Degree and works as an instructor at Bowling Green State University Firelands in Huron, Ohio. She has coauthored a chapter in the book *The Move to Community Policing*, and regularly conducts seminars to raise awareness of identity theft issues.

HV 6675 .H64 2010
Hoffman, Sandra K.
Identity theft